Herbert Kaspar/Bob Shell

**Canon EOS-1N**

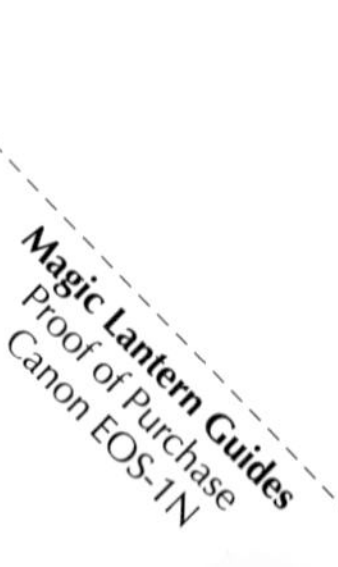
Magic Lantern Guides
Proof of Purchase
Canon EOS-1N

Magic Lantern Guides

# Canon EOS-1N

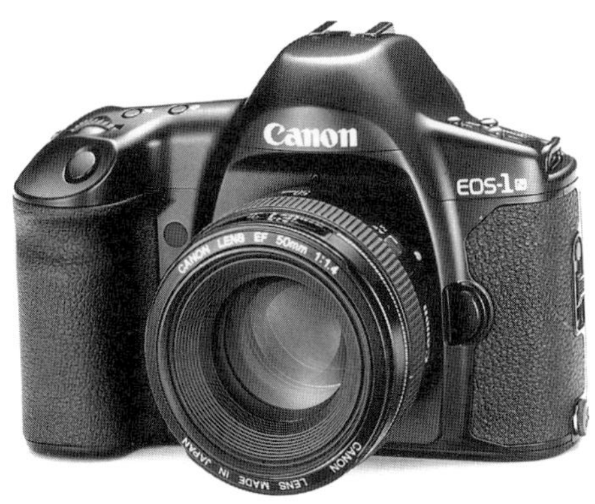


Herbert Kaspar/Bob Shell

**Magic Lantern Guide to**
**Canon EOS-1N**

A Laterna magica® book

First English Language Edition 1995
Published in the United States of America by

**Silver Pixel Press®**
Division of
The Saunders Group
21 Jet View Drive
Rochester, NY 14624

From the German edition by Herbert Kaspar
Edited by Bob Shell
Translated by Phyllis M. Riefler-Bonham

Printed in Germany by Kösel GmbH, Kempten

**ISBN 1-883403-15-4**

 *Product photos and diagrams were provided by Canon GmbH; all other photos were supplied by Per-Andre Hoffmann, unless otherwise noted. We would like to thank Chuck Westfall of Canon U.S.A., Inc., Camera Division, for offering his technical expertise to this book.*

# Contents

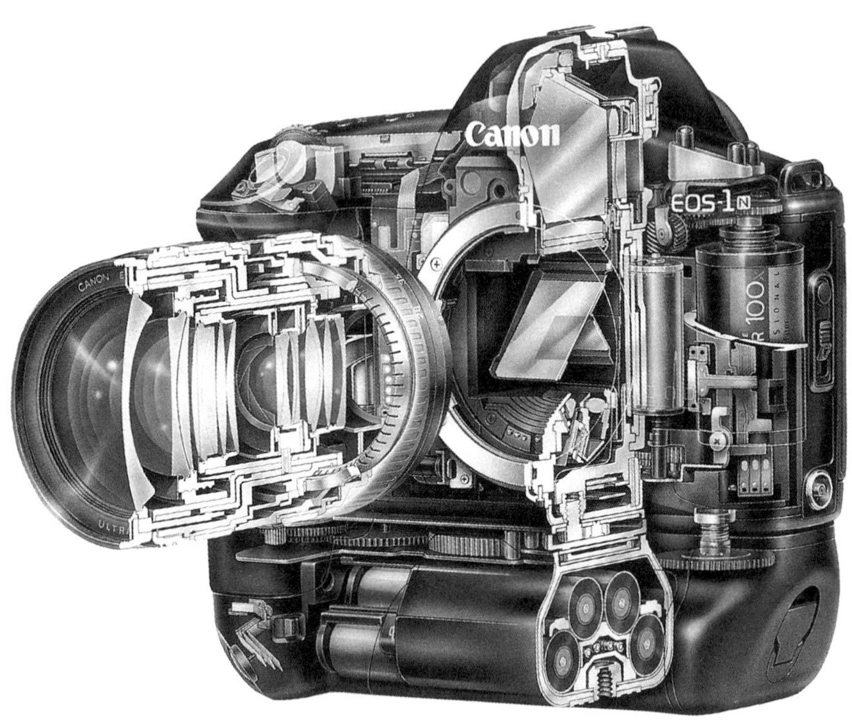


The EOS-1N—A view of the interior mechanism.

# Foreword

Canon introduced the original EOS-1 professional camera in 1989. Its rounded body style, ergonomic design, and many advanced pro-level features set it apart from the cumbersome, boxy autofocus cameras of its day and laid the groundwork for present-day SLR camera design. Five years later Canon launched the EOS-1N, a further refinement of this flagship model. Its innovations and new features include improved shooting speed and focus prediction, an enhanced multiple-zone TTL flash sensor, substantially quieter film rewind, and the Advanced Multi-BASIS AF sensor. The EOS-1N was an immediate hit with even the most skeptical audience—professional photographers.

This *Magic Lantern Guide* is intended to make using the EOS-1N camera easier. It explains the use of its many features and functions and offers insight on what feature is appropriate for any given situation. Since an understanding of photographic principles is also necessary for achieving success with the EOS-1N, explanations of these principles and their application in advanced 35mm photography are found throughout this book. For expanded information on Canon autofocus lenses for use on the EOS-1N, we recommend that you also read the *Magic Lantern Guide to Canon Lenses* by George Lepp and Joseph Dickerson.

While this text is designed to progress logically, describing the basic use of the camera as well as advanced techniques, it is not necessary to read this book's chapters in sequence. Each chapter covers a particular aspect of the EOS-1N and can be read and referred to as needed.

***Note:*** Per-Andre Hoffmann, a professional photographer living in Stuttgart, Germany, supplied many of the photographs in this book. His specialty is travel photography. Mr. Hoffmann takes pictures of the world's most beautiful spots for government tourist offices, travel agencies, hotels, and airlines. His pictures have been published in such highly respected journals as *GEO, stern,* and *National Geographic.*

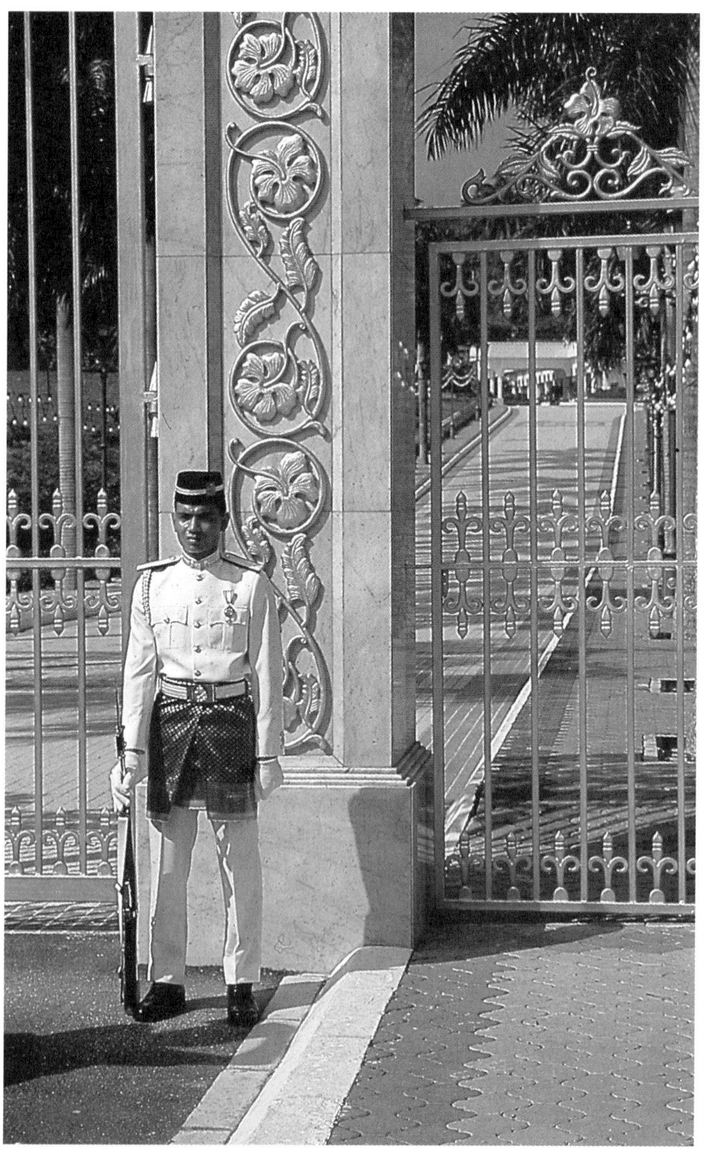

The Canon EOS-1N's sophisticated metering system measures differences in luminance in 16 areas of the photograph to produce extremely accurate exposures. Photo by Bob Shell.

# Preparing to Use the EOS-1N

Before indulging in the joy of taking pictures with a camera such as the EOS-1N, some preparation is required. Nothing will function without battery power, film needs to be loaded, a lens must be mounted, and adding a camera strap is a good idea.

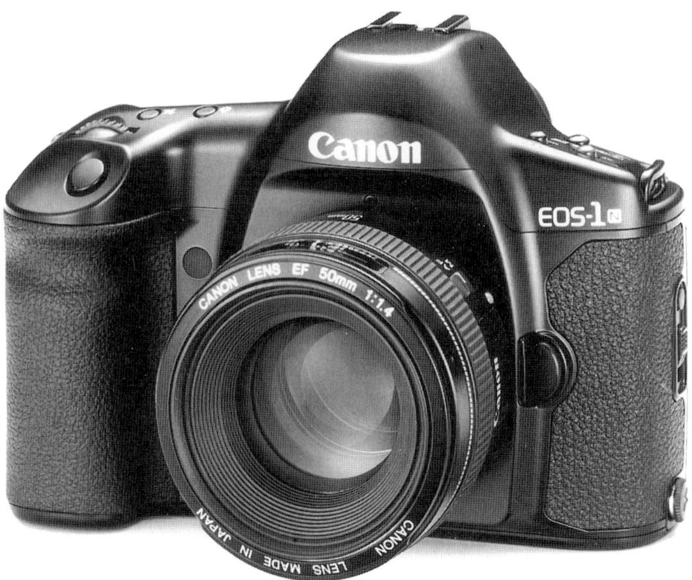


**Canon's new professional model, the EOS-1N, is sturdy and durable, with conveniently located controls.**

## Power Supply

The EOS-1N camera is powered by a standard 6-volt lithium battery (2CR5 type), which is housed in the grip/battery chamber. All you need is a coin to turn the grip screw, making it easy to load and unload the battery. You no longer need to pry open little caps or covers with your fingernails. A BP-E1 Battery Pack is also available to power the EOS-1N. See the *Accessories* chapter for more information.

### Loading and Unloading the Battery

To load the lithium cell, first remove the grip/battery chamber, using a coin to loosen the screw on its base. Slide the grip/battery chamber down and press the battery into the chamber so that the metal terminals on the battery align with the metal contacts in the back of the chamber.

To remove the battery, again remove the grip/battery chamber from the camera. Holding the battery chamber in your left hand, pull the gray battery ejector lever to the left with your left thumb. This will pivot the battery out of its chamber so that it can be removed. Be aware that it fits very snugly.

### Checking the Battery

You should always know what the status of your battery is before taking your camera out on a shoot. To check your battery, set the main switch to "A" (on). Then open the palm door and press the gray battery check button. The letters "bc" (battery check) will appear in the LCD panel. If three sets of four dashes (---- ---- ----) are displayed on the LCD, your battery is good. If two sets of four dashes (---- ----) are displayed, power is diminishing and you should have a spare battery on hand. If one set of four dashes (----) is blinking in the LCD, the battery is very low and will soon run out of power. The letters "bc" will blink when the battery is nearly drained (or when the camera detects a malfunction). If no dashes are displayed, the battery is drained and must be replaced.

If "bc" blinks and (after pressing the battery check button) the dashes on the LCD indicate the battery's power level is sufficient, unload the battery, wipe the terminals and the contacts with a clean, dry cloth, and reinstall the battery. If "bc" is still blinking, press the shutter button. If that does not correct the problem, the camera should be serviced by an authorized Canon service center.

## Film Functions

### Loading the Film

The EOS-1N can be loaded with film just as easily as any other camera with a built-in motor. First, open the camera back by pressing in the back cover lock release button and sliding the back cover latch down. Drop the film cassette into the left-hand chamber and pull the film leader to the right until it reaches the orange index mark. Engage the film perforations with the lower teeth of the sprocket. Then snap the back closed. The built-in motor will advance the film automatically to its starting position. A film cassette symbol emitting a row of traveling dots resembling a film strip will be displayed on the LCD panel. If the film has been loaded successfully, "1" will appear in the LCD's frame counter field, the apparent motion of the displayed film strip will stop, and the dot below the "0" index on the exposure scale will blink. This blinking dot indicates that an exposure compensation factor has not been entered. If the entire row of dots following the cassette blinks, it means that the film was loaded improperly and you need to start all over.

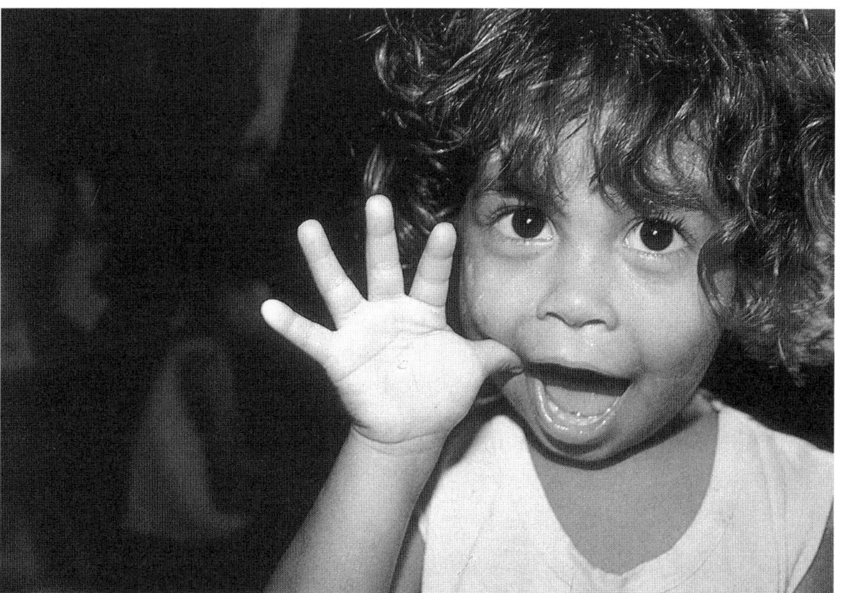

**When lighting is poor, use flash with either ISO 200 slide film or ISO 400 color negative film for best results.**

**Setting the Film Speed**

Regardless of whether you use a color negative, black-and-white negative, or color slide film in your EOS-1N, the sensitivity or speed of the film is an important consideration. The ISO value, together with the subject's brightness, determines acceptable combinations of shutter speed and aperture.

Like most modern SLR cameras, the EOS-1N is equipped with an automatic DX system that reads film speed information from appropriately marked film cassettes into the camera's central processing unit (microprocessor). Film speeds between ISO 25 and ISO 5000 can be handled by this automatic feature. If you want to set a different speed for a film within this range or if you are using a film with an ISO value outside this range, simultaneously press the AF mode selector and the metering mode selector (connected by the ISO symbol) on the upper left-hand side of the body. Then turn the main dial until the desired value is indicated on the LCD panel and release the two buttons. Remember, however, the automatic DX feature will again be active the next time you load film.

If you want to set the film speed manually over a prolonged period (for example to expose your ISO 100 speed slide film at ISO 80 because you like super-saturated colors), you can disable the automatic DX feature by activating Custom Function 3, setting 1. Once you have done this, the manually set film speed is retained unless you change it or you switch off this Custom Function.

**Film Transport**

Early on Canon recognized the advantages of motor-driven film transport and offered two types of motor drives for the F-1 camera. The AE-1's accessory winder A made this convenience available to amateur photographers. And with the T50 camera, Canon made the leap to the integrated winder.

An extremely quiet motor drives the EOS-1N's film transport system. Not only does the camera automatically load film, but when pictures are taken, the film advances automatically. The basic EOS-1N system allows you to choose between single-frame advance mode and continuous advance mode. If single-frame advance is selected, the film will be advanced by one frame after each exposure. Then the motor will stop, even if you hold the shutter button down. In continuous advance mode, film advance and exposure operations will continue as long as the shutter button is pressed down. The maximum film advance rate is 3 frames per second (fps). This frequency is achieved with relatively fresh batteries, using a shutter speed not exceeding 1/250 second, and using One-Shot autofocus mode.

The Power Drive Booster E1 can be attached to the EOS-1N. It offers single-frame advance, low-speed continuous advance, and high-speed continuous advance modes. See the *Accessories* chapter for more information about the Power Drive Booster E1.

**Rewinding the Film**

Rewinding the film back into its cassette is controlled by a separate motor, which can be engaged automatically (when a roll has been completely shot) or manually. This operation can be either quiet and fast or extremely quiet and slightly less fast.

The default rewind mode is at high-speed, starting automatically after the final frame of film has been exposed. To disable the automatic feature you can select Custom Function 1, setting 1 (F-1, 1). (See the *Custom Function* chapter for more information on how to set Custom Functions.) High-speed rewinding is then triggered by pressing the rewind button in the center bottom of the camera back. This is useful when you want to switch film in the middle of a roll. Rewinding a 36-exposure roll of film takes approximately 7 seconds, provided that the batteries are fresh.

Custom Function 1, setting 2 (F-1, 2) produces automatic silent rewinding upon reaching the end of a roll. Setting F-1, 3, produces silent manual rewinding when the film rewind button is pressed. (Automatic rewind is disabled.) At these settings, it takes approximately 20 seconds for a 36-exposure roll to rewind.

Considering the already low noise level of the rewind motor (approximately 1/8 that of the older EOS-1), the sound generated during the silent rewinding operation is reduced even further. Unless you are a photojournalist working under critical time constraints, Custom Function 1, setting 2 (F-1, 2) is recommended to spare your neighbors' ears and nerves, and you can use the 20 seconds while the film is rewinding to remove the next roll from its container. When pictures are taken in a church or synagogue, for example at a wedding, a setting of F-1, 3, is recommended because it allows you to control when the film will be rewound. This ensures that the EOS-1N will not make noise during the most sacred moments of the ceremony. (In a location where everyone is silent, even quiet film rewinding noise can be heard clearly!)

Another rewinding option is offered with Custom Function 2, which allows you to determine whether the film will be pulled entirely into the cassette (using F-2, 0, the default setting) or whether the film leader will remain outside (using F-2, 1). The latter is recommended only to those who process their films in their own laboratories or who want to rewind the film mid-roll, needing to reload the film at a later date.

## Mounting and Removing the Lens

The EOS-1N is designed with a fully electronic mount that accepts EF lenses. To attach a lens, hold it perpendicular to the camera and align the red dots on the lens and body. Place the lens squarely on the mount and turn the lens clockwise until you hear the quiet click of the lens catch. Set the focus mode switch on the lens to the desired focus mode, "AF" (autofocus) or "M" (manual focus operation).

To remove the lens, press the lens release button and rotate the lens counterclockwise until it releases from the body. When a lens is not on the camera, we strongly recommend that you use lens caps. (Do not touch the mirror inside the camera body!) Although dust, fingerprints, or scratches on the front or rear lens elements may not make a lens useless, they will impair its imaging performance.

## Adapting the Eyepiece

### Corrective Lenses

The EOS-1N's eyepiece is designed to allow the photographer to view the entire viewfinder. Still, for many who wear eyeglasses it is not possible to see the center of the image and its corners equally well. Canon offers two options for using the EOS-1N without eyeglasses.

**The EOS system is extensive, offering camera bodies, accessories, and lenses to suit almost any situation. The EOS-1N mounted with an EF super telephoto lens captured this detail of New York's Chrysler Building from a distance.** 

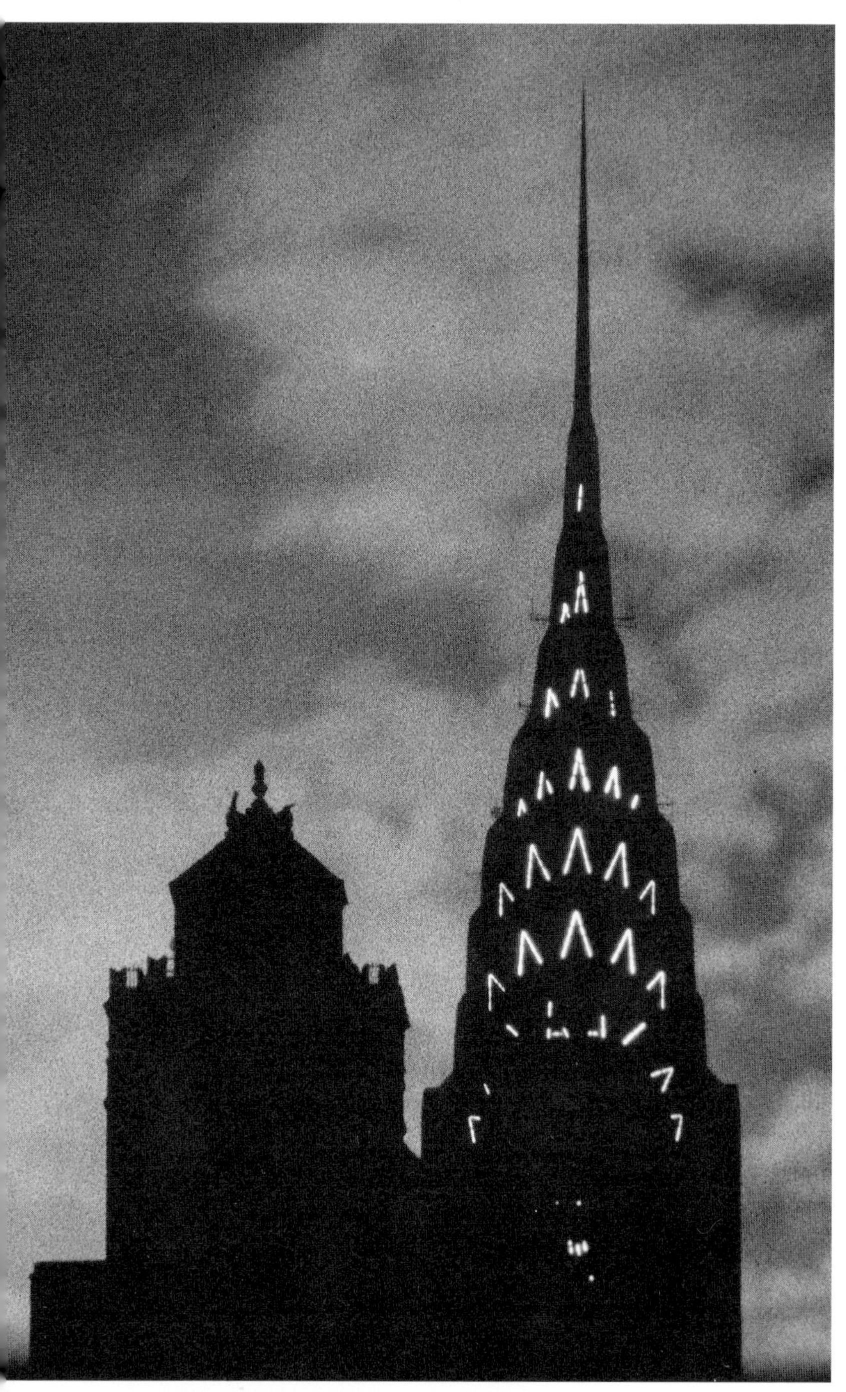

The EOS-1N's eyepiece is equipped with a dioptric adjustment dial (a knurled dial located behind the eyecup frame) that allows a correction within a range of -3 and +1 on a diopter scale. The default setting is -1. To adjust the eyepiece's diopter, first take the eyecup frame off the camera by pressing in on both sides of the eyecup. Then slide the eyecup assembly up and off the eyepiece mount. Do not use force, as doing so could break the fragile mounting pins! The dioptric adjustment dial is located to the left of the eyepiece. Now take the lens off the camera and place the camera body to your eye. Rotate the dial until the focusing points and fine spot metering area on the viewfinder are sharp and can be seen clearly. Replace the eyecup frame by gently sliding it down over the eyepiece.

You can also use one of Canon's ten available corrective lenses (Dioptric Adjustment Lens E), which come in strengths of +3 to -4 diopters. Their corrective effect can be combined with the camera's stepless dioptric adjustment dial. To install an accessory Dioptric Adjustment Lens E, you must exchange the eyecup for another (Rubber Frame Ec) that will accommodate the accessory lens.

### Eyepiece Shutter

If you are not looking through the viewfinder when making an exposure, for instance if the camera is mounted on a tripod or you are using the self-timer, you should first close the eyepiece shutter. To do this, pull the lever above and to the right of the eyecup over to the right. The eyepiece shutter prevents light from entering the viewfinder system from the back and reaching the exposure metering cells—which could result in metering errors.

## Carrying Your Camera

### Camera Straps

The EOS-1N comes with a Domke® Gripper™ strap (in the U.S. only) made especially for Canon. It is a nice little luxury supplied by Canon. The strap is high quality; you wouldn't want to trust your expensive camera to anything less. Rubber threads woven into the strap prevent it from slipping off your shoulder. Swivel hooks keep the strap from twisting. Of course, any strap of your choice can be attached to the eyelets on either side of the top of the camera.

For the safety of your camera, adding a strap is a must! You can wear it around your neck or over your shoulder. Some photographers wrap the strap securely around their right wrist and keep their hand on the camera's grip. Just don't get in the habit of dangling your camera by the strap. It is more likely to be damaged or become an easy target for thieves. If you are out in poor weather or if you do not want to draw unwelcome attention to your EOS-1N, just sling your camera over your shoulder and put on a roomy jacket or windbreaker.

**Camera Bags and Cases**

There are numerous types and sizes of camera bags and cases available. The type of bag or case you buy depends on the sort of photography you do. You may even have a need for more than one bag or case. Canon offers two semi-hard cases for the EOS-1N, the EH2N-L and the EH2N-LL, sized to fit the camera with a variety of lens lengths.

For storing or transporting all of your equipment, a bag must be adequately large to hold the camera and all its accessories. Buy one that is larger than you currently need so that it can hold any new equipment you might purchase in the future.

Choose a lightweight, durable camera bag with lots of pockets for carrying just the essentials. A waist pack (such as the Orion II AW from Lowepro® or the Domke OutPack® Waist Pack) or a backpack (such as the Domke OutPack Photo Backpack) are convenient alternatives for taking camera equipment with you hiking or cross-country skiing. Make sure that the compartments are covered by overlapping flaps so that water cannot enter from the top. A completely waterproof bag cannot be made, but the bag you choose should at least be adequate to keep the equipment dry in a rain shower. Only then can you take the camera along confidently when the clouds are threatening rain. The bottom of the bag should be reinforced so it can support a heavy load without bending. A variable interior with moveable inserts is the most versatile. The equipment dividers should be padded to protect valuable equipment from banging against one another. Dividers with sewn-in bottoms prevent equipment from "wandering" and make it quick and easy to move equipment from one bag to another.

# EOS-1N Body

At first glance, the new EOS-1N may appear to be the same, "good-old" EOS-1. However, a second, more careful look reveals distinct differences, showing that new ideas were incorporated in redesigning this professional model.

Pick up an EOS-1N and you will perceive that its form and function have been combined to make it practical. Like the EOS-1, the EOS-1N has a sturdy body, a feature of great importance. Its exterior consists of polycarbonate reinforced with glass fibers, making it extremely resistant to wear and tear. In addition, its major components, such as the bayonet-mount assembly, are still crafted in metal for precise lens alignment and perfect focus.

Canon specifies a working temperature range from 14°F to 113°F (-20°C to +45°C). At these temperatures the relative humidity can be as high as 85% without adversely affecting camera operation. In order to ensure that the EOS-1N can be used in all types of weather and locales, the body offers maximum protection against dust and moisture penetration. Dust and moisture cannot enter the interior of the EOS-1N through the camera controls. There is a very narrow slot around the main dial where water could enter, but Canon has given the dial a waterwheel design so that when it is rotated, the dial "shovels" the water droplets back out. Although caution is always advised when using delicate photographic equipment, if your EOS-1N is subjected to a downpour, don't panic. However care should be taken to dry off the camera as soon as possible. And of course, this does not mean that you can take your EOS-1N underwater! Special underwater housings must be used.

## Camera Controls

The familiar mode-selection (command) dial on most EOS models is not found on the EOS-1N. Instead, the EOS-1N uses the EOS-1's push-button controls, which were inherited from the T90 and earlier EOS models (the EOS 650, EOS 620, and EOS 630). The fact that the push-button controls have been retained from the design of

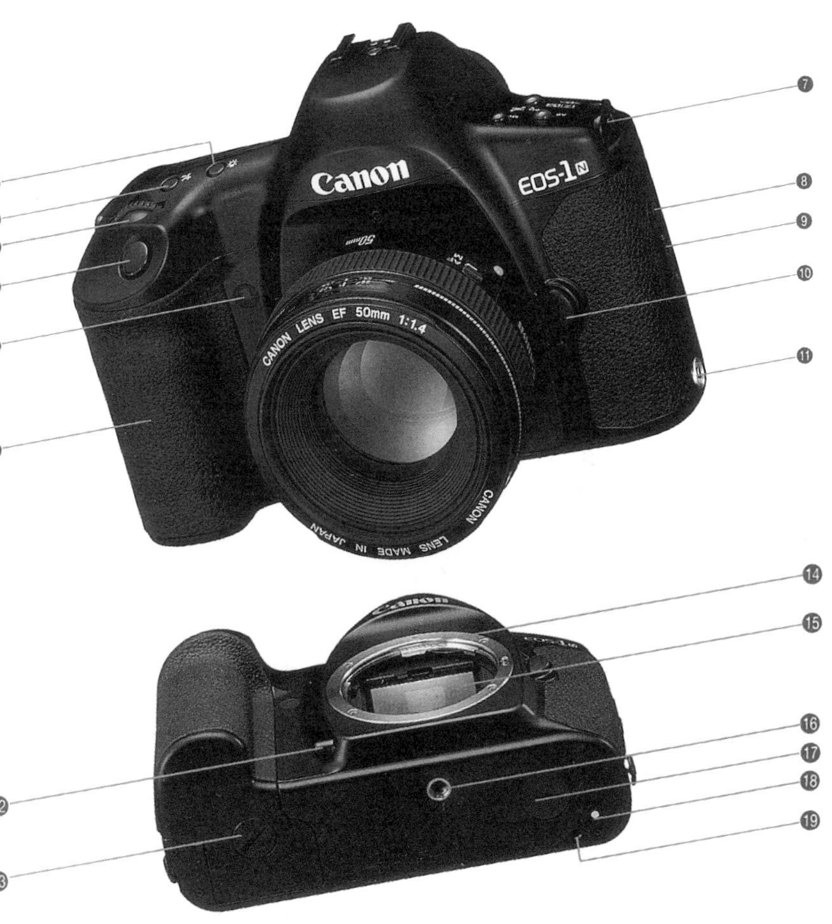


1. LCD panel illumination button
2. Exposure compensation button (+/-)
3. Main dial
4. Shutter button
5. Self-timer indicator
6. Grip/Battery chamber
7. Strap eyelet
8. Back cover lock release button
9. Back cover latch
10. Lens release button
11. PC terminal
12. Depth-of-field preview button
13. Grip screw
14. Lens mount
15. Mirror
16. Tripod socket
17. Booster coupler cover
18. Booster coupling pin
19. Booster/Battery pack attachment hole

the EOS-1 underscores Canon's commitment to meeting the needs of the professional with this camera. Those who are replacing the EOS-1 with an EOS-1N will not have to relearn the controls, and those using both models can readily switch between bodies!

***Note:*** The terms "left" and "right" are used to describe the locations of the various camera controls. They refer to the position of the control when the camera is held in the shooting position.

### Main Switch

The EOS-1N's main power switch is located on the back of the camera near the base. This switch is not as unimportant as its unusual location might lead you to believe. Be sure to remember to switch your camera off when you are done using it, because when the EOS-1N is put aside with the switch turned on, the LCD panel remains active, and even this minimal use of power will eventually drain the batteries.

The main switch has three settings: "L" for locked or off, "A" for on, and the third position is denoted by an icon for sound waves standing for "on, with audible signals activated." In the latter position, audible beeps are emitted by the camera when focus has been confirmed in One-Shot autofocus mode or in manual focus mode. Unless you are alone and want to take a self-portrait, it is best to do without the nerve-wracking beeps, in our opinion.

### Main Dial and Quick Control Dial

The EOS-1N has two input dials, both of which are of considerable importance for handling the camera quickly and easily. The camera is designed so that the photographer's right forefinger falls naturally on the main dial, which can be rotated in click-stops in both directions. This allows you to select specific settings for a certain function (such as focusing point, metering mode, autofocus mode, shooting mode, or custom function, which are first chosen by pressing the corresponding button). Once all possible options for that function have been displayed by turning the dial, the cycle will begin again. However shutter speed and aperture numbers are not subject to such a cycle. Once the greatest or smallest value has been reached, the dial will continue to turn in a given direction, but no further change in value will occur. This prevents gross exposure errors from occurring, caused by

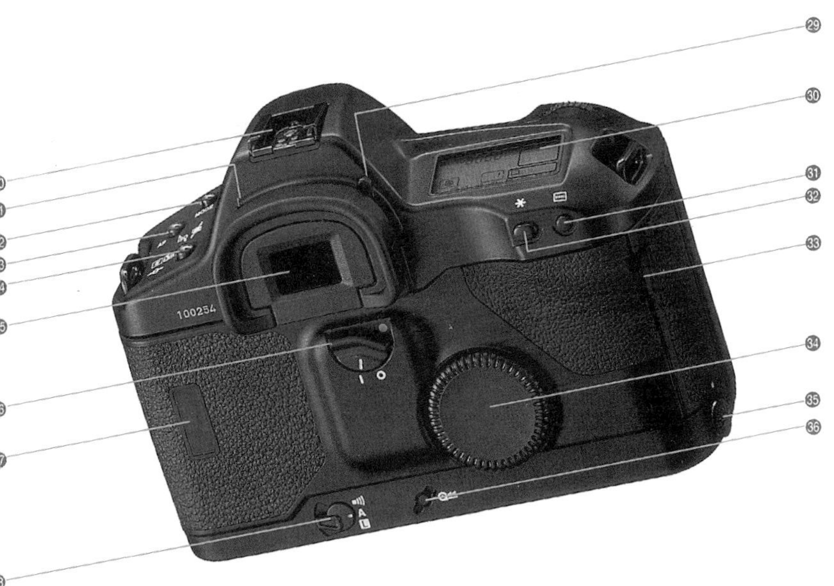

20. Accessory shoe
21. Dioptric adjustment dial
22. Shooting mode selector (MODE)
23. AF mode selector (AF)
24. Metering mode selector/ Flash exposure compensation button
25. Viewfinder eyepiece
26. Quick control dial switch
27. Film window
28. Main switch
29. Eyepiece shutter lever
30. LCD panel
31. Focusing point selector
32. AE lock button (*)
33. Palm door
34. Quick control dial
35. Remote control socket
36. Film rewind button

accidentally turning the dial too far and setting the largest rather than the smallest aperture.

The thumb-operated quick control dial may, at first glance, appear strange, but after you have taken a few shots with the EOS-1N, you will not want to be without it. Because its thumb-wheel design allows for convenient and fast exposure adjustment, it is so tempting to use that the yield of successful pictures is increased. (This is truly a great feature of the EOS-1N exposure metering system, but of course it cannot recognize whether a slight overexposure or underexposure will create a better mood than an

**The EOS-1N's quick control dial makes it easy to enter exposure compensation without taking your eye away from the viewfinder. A slight minus exposure correction was made to render these palm trees as silhouettes.**

exposure that the camera recommends. Therefore, the system still requires the photographer's judgment despite its sophisticated design.)

Furthermore, depending on the shooting mode selected, this dial can be used as a complement to the main dial (to set the aperture while the main dial is used to set shutter speed in Manual mode, for example). If desired, it can also be used for tasks that would normally require an adjustment of the main dial (such as setting the aperture in Bulb mode). In that case, it is a matter of convenience as to which dial is used. Only the quick control dial, however, is able to adjust the flash exposure compensation value (while the flash exposure compensation button is pressed).

The quick control dial has its own On/Off switch (labeled with an "I" and "O") located above it on the camera back. This switch is large and can be easily manipulated while you hold the camera to your eye. Turn it to "O" to deactivate the quick control dial and prevent inadvertent changes of exposure, shutter speed, or aperture. Turn it to "I" to activate the dial only when needed.

### Shutter Button

The shutter button is located directly in front of the main dial in a small recess and is normally activated with the right forefinger as well. Of course, it is also possible to move the main dial with the forefinger and press the shutter button with the middle finger.

It has two stages of operation. Pressing the button halfway down activates the autofocus and metering systems. It also locks focus (in One-Shot AF mode only). Pressing the button all the way down releases the shutter and makes the exposure.

### Other Camera Controls and Their Uses

***Top left:*** Three function selector buttons are provided on the upper left side of the body. These are used to set the exposure mode, autofocus mode, metering mode, or flash exposure compensation value. Appropriate adjustments are then made with the main dial, which is located just behind the shutter release button on the top of the camera. (The quick control dial on the camera back can be used in special cases.)

The three selector buttons can be pressed individually or in sets of two. To change the exposure mode, press the **shooting mode selector** (marked "MODE") while at the same time rotating the main dial. The following modes are available in sequence: Aperture-Priority AE ("Av"), Depth-of-Field AE ("DEP"), Manual exposure ("M"), Shutter-Priority AE ("Tv"), Bulb ("buLb"), and Intelligent Program AE ("P"). The cycle is repeated as the dial is rotated.

The **AF mode selector** (marked "AF") is used to select the automatic focus mode. While pressing the AF mode selector, turn the main dial to select the desired AF mode: autofocus with focus priority ("ONE SHOT") for stationary subjects, or shutter release priority ("AI SERVO") for continuous focus of moving subjects. This button will not function if manual focus is selected on the lens. See the *Focus* chapter for more information.

The third button has dual functions as the **metering mode selector** and **flash exposure compensation button.** It is marked with two symbols, one representing metering modes and the other, flash exposure compensation. When this button is pressed and the main dial is turned, you can select the metering mode from a number of options: 16-zone evaluative, partial, and fine spot metering. (Center-weighted average metering is also available by using Custom Function 8, setting 1. However, the evaluative metering symbol will appear in the camera's LCD panel.)

When this button is pressed and the quick control dial is turned, you can enter flash exposure compensation values, which will appear on the LCD panel.

By pressing this button and the AF mode selector while simultaneously turning the main dial, the film speed (ISO) can be changed. Pressing it with the MODE button while turning the main dial allows you to select the number of multiple exposures you wish to take (a maximum of nine) on one frame of film.

The crossed circle engraved on the camera behind the pre-selection buttons is the **film plane indicator,** identifying the exact position of the film plane. This is important when the precise distance from lens to film must be determined, such as in extreme close-up photography when a bellows is used. Incidentally, all distance data on the lenses relate to the film plane.

***Top right:*** Behind the shutter button and main dial are two control buttons, located on the top right of the body. In the area near the right forefinger is the **LCD panel illumination button,** marked with a light-bulb symbol. When this button is pressed, the LCD panel lights up for approximately six seconds to assist you in making camera settings in dimly lit locations. The blue light illuminates the LCD panel quite well but does not influence exposure readings. In a pinch, you could use it to read the film speed on a roll of film, though. To turn the light off before the six-second duration expires, press the button again. To extend the length of time the LCD is illuminated, press any function button (such as the shooting mode, metering mode, or AF mode selector) while the LCD is still lit. The light will turn off automatically approximately two seconds after an exposure has been made.

Next to the LCD illumination button is the **exposure compensation button,** marked with a +/- symbol. After this is pressed, the main dial can be used to enter an exposure compensation value. The surface of this button is flush with the body, making it somewhat difficult to use. This is not a flaw in the design, but intentionally positioned. Its placement prevents you from accidentally setting an exposure compensation factor, yielding unexpectedly poor results.

***Front:*** On the front of the camera are two, rather large buttons. The one to the left of the lens is the **lens release button.** It must be pressed in to remove the lens. The other, to the right of the lens, is the **depth-of-field preview button,** which stops the lens down to the shooting aperture. This allows you to view the image's range of apparent focus before the photo is made. Exposure settings lock when the depth-of-field preview button is pressed in. Also, this button will not operate while the camera is autofocusing.

***Back:*** Two additional buttons are on the top right side of the camera back. Use your right thumb to press the **autoexposure lock button,** which is marked with a star (*). This allows you to lock an exposure setting separatetly from the autofocus operation. See page 67 for more information about AE lock.

To its right is the **focusing point selector,** indicated by five rectangular dots surrounded by a larger rectangle. When this button is pressed, the main dial is used to activate one specific autofocus sensor (focusing point) or all five sensors, which lets the camera's autofocus system select the appropriate focusing point. The selected sensor/s will be illuminated in red in the viewfinder and will also be displayed on the camera's LCD panel for six seconds, or until the shutter release is pressed partway. See the *Focus* chapter for more information.

The function of these two buttons can be changed by activating the Custom Function features. See the *Custom Function* chapter for more information.

The **film rewind button** is located at the center bottom of the camera's back and is designated with a cassette symbol. It is used when you need to rewind the film before reaching the end of the roll.

***Right side:*** The camera has a number of adjustment buttons that are used infrequently. They are located under a spring-loaded "palm door" on the right side of the camera. This configuration makes the EOS-1N less complex and easier to handle, despite its many advanced technical features.

The uppermost button under the door is the **Custom Function set button** ("CF"), which offers 14 individual functions. When used in conjunction with the main dial, you can adjust your EOS-1N to your own preferences. Also, this button is slightly recessed to prevent changing a preferred setting accidentally.

The gray button with a drawing of a battery beneath it is the **battery check button.** Pressing it will cause the battery's status to be displayed on the LCD panel. See page 14 for more information.

Select the drive mode or the self-timer duration by pressing the blue **film winding mode selector** (marked "DRIVE") and then turning the main dial. The selected film advance mode (single-frame or continuous advance) or self-timer duration (10 or 2 seconds) will be displayed in the blue-framed window on the LCD panel. See page 16 for more information about drive modes and page 96 for more on self-timer operation.

By pressing the gray battery check and blue film winding mode buttons simultaneously, you can then use the main dial to select automatic exposure bracketing in 1/3 stops, up to a maximum of +/- 3 EV. You have six seconds after pressing the button (or pair of buttons) to make your motor drive and/or autoexposure bracketing selections. See page 69 for more on autoexposure bracketing.

The white button inside the palm door is the **clear button** (marked "CLEAR"). This is used to return your EOS-1N to its default settings. The shooting mode will default to Program AE, autofocus mode will default to One-Shot AF, metering mode will default to 16-zone evaluative metering, and the drive mode will default to single exposure (single-frame film advance). Custom Functions set will not be affected, however. This button is useful for times when you have made all kinds of adjustments and no longer remember what you've done!

***Note:*** If you have set Custom Function 8, setting 1 for center-weighted average metering and the metering mode is set to either partial or spot metering, the metering mode will not be affected when the clear button is pressed.

To reset all Custom Functions to their default (0) settings, press the Custom Function set button and then press the clear button.

***Additional camera controls:*** Hidden on the sides of the body behind tiny screwed-on covers are a **remote control socket** (right) and a standard **PC terminal** (left). A thumb's width above the PC terminal is the **back cover latch.** To prevent anyone from accidentally opening the back and ruining the film in the camera, the **back**

**cover lock release** (a button) and the back cover latch (a slide switch) must be manipulated at the same time. With a little practice, it is possible to do this with one finger.

The last two operating controls to be mentioned are the eyepiece shutter lever and the dioptric adjustment dial. The **eyepiece shutter lever,** located to the right of the eyepiece, operates an eyepiece blind and is visible even when the eyecup is attached. This prevents extraneous light from entering through the eyepiece when the camera is not positioned at the eye (for instance, when it is mounted on a tripod). The **dioptric adjustment dial** is a small wheel that is only visible when the eyecup is removed. It is used to adjust the eyepiece to compensate for imperfect vision. This allows most people with eyeglasses to take pictures without wearing them. See pages 18 and 20 for more information about these two controls.

## Information Displays

Of course, it is possible to let the EOS-1N work fully automatically all the time and achieve good results. As a rule, however, it is important to know what the camera is doing. For this, the EOS-1N offers ample information.

### Viewfinder Display

The most important information for the photographer is how the subject relates to the rest of the picture. The EOS-1N's viewfinder shows nearly 100% of the slide or negative area and is superior in this respect to most cameras on the market.

The information in the viewfinder is backlit to enhance visibility in all conditions. This does not interfere with the view of the image, though. Along the bottom of the viewfinder at the very left, an "M" appears on the LCD when the camera is set for Manual exposure mode. To the right of the Manual exposure indicator is a star (*). When the star is lit, AE lock is activated; when it blinks, an autoexposure bracketing series has not yet been completed.

Large and clearly legible LED numbers indicating shutter speed and aperture appear in the center of the LCD panel at the base of the viewfinder. If these numbers blink, it is a warning of impending exposure error. The maximum aperture and/or the maximum

**The EOS-1N's viewfinder displays information clearly, offering all you need to know to make an exposure without having to remove your eye from the eyepiece.**

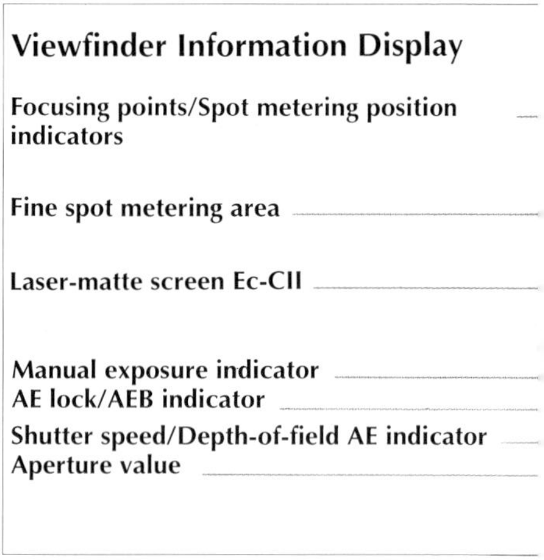

## Viewfinder Information Display

**Focusing points/Spot metering position indicators**

**Fine spot metering area**

**Laser-matte screen Ec-CII**

**Manual exposure indicator**
**AE lock/AEB indicator**
**Shutter speed/Depth-of-field AE indicator**
**Aperture value**

shutter speed will blink to warn you of potential underexposure; the minimum aperture and/or minimum shutter speed will blink to warn you of potential overexposure.

To the right of the aperture display is a +/- symbol indicating exposure compensation. This symbol appears when either ambient light or flash exposure compensation settings are set. The lightning-bolt icon (called the "flash charge completion indicator") to the right of the exposure compensation symbol lights up when a dedicated flash unit is ready to fire.

And farther to the right is the in-focus indicator, a large, green, LED dot. If the dot is lit continuously and the camera is in One-Shot AF mode, it indicates that automatic focus has been achieved. If the dot is blinking, then focusing cannot take place. In AI Servo AF mode this display does not light. For more information on focusing, see the *Focus* chapter.

The exposure level scale running vertically down the right side of the viewfinder display expands on the exposure displays on the LCD panel and makes detailed data available to the photographer. The scale consists of a series of small squares and slightly larger rectangles. Each square corresponds to 1/3 stop or EV (Exposure Value), while each rectangle represents 1 stop or EV. The triangle in the center of the scale (correct exposure indicator) represents "0," or correct exposure. One or two arrows will light to the right of the scale. If an arrow points to the triangle, exposure will be

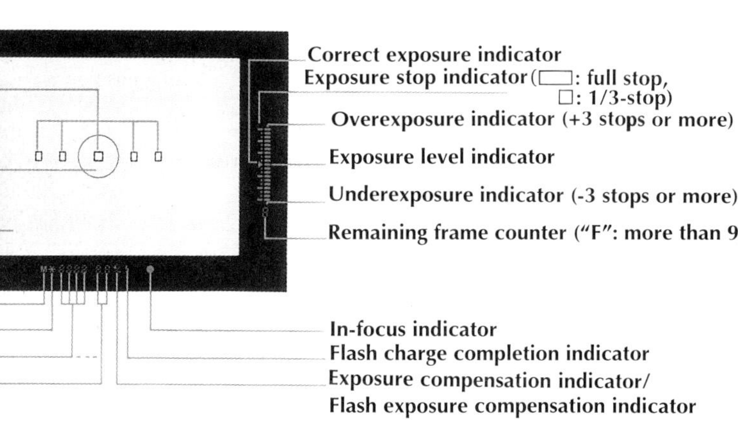


correct. Arrows pointing at the squares or rectangles on the scale indicate improper exposure, as well as the extent of the error. When the AE lock button is pressed, the exposure level scale can help you determine the range of contrast in a scene. After a meter

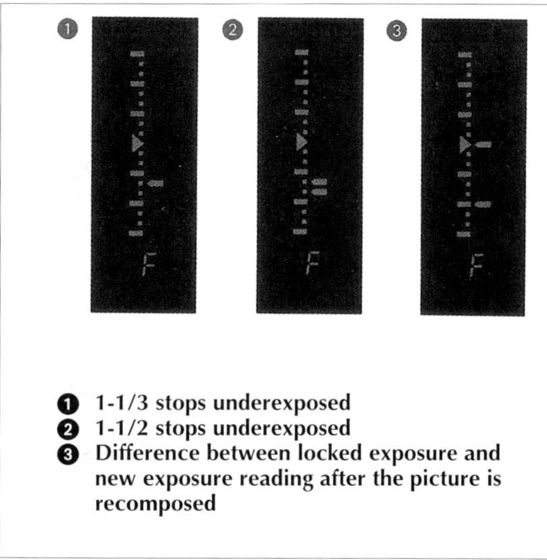

❶ 1-1/3 stops underexposed
❷ 1-1/2 stops underexposed
❸ Difference between locked exposure and new exposure reading after the picture is recomposed

**The exposure level scale to the right of the viewfinder offers detailed information about underexposure, overexposure, or the difference between two spot metering readings. The triangular index represents "0," or correct exposure.**

reading is locked in and the photo recomposed, a second arrow will indicate the degree of difference between the current exposure value and the set value.

Above and below the exposure level scale are arrows that light and point up or down when over- or underexposure (respectively) of more than 3 EV is expected or when a meter reading deviates from the stored reading to that extent.

Beneath the exposure level scale is a number that counts the last nine frames of a roll of film so that you can prepare for the upcoming change of film. (This function works only with DX-coded film.) If more than nine shots remain in the roll, an "F" will be displayed in this location instead of a number.

### LCD Panel

The second source of information is the LCD panel on top of the camera. The LCD panel provides only the information pertinent to the current settings, despite the multitude of possible data displays. Among the information that can be displayed are: shooting mode, shutter speed, film speed, Custom Function setting, focusing point, AF mode, film winding mode, battery check, frame counter, flash exposure compensation, metering modes, aperture, and much, much more. With such a large, diverse amount of information included on this camera's LCD, we felt it would be more useful to refer to it when it is pertinent to various functions described throughout this book. Therefore, please refer to the illustration on page 35 as well as related explanations to better understand the data displayed on the LCD panel.

The LCD panel can be illuminated for better legibility by pressing the LCD panel illumination button (light-bulb symbol). The light will go off six seconds after the illumination button has been pressed or two seconds after the shutter button is pressed.

## Motor Drive

The EOS-1N's motor drive is capable of advancing the film one frame at a time or continuously. You can switch between single-frame or continuous advance modes by turning the main switch to "A" (which turns the camera on), opening the palm door on the right side of the camera, and pressing the blue film winding mode

## LCD Panel Display

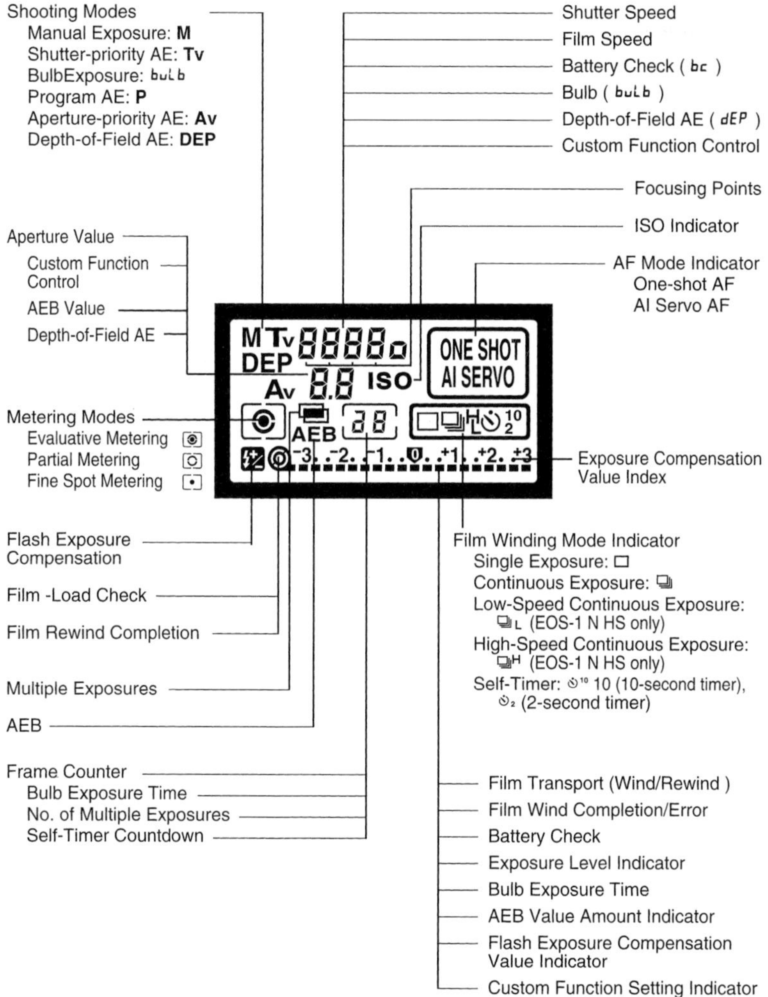


**Though this diagram shows most of the information that could be displayed on the LCD panel, in fact, only information relevant to the current exposure will be displayed on your camera's LCD.**

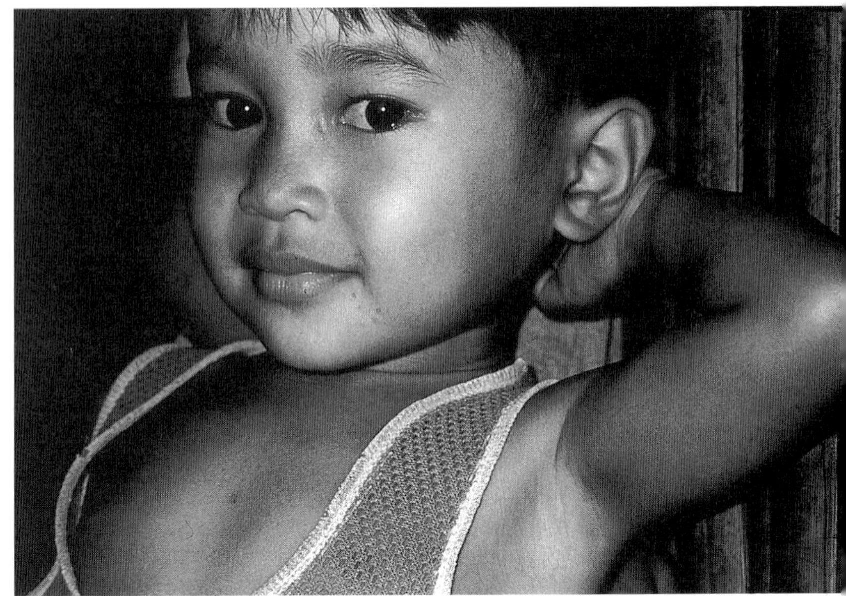

**The LCD illuminator is a useful feature when making flash exposures in a dark room.**

selector (DRIVE). Next, rotate the main dial until the appropriate symbol—a single rectangle (single-frame advance) or several overlapping rectangles (continuous advance)—is displayed in the blue-framed window of the LCD panel.

In single-frame advance mode the motor advances by one frame after the shutter button is pressed down completely, making one exposure. (If you hold the shutter button down in One-Shot AF mode with evaluative metering, the focus and exposure values will remain in memory, provided you have not changed the default settings by using Custom Function 4!)

In continuous advance mode the motor works at a maximum frequency of 3 frames per second (fps), and will continue to make exposures as long as the shutter button remains depressed. The shutter speed and the AF mode determine the exact frequency. Shutter speeds longer than 1/250 second slow down the motor, which must wait until the exposure has been completed. In AI Servo AF mode, the EOS-1N automatically resets the focus for

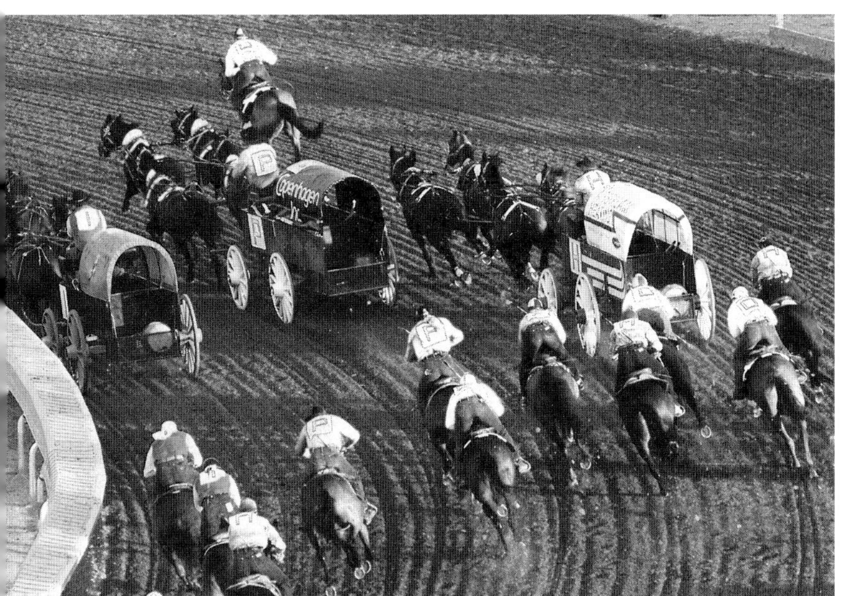

**To shoot fast-paced action like these galloping horses, use continuous film advance mode so you won't miss the definitive moment when your horse pulls ahead. Photo by Peter K. Burian.**

each exposure to the portion of the subject that is captured by the active metering area. This can result in exposing fewer than 3 fps. Should 3 fps not be fast enough, you can modify your EOS-1N to operate faster using the Power Drive Booster E1, which can increase film transport up to 6 fps. For more information, see the *Accessories* chapter.

# EOS-1N Focusing System

Of course some out-of-focus pictures are considered to be good pictures. However the proverb "a chain is only as strong as its weakest link" still holds true. As a rule, we expect a successful photo to be in focus. And more lies behind this assumption than you might think. Whether a picture appears "sharp" or "not sharp" is a function of many factors, not the least of which is the mechanics of focusing through changing the distance between the lens and the film plane or the lens and the subject. With the EOS-1N, you can focus manually or use its autofocus function.

In addition to focusing, there are other aspects affecting the apparent sharpness of an image. The resolving power, or the ability of the lens and the film to retain separation between neighboring subject elements, affects the appearance of sharpness. Both the lens' and film's capacity to record contrast determine whether tones are reproduced correctly; images with poor contrast appear less sharp. The level of sharpness that the lens and film are able to reproduce determines whether the transition between tones is clearly delineated or blended softly at the edges. The grain structure (granularity) of the film determines whether surfaces that are uniformly smooth can be reproduced accurately or whether they will appear to be grainy. (Actual grain can be found only in black-and-white films where large silver salt crystals are noticeable. The "grain" exhibited by color films is formed by small dye clouds deposited on the silver salt crystals during development.)

The construction of Canon lenses assures that the many possible optical aberrations (such as chromatic and spherical aberration, coma, or field curvature) do not affect the lenses' reproduction quality. To do this, engineers have combined lens elements in a number of different ways. Each element is constructed with individualized specifications, depending upon the function it serves in the lens assembly. The elements can be made with different cross-sections, from different types of glass or other special materials such as "grown" crystals, or with different radii of curvature—some even deviating from the conventional spherical design (these are known as aspherical lenses).

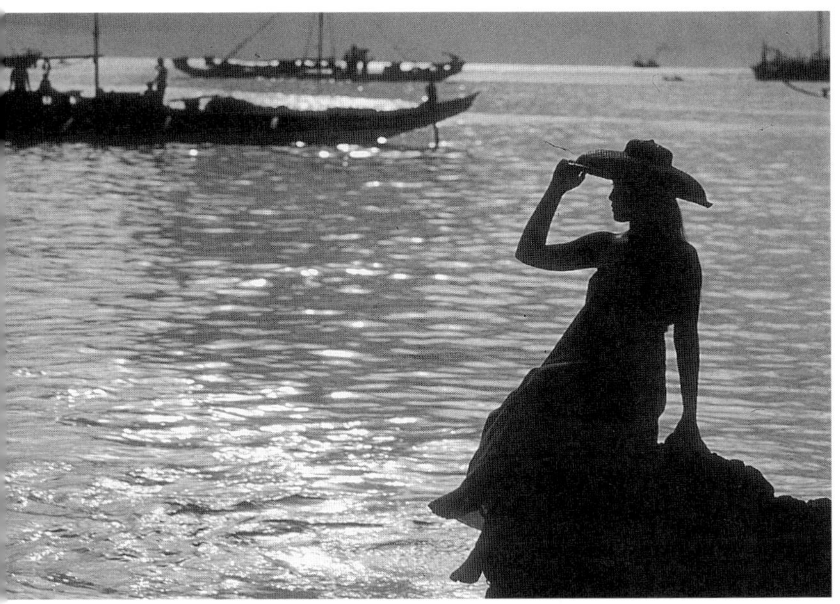

**There was enough ambient light in this scene to give the woman's dress adequate contrast for the camera's AF system to focus on. After focus was achieved, the photographer underexposed the image slightly to produce a silhouette without defining the dress' detail.**

Movement of the camera (camera shake) during exposure results in the loss of sharpness. A fast shutter speed or a stable tripod will prevent this problem. Movement by the subject or panning the camera during exposure results in "motion blur," so-called because it causes the image to be streaked or blurred. A fast shutter speed will help counteract this effect, although using a tripod and slow shutter speed can produce an artistic effect.

In any case, we suggest that other than taking full advantage of the sophisticated focus system of the EOS-1N, you should use a good lens, a sturdy tripod, and a reliable photofinisher to do justice to your images!

## Autofocus Sensors

The EOS-1N camera has five separate autofocus sensing areas. This makes it easier for the photographer to control what part of the scene is actually in focus. The heart of the EOS-1N's autofocus is the new "Multi-BASIS" (Base-Stored Image Sensor), which consists of five individual autofocus areas aligned horizontally along a central axis. The sensors are located in a row on the bottom of the mirror chamber, where they receive light reflected by a secondary mirror. This mirror is mounted on the back of the main mirror, which allows a small amount of light to pass through its semi-silvered surface. This is not noticeable in the viewfinder.

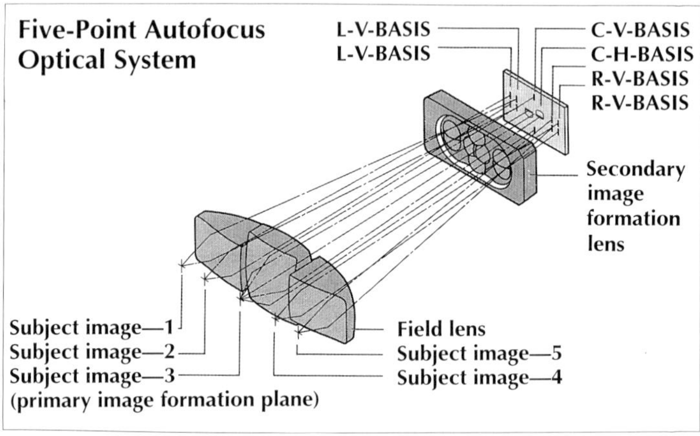


**The EOS-1N features a wide-area autofocus system with a Multi-Base-Stored Image Sensor (Multi-BASIS), five focusing sensors, and TTL cross-type secondary image registration to create high-precision focus.**

Each of the four outer autofocus areas is associated with a vertically arranged CCD array. These sensors respond to horizontal lines of contrast. This is useful for landscape shots because the horizon line can be used for focusing. As long as a lens has an aperture of f/5.6 or larger, these four outer sensors will activate. Since there are no EF lenses slower than f/5.6, this is generally not a problem. However, adding a tele-extender reduces the effective aperture of a lens by one to two stops. If the maximum effective aperture is smaller than f/5.6, the autofocus sensors will not receive enough light to function.

The central autofocus area has a cross-type sensor featuring horizontal and vertical axes, or components. The main benefit of a cross-type sensor compared to a conventional single-axis sensor is its superior subject recognition capability. This is especially useful in action photography using predictive autofocus, when consistent, reliable data is crucial for maximum performance.

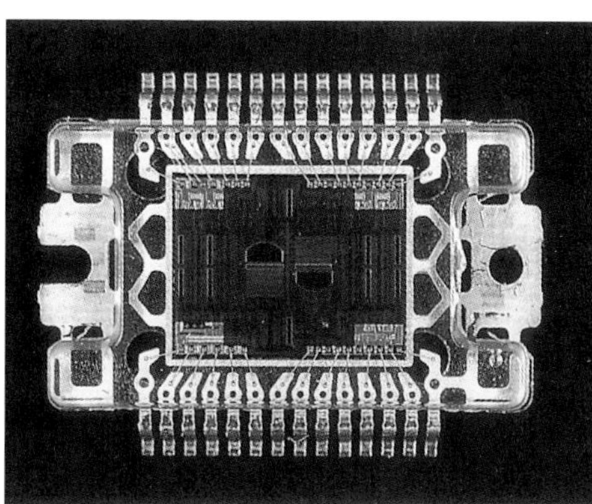

**The Multi-Base-Stored Image Sensor (BASIS). Note the cross-type CCD sensor in the center and the CCDs located to either side of it.**

The horizontal component of the EOS-1N's central autofocus sensor is used for EF lenses with maximum apertures as small as f/5.6, but unlike most other EOS cameras with cross-type sensors, the vertical component of the central sensor is activated with EF lenses whose maximum aperture is f/2.8 or larger. Because the base-length of the vertical component is much wider than the base-length of the horizontal component, focusing precision is improved by as much as three times when using fast lenses. In other words, though either component is capable of setting the focus within a tolerance determined by depth of focus, the vertical component is approximately 67% more accurate than the horizontal component.

## Autofocus Modes

The EOS-1N features two different AF modes: One-Shot AF and AI Servo AF. Under close scrutiny, however, there is a third option:

AI Servo with Focus Prediction Control. But this mode occurs automatically, without letting you know! Selecting the EOS-1N's AF mode is extraordinarily easy, provided you stick to the basic functions. Simply press the AF selection button and rotate the main dial until either "One-Shot" or "AI Servo" is displayed in the AF window on the LCD monitor.

By combining the selected AF mode with different exposure metering modes (16-zone evaluative, center-weighted average, partial, or fine spot), film winding options (single or continuous advance), and the three Custom Function 4 settings, many different options are available. You can initiate automatic focusing, store focusing and exposure metering values in memory, and obtain information regarding the difference between stored and current exposure values.

**One-Shot Autofocus**

One-Shot AF mode's distinguishing characteristic is focus priority—an exposure cannot be made until focus has been achieved. In conjunction with this, the focus value is stored (i.e., focus is locked) until the exposure is taken if you maintain pressure on the shutter button. Because of this, if the camera or subject moves after focusing and before you have taken the exposure, your shots may be out of focus despite focus priority.

When a fast lens is used on the EOS-1N, the obvious choice of focusing point is the central one, with its more versatile cross-type sensor. The photographer needs only to lock the focus and recompose the image as desired, making certain that the camera-to-subject distance doesn't change. Of course, it is possible to use any of the five focusing points thanks to the manual or automatic focusing point selection option.

Which subjects are best shot in One-Shot AF mode? Subjects that don't move! Some EOS-1N owners will work almost exclusively in One-Shot AF mode, photographing architecture, flowers, landscapes, still lifes, or other static subjects. Usually in these cases single-frame advance is used, unless a series of pictures is to be taken in rapid succession. When shooting a series in One-Shot AF mode (using continuous advance mode), the focus distance setting for the first frame will be maintained for all subsequent shots.

When One-Shot AF is used with continuous advance, the EOS-1N

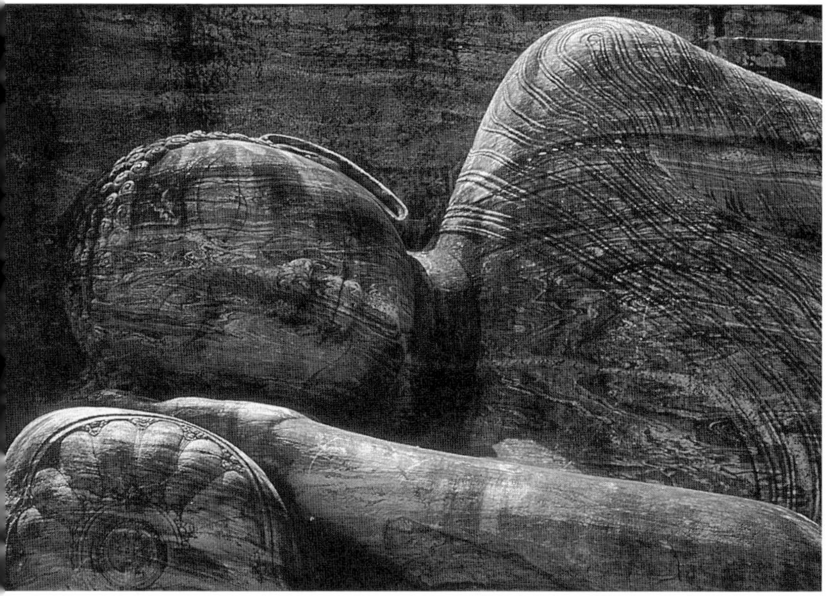

**Photographers who shoot still lifes, architecture, and other stationary subjects will appreciate the EOS-1N's One-Shot AF mode.**

can take approximately 3 frames per second (fps). With the Power Drive Booster E1 attached, it can take 3 fps when set on low ("L") and up to 6 fps when set on high ("H").

**AI Servo Autofocus**

In this mode when the shutter button is pressed partway, the lens readjusts continuously to focus on whatever lies within the active focusing area. Pressing the shutter button will not lock focus. Therefore, if the shooting distance changes between the time the AF system is activated and the exposure is made, focus will be readjusted. (Exposure is determined just before the exposure is made.) Of course, changes in distance must not occur too quickly because the autofocus might not be able to adjust fast enough and blurry pictures could result. Also, if you are taking exposures faster than the camera can adjust the focus, your pictures will not be sharp.

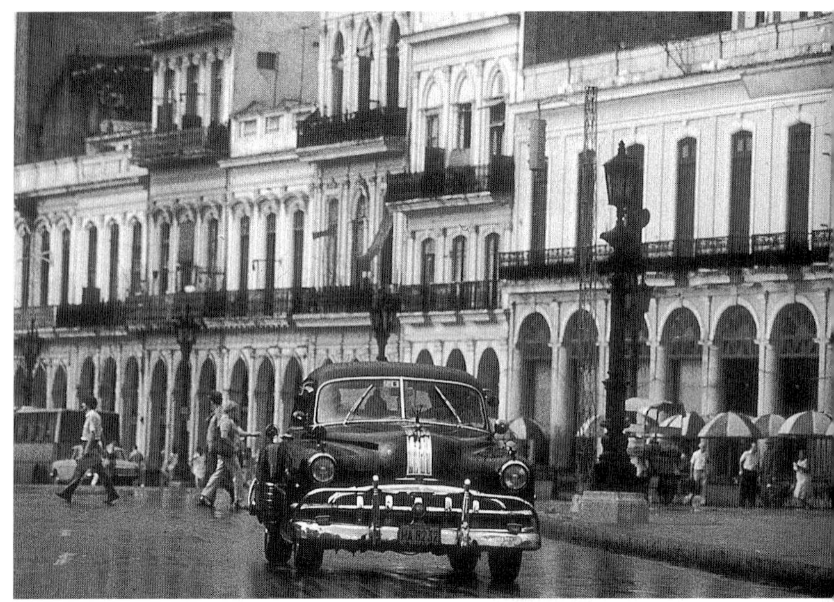

**Subjects moving toward the camera are kept in focus with AI Servo AF mode.**

AI Servo autofocus mode should be used for all types of moving subjects: children playing, studio models, sports competitors, wildlife. AI Servo is frequently used in combination with continuous advance mode for making a series.

In AI Servo mode using Custom Function 4, setting 1 (F-4, 1), automatic focusing is activated by pressing the AE lock button (*), and exposure will lock when the shutter button is pressed partway down. When setting F-4, 2 is used, autofocus is active until the AE lock button (*) is pressed, at which time focus locks. Those who have good reflexes can select the focusing point manually using the quick control dial when Custom Function 11, setting 2 is set. (The active focusing point will light red in the viewfinder.) Using this technique, the subject can be tracked across the image area by changing the focusing point rather than by panning the camera itself. If spot metering is activated and Custom Function 13, setting 1 is selected, the exposure will be adjusted for the subject that falls within the selected focusing point.

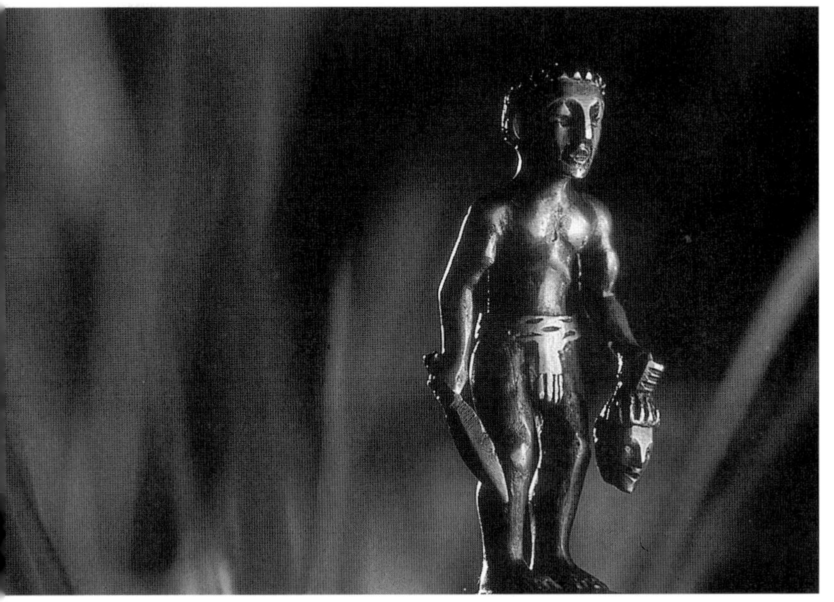

**Custom Function 4, setting 1 is a good solution when you need to lock exposure and focus settings separately.**

## AI Servo with Focus Prediction Control

With the EOS-1N, as with any camera, a brief moment passes between the time the shutter button is pressed and the exposure is actually made. In this moment the aperture is stopped down, the mirror tilted up, and the first shutter curtain set in motion. In this brief moment a moving subject can leave the focusing point, causing the picture to be out of focus. To prevent this, the EOS-1N is capable of preliminary automatic focus computation, which Canon calls "Focus Prediction Control." This feature calculates where a subject will be at the moment of exposure (provided it is moving at a uniform speed and not changing direction) and adjusts the focus accordingly, coordinating focus and exposure with the subject's location.

If automatic focusing point selection mode is set, the camera's AF sensors can follow the subject across the image area. (Press the focusing point selector and turn the main dial until all five focusing point boxes glow red in the LCD.) The center focusing

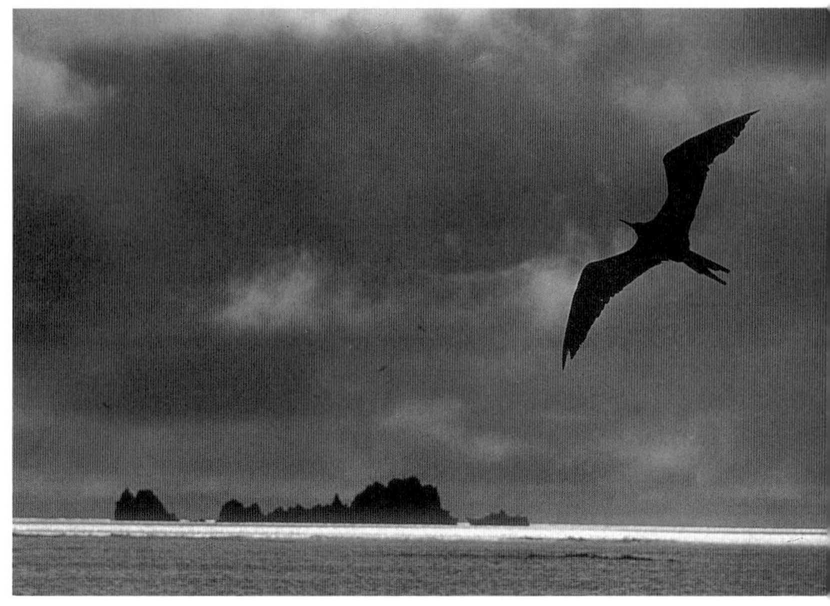

**The EOS-1N's automatic focusing point selection and Focus Prediction Control features are helpful with subjects that are moving across your field of view.**

area must be directed at the main subject when focus is initially adjusted. If the subject later moves to another focusing point, the automatic system will follow it, and both the focusing point and the focus itself will be readjusted. This is true for motion directed both toward the camera as well as away from it.

If evaluative metering has been selected, the exposure will be adjusted to the main subject while also assessing the background in determining the correct exposure value. If you are taking a series and you want the exposure to remain constant while the main subject moves before a background of varying brightness, it is best to leave focusing to the automatic system and set the exposure manually for the entire series. This prevents changes in exposure from one frame to the next.

In continuous advance mode, focus tracking and Focus Prediction Control are the two prerequisites for making successful high-speed exposure series. The EOS-1N in AI Servo AF mode can take

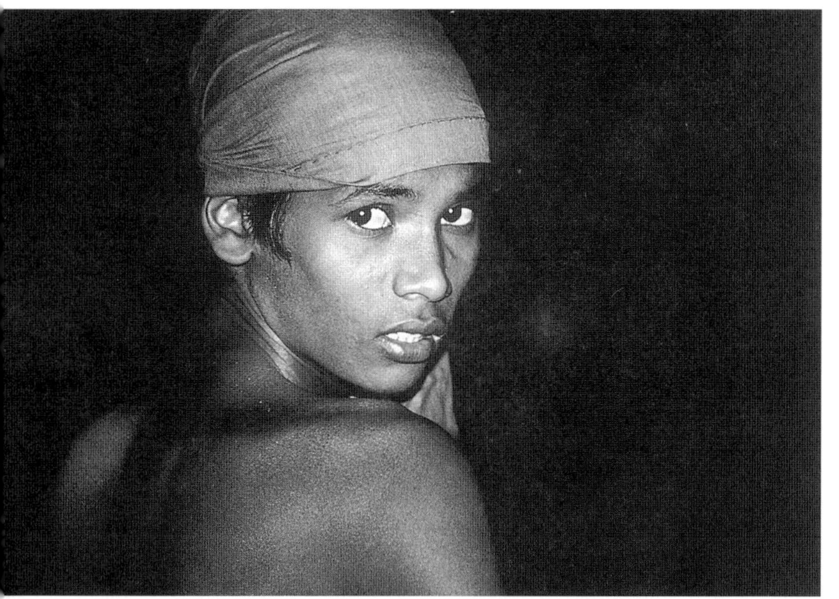

**The EOS-1N's five-point autofocus system allows you to choose the area of the frame in which autofocus will be active. This advanced system is very useful for shooting off-center subjects without having to recompose the photograph.**

about 2 fps. With the Power Drive Booster E1 attached, the EOS-1N in AI Servo AF can take approximately 2.5 fps set at low (L) and up to 5 fps at high (H) with continuously adjusted focus and, if required, Focus Prediction Control.

## Autofocus Area Selection

Yes, it is nice that the EOS-1N offers the photographer the opportunity to work with five autofocus areas (or focusing points), however this does not mean that you must switch continually from one focusing point to another. Your subject matter should be the determining factor in selecting the appropriate focusing point.

### Manual Focusing Point Selection

To select an autofocus area manually, first press the focusing point

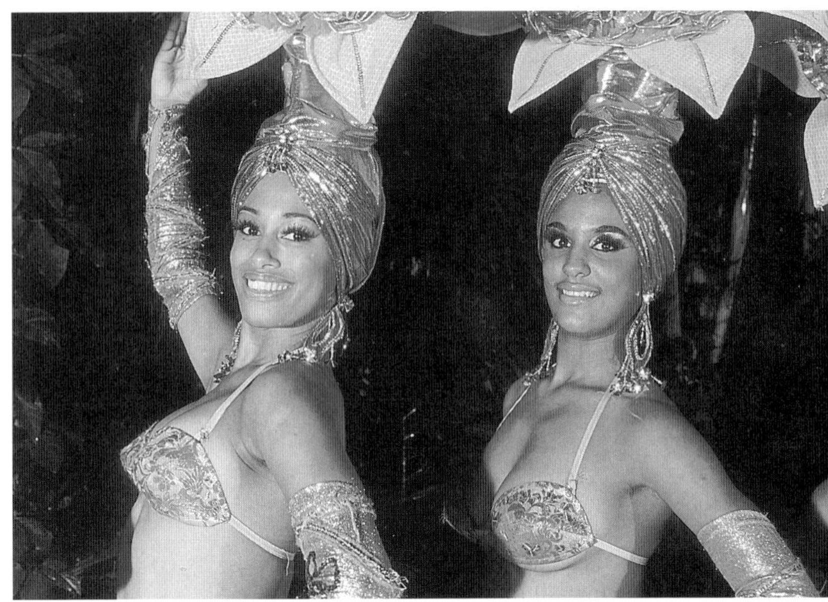

**When the camera is set to automatic focusing point selection, its five-point AF system evaluates the scene and opts to focus on the closest target, the dancers.**

selector (the button farthest right near the top of the camera back). The last focusing point selected will be displayed as a box on the LCD panel, or, if automatic autofocus area selection was the last to be active, all five boxes will be displayed. Now rotate the main dial until the desired focusing point is displayed. In the viewfinder, the focusing point you have chosen will be lit in red. The focusing point will be set after six seconds elapse without it being changed or as soon as the shutter button is pressed halfway.

**Automatic Focusing Point Selection**

If you activate all five focusing points, the choice of which one to activate is left up to the camera. In One-Shot AF mode, the automatic system compares the distances of the areas captured by the five AF sensors and focuses on the one closest to the camera.

In AI Servo AF mode, you must first aim the center focusing point at the main subject. If the subject is in motion, the focus will then be adjusted automatically as the subject's position changes to a new AF area. Focus Prediction Control assesses a moving subject's speed and direction to determine where it will be at the instant of exposure. If continuous advance mode is active, the first exposure in the series will be made with shutter release priority, meaning that the picture will be taken whether or not focus is achieved. Focus takes priority for subsequent exposures in continuous advance mode.

**AF Custom Function Settings**

A focusing point can also be selected in a variety of ways by choosing Custom Function 11. When set on F-11, 0, the normal selection method (pressing the focusing point selector and turning the main dial) is active. Using settings F-11, 1 and F-11, 2, a focusing point can be selected by pressing the exposure compensation button and turning the main dial. In both cases the focusing point selector and main dial are used to enter exposure compensation factors.

In F-11, 2, you can use the quick control dial to select the focusing point. However, if this option is chosen, the focusing point display will not appear on the LCD panel. The selected focusing point can instead be seen glowing red in the viewfinder. It therefore makes sense to use the quick control dial to select the focusing point only while the camera is at your eye and the exposure meter is activated (by pressing the shutter button partway). Furthermore, the quick control dial can be used to select the focusing point and track the subject when AI Servo is active in continuous advance mode.

**Deciding Which Focusing Point to Choose**

For most exposures taken with One-Shot autofocus mode, using the central focusing point is sufficient. If high-speed lenses are used, this focusing point is recommended because the AF sensor's vertical component responds best to lenses with maximum apertures of f/2.8 to f/1.

If the central focusing point is selected, you can initiate focus on the portion of the subject that you want to be sharp by pressing the shutter button halfway. You can lock the focus by maintaining pressure on the shutter button, then compose the image as you like. Finally, fully depress the shutter button to take the picture.

Although it is a little cumbersome to describe, in actual practice this procedure happens very fast and quite reliably.

Activating one of the other four focusing points offers a significant advantage only when the most important element of the subject is located precisely at that particular point. For example, if you are taking a portrait of a person standing and are holding your camera in a vertical position, you would want to select the uppermost focusing point because the central focusing point would be at the person's waist. A look through the viewfinder will indicate whether it is ever worthwhile to switch to one of the outer focusing points.

Automatic focusing point selection is the best choice if moving subjects must be rendered sharply in your pictures. The automatic focusing point selection feature is often used in conjunction with AI Servo autofocus mode because focus is adjusted continuously, taking into account the subject's movement between the time the shutter is triggered and the time the shutter cycle is completed.

### Focusing Point Illumination

In most instances, the active focusing point/s will flash red in the viewfinder once focus has been achieved. In One-Shot AF, whether automatic focusing point selection or manual selection is used, the active focusing area/s will flash red. And, if a focusing point has been manually selected in AI Servo mode, it will also glow red once the subject is in focus. But in AI Servo AF mode with automatic focusing point selection, the active focusing point/s will not light up. If you find these flashing red frames annoying, you can deactivate them by choosing Custom Function 10, setting 1.

# Exposure Metering

## Exposure Values

The combination of shutter speed and aperture required for correct exposure is determined by two factors: the film's sensitivity (ISO rating, or film speed) and the light reflected by the subject or scene being photographed. The ISO rating is an indication of a film's sensitivity to light. The higher the film speed, the more sensitive the film, and the less light is required for exposure. Therefore, all things being equal, film with an ISO rating of 400 requires less light for exposure than an ISO 50 film.

The subject or scene, in turn, exhibits a certain brightness. In general, a smaller aperture and a faster shutter speed would be used to expose the same scene with ISO 1000 film compared to those used when using ISO 50 film. Both factors can be expressed in one value—the Exposure Value (EV).

For each exposure value, many different shutter speed and aperture settings can be combined to yield an equivalent exposure. This means that by increasing one factor by one increment and decreasing the other by the same amount, exactly the same exposure (or quantity of light striking the film) will be maintained. As you increase the aperture size by one stop (e.g., from f/16 to f/11) and halve the exposure time (e.g., from 1/30 second to 1/60 second), the overall exposure remains the same. Conversely, doubling the exposure time and decreasing the aperture size by one stop maintains equivalent exposure. Exactly the same amount of light will expose the film as before.

## Metering

Exposure metering determines the combination of shutter speed and aperture that is correct for the film's sensitivity and the subject's brightness. To achieve this, the EOS-1N is equipped with a silicon photocell that converts light to power, which is in turn measured by an amplifier circuit. The EOS-1N's silicon photocell is sensitive enough to respond when an exposure value of barely 0 is registered using 16-zone evaluative or partial metering (using ISO 100 film with a shutter speed of 2 seconds and an aperture of f/1.4). In these two metering systems, the maximum brightness level that can be metered is EV 20. However, when the camera is set to fine spot metering, only a small portion of the silicon cell is used. Therefore the metering range begins at EV 3, but still extends to EV 20.

The EOS-1N's exposure meter is calibrated to calculate exposure for a subject of 18% reflectance. Manufacturers have made this 18% reflectance the standard because it is the average reflectance of most scenes. The average scene is composed of equal portions of dark and light tones that average out to middle, or 18%, gray. Hence, the exposure meter works well in most instances. The shutter speed-aperture combinations determined by the exposure meter will assure that a middle gray subject will be reproduced as middle gray by the film.

Problems arise when the subject is predominantly composed of extremely light or extremely dark details (illuminated buildings at night or backlit subjects, for instance) or when the subject is almost entirely very dark (a black cat on a black velvet cushion) or very light (a bride with white flowers in front of a white wall). Erroneously exposed pictures frequently result because the meter calibration is set to render the subject as 18% gray. If the subject is mostly light-colored, added (plus) exposure will produce a better result. Without this addition, the subject will be rendered as middle gray. If the subject is extremely dark, less (minus) exposure will prevent the subject from being washed out. See page 63 for more information on exposure compensation.

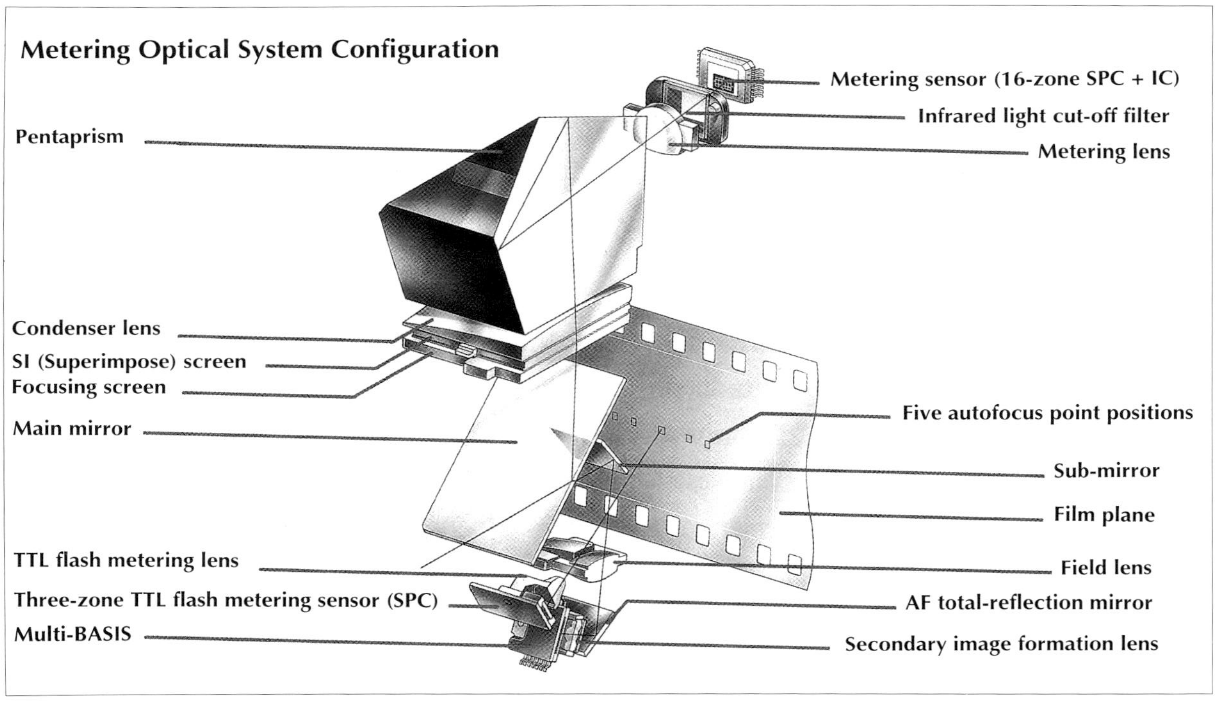


The metering system for focus, exposure, and flash exposure.

## Metering Modes

### 16-Zone Evaluative Metering

The EOS-1N features evaluative metering covering 16 metering zones. By looking at the metering array you can see that each of the five focusing points is associated with a metering zone, that four large L-shaped zones surround the outer edge of the metering area, and that there are no metering areas along the image's edge.

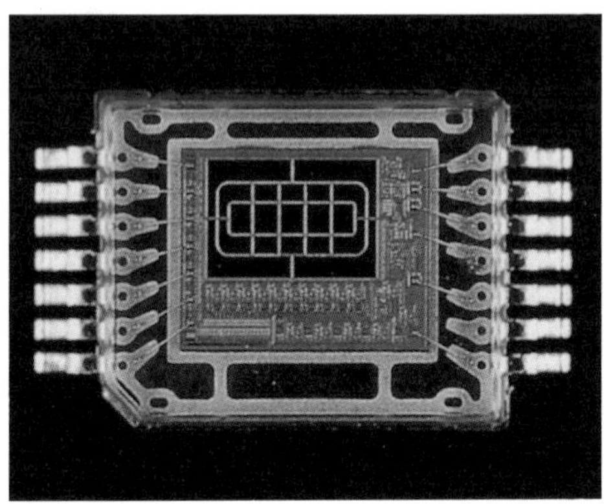

**The heart of the camera's metering system is the 16-zone silicon photocell (SPC) sensor. A microprocessor then uses complex algorithms to compare differences in brightness between the zones, allowing the camera to recognize a wide range of lighting situations.**

As a result, the center—the conventional location of the main subject—is measured in a more precise manner than the periphery, which is usually just the subject's environment. For example, the perimeter of the scene, frequently the sky, will not be considered in calculating the exposure.

What is the advantage of having 16 metering areas instead of one? By evaluating the pattern resulting from readings made by each zone, the camera's computer can "recognize" whether the subject is backlit, situated in front of a dark background, or if the lighting conditions are balanced. Depending on the resultant pattern of light readings, some metering zones are more heavily weighted, others are given less weight, and some are not considered at all.

The evaluative metering system also takes into account the part of the scene where the autofocus area is aimed or where the focused-on subject is located. This occurs regardless of whether the AF sensor area (focusing point) is selected manually or automatically. If the autofocus area is selected automatically, the

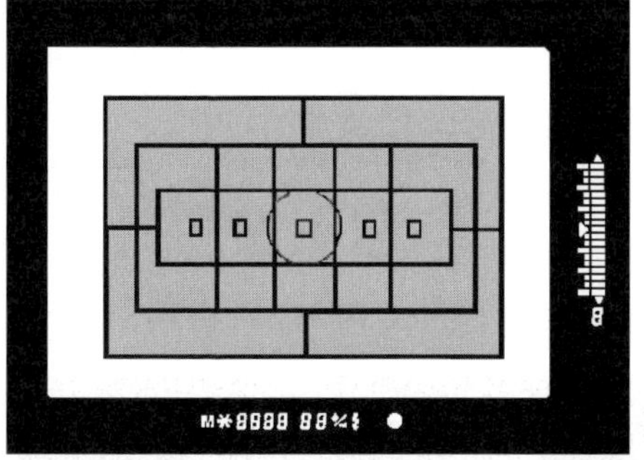

This is how the metering pattern of the EOS-1N is configured. Be aware that the outermost edge of the image area is not metered at all.

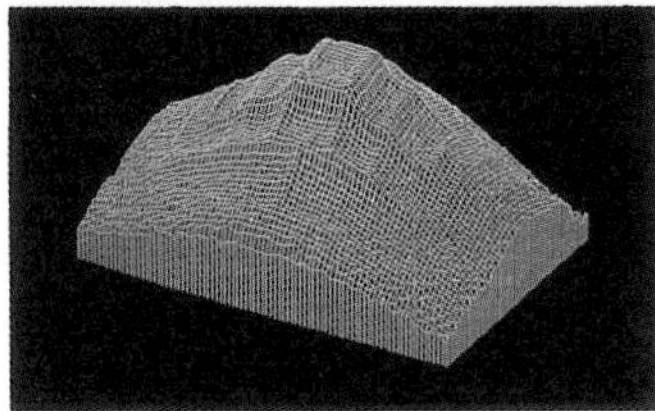

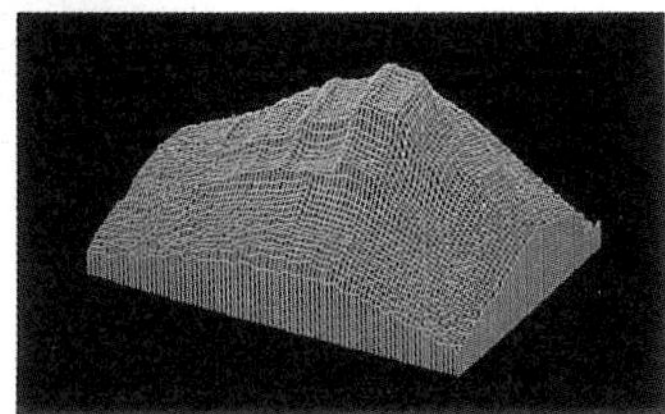

**In calculating exposure, the weight given each metering zone depends on the focusing point selected.**

combination of evaluative metering and five-point autofocus (called Advanced Integrated Multi-Point Control System, or AIM) works well, allowing fast and fairly reliable picture-taking.

Why only fairly reliable? The automatic exposure evaluation of 16-zone evaluative metering is not infallible. In particular, under conditions of extreme contrast (if the sun is in the picture, or a small, bright, main subject is located in front of a black background), erroneous exposures are still possible despite the AIM system. It is important to remember that there is no indication of whether adequate correction is automatically taking place in the meter-determined exposure settings. In extreme lighting conditions, partial or spot metering would probably be a better choice for the discriminating photographer.

To activate 16-zone evaluative metering on the EOS-1N, press the metering mode selector while rotating the main dial until a bold black dot surrounded by two semi-circles appears in the metering mode field on the LCD panel.

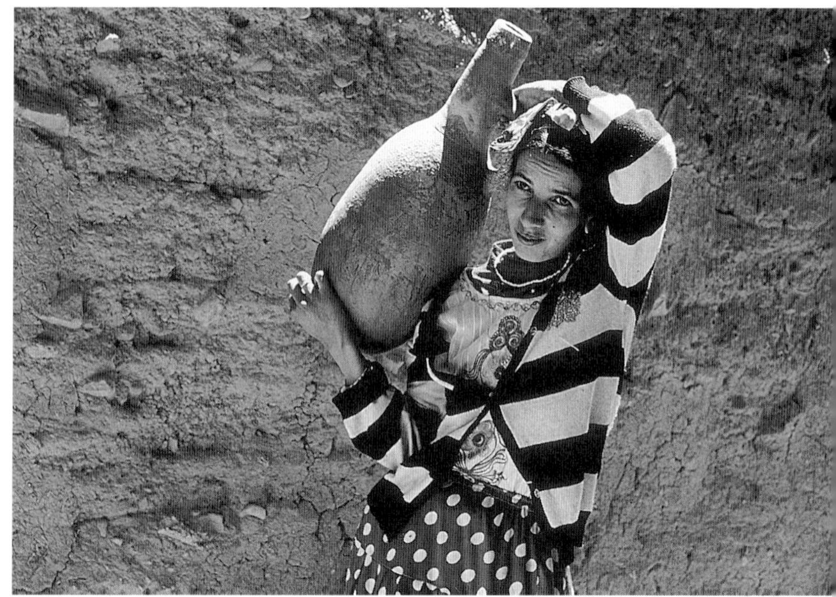

**The AIM system (Advanced Integrated Multi-Point Control) calculates the exposure primarily for the area captured by the active AF sensor.**

In many situations you may not want to take advantage of the automatic exposure compensation function that automatically occurs in the evaluative metering mode. Since you never know whether the combination of shutter speed and aperture suggested by the EOS-1N includes an exposure compensation factor or not, you can change from evaluative metering to center-weighted average metering by using Custom Function 8, setting 1.

### Center-Weighted Average Metering

Quite a few top-of-the-line cameras offer center-weighted average metering. This is probably because there are many photographers who grew up with center-weighted metering and know it well.

To use center-weighted average metering, you must first select Custom Function 8, setting 1. Next, press the metering mode selector. While it is still pressed, rotate the main dial until a black dot

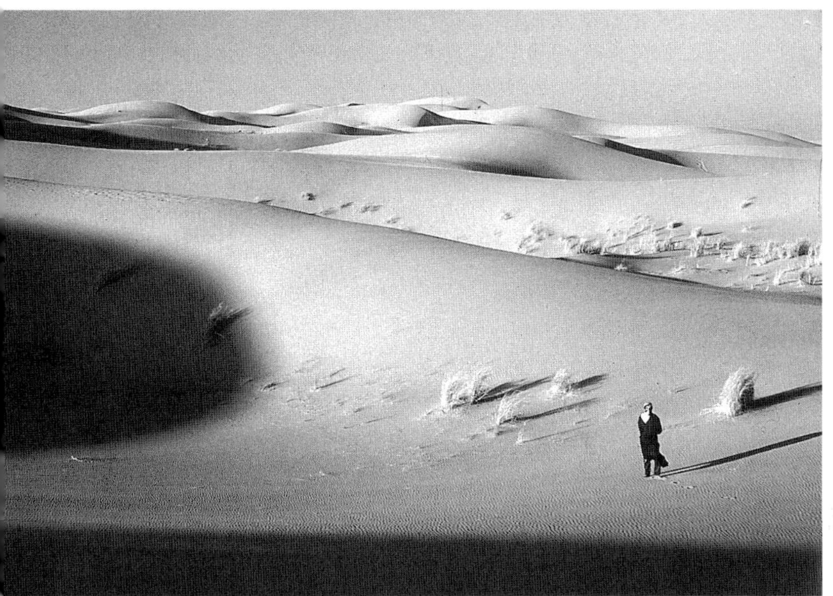

**Sixteen-zone evaluative metering recognizes the shadow on the left side of the picture as being darker than the other metered areas. It takes this into consideration in its computations, and creates a well-balanced exposure.**

surrounded by two semi-circles appears in the metering mode field on the LCD panel. This is the same symbol that appears when 16-zone evaluative metering has been selected. To switch back to evaluative metering, you must set Custom Function 8, setting 0. See page 119 for more information.

Center-weighted average metering uses all 16 metering areas, but more emphasis is given to the central areas than to the peripheral areas. (The outer edge of the image is not taken into account in this metering mode.) Since this system is usually chosen when the subject is in the center of the frame, we recommend that you select the central focusing point manually in order to assure that metering and focus are linked to the same subject detail. (If you let the camera select a focusing point automatically, it can select any of the five focusing points, not necessarily the central one.) And you can gain even more control by selecting Custom

Function 4, setting 1, by measuring and locking focus and exposure separately (using the shutter button and AE lock button). This will ensure greater accuracy when shooting difficult subjects.

Using the quick control dial to quickly enter an exposure compensation value works well with center-weighted average metering. Exposure for backlit subjects can be adjusted with a quick clockwise turn to achieve the desired additional (plus) exposure compensation. The compensation value will be indicated by the position of the arrow on the exposure level scale (to the right of the viewfinder), and the +/- symbol (at the bottom of the viewfinder) will indicate that exposure compensation is in effect.

Should center-weighted average metering with exposure compensation not be adequate for situations requiring more precise exposure, there are still two other options: partial and spot metering. And don't forget the automatic exposure bracketing feature! This may be the only solution to capturing a subject with the best possible exposure when you don't have time to make adjustments.

## Partial Metering

Partial metering has been a feature of Canon cameras for a very long time. Some of Canon's very first SLR cameras offered partial metering, which reads an area smaller than center-weighted average metering but larger than fine spot metering. The EOS-1N is no exception, featuring Canon's typical partial metering system as well.

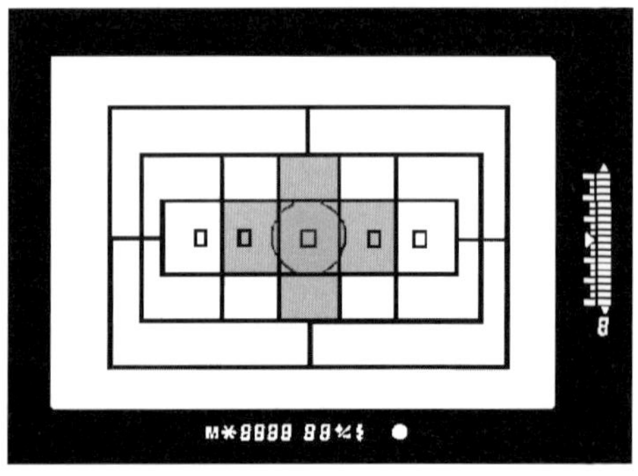

**Partial metering activates a cross-shaped metering area consisting of the three central horizontal areas and the two areas located above and below the center area.**

Set your EOS-1N's exposure meter on partial metering mode by pressing the metering mode selector while turning the main

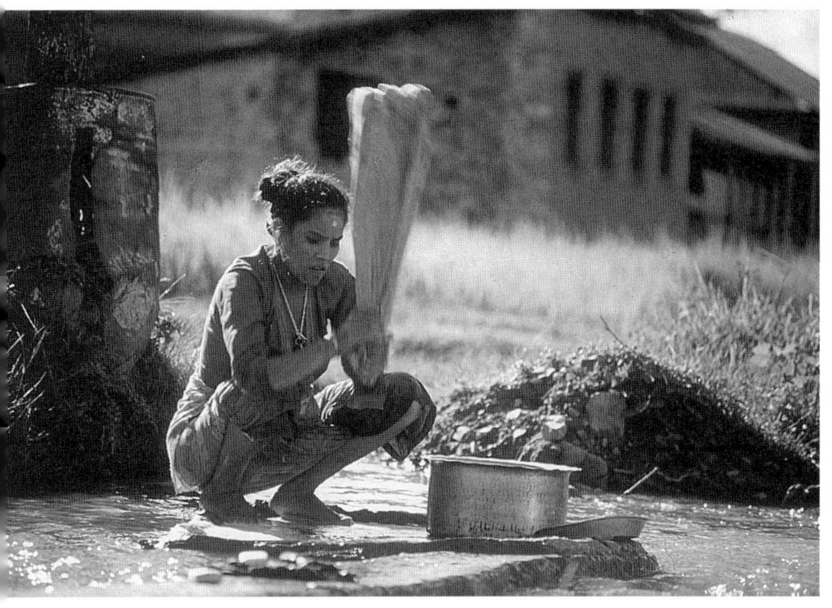

**Using partial metering for shooting this scene of a woman dressed in neutral colors resulted in correct exposure of the main subject against a slightly lighter background.**

dial until two semi-circles (without a dot) appear in the metering mode field on the LCD panel.

In partial metering mode the EOS-1N uses four of the 16 metering zones—the central three running horizontally and the two halves of the metering zone located above and below the central zone. This cross-like metering concentration covers approximately 9% of the total image area. This metering area is not delineated in the viewfinder, however it is approximately as wide as the three central focusing points that appear in the viewfinder.

Partial metering lets you focus and adjust the exposure on dominant image details or larger subject zones whose reflectance is approximately 18%. The advantage of partial metering over center-weighted average metering in situations such as these is that it allows you to ignore unimportant subject details in metering for correct exposure. Its advantage over fine spot metering is that it allows you to meter and shoot faster because its larger metering area need not be aligned as precisely.

By selecting Custom Function 4, settings 0 or 1, you can measure and store exposure and focus values together or separately (using the shutter button and AE lock button), as needed.

If you are working in partial metering mode, you should select the central focusing point manually so that exposure and focus are adjusted for the same subject. You can also expect good results by activating automatic focusing point selection and making sure that the subject is captured by one of the three central focusing areas. This is of particular importance when moving subjects are being photographed.

### Fine Spot Metering

Many experts swear by it, and many beginners agonize over it. Fine spot metering allows you to master many tricky lighting situations, but it has its drawbacks. Activate the EOS-1N's fine spot metering mode by pressing the metering mode selector and rotating the main dial until only a bold dot appears in the metering mode field on the LCD panel. Normally only one—the one in the center—of the 16 metering zones is enabled. The fine spot metering area is indicated by the circle engraved in the viewfinder. However, by selecting Custom Function 13, setting 1, it is possible to link the spot metering system with a manually selected focusing point.

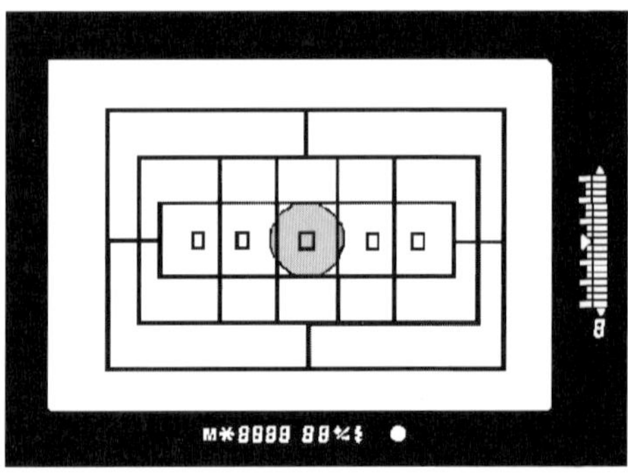

**The EOS-1N offers two spot metering options that can be selected using Custom Function 13: metering linked to the fine spot metering area (circle etched in the viewfinder), or metering linked to one of the focusing points.**

A focusing point can be selected manually, not only by pressing the focusing point selector and turning the main dial, but also by using the quick control dial if Custom Function 11, setting 2 is set. The selected focusing point will be lit in red in the viewfinder. This custom setting allows you to respond quickly to moving subjects and adjust the exposure fast for a small object or detail. If the fine spot metering area is set to read the center of the image, only 2.3% of the viewfinder's image area is used for exposure metering. If metering is linked to one of the outer focusing points, then 3.5% of the image area is used in this mode.

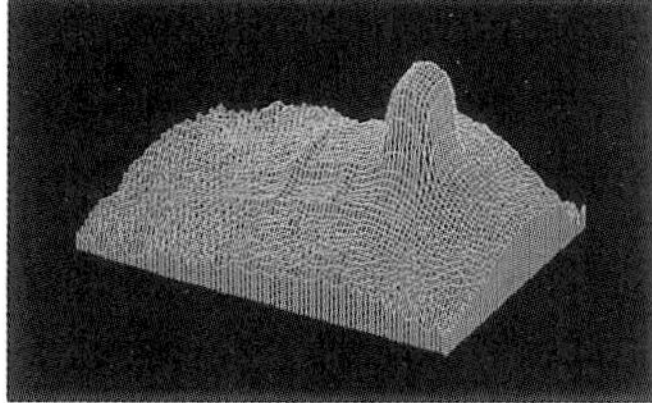

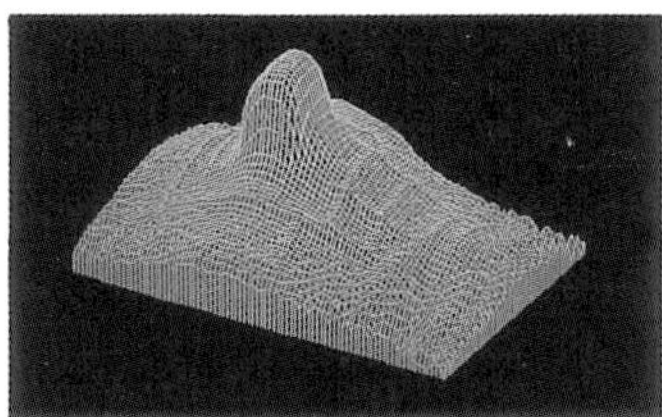

**If Custom Function 13, setting 1 is activated, a spot meter reading will be made of the area corresponding to the selected focusing point.**

If you want to enter an exposure compensation factor to check the effect of an extremely light or dark background on the total exposure from the very beginning, you will want to use the quick control dial. Therefore, set Custom Function 11, setting 0, and select your focusing point the conventional way, by pressing the focusing point selector and rotating the main dial.

Automatic focusing point selection is not recommended in conjunction with fine spot metering because the spot metering area is linked with the central focusing point. If the subject you wish to focus on is not covered by the central focusing sensor, an error in exposure could occur.

It is best to use spot metering when the subject contains at least one detail that has a reflectance corresponding to that of medium gray (18%). The narrow spot meter adjusts the exposure based on this detail.

Successful pictures are not washed out by light or drowned by shadows. To determine whether either case is possible for the situation you are shooting, spot meter the lightest and the darkest detail of the subject and note these values. If there are five or fewer stops between these two values, the exposure will be accurate. If the difference amounts to more than five stops, you need to decide

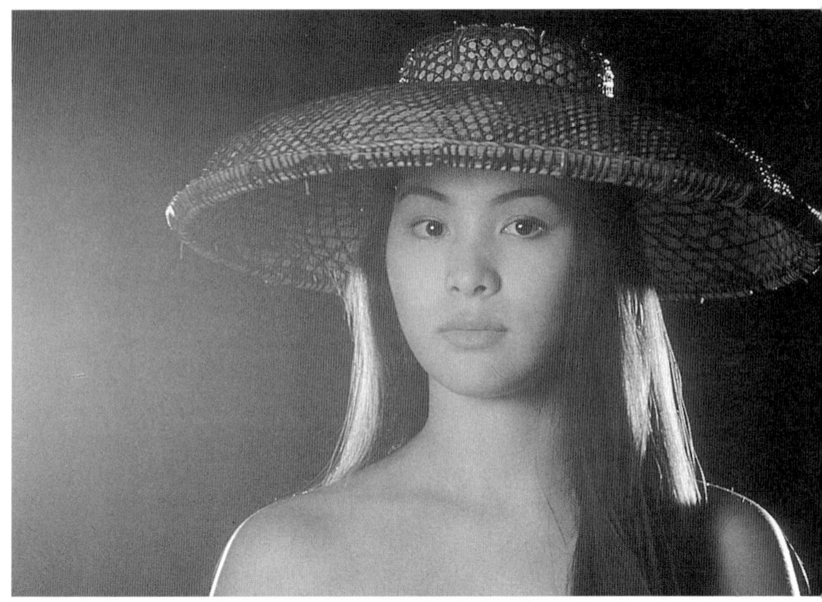

**Spot metering this woman's face ensured that the dark background was excluded from the exposure meter reading, resulting in a well-exposed portrait.**

whether you want to record detail in the highlights or shadows. Of course, you can lighten shadows (with flash, a reflector, or white cloth, for example) or, in some cases, use a graduated neutral density (ND) filter to reduce the contrast between light and dark subject details (ND 2x reduces the contrast by one stop, ND 4x by two stops). Graduated neutral density filters are best when there is a somewhat recognizable delineation between the light and the dark image areas because these filters are divided into a lighter and a darker half. Cokin® graduated neutral density filters offer versatility because they can be rotated or adjusted within the filter holder.

Another method of using fine spot metering (or even partial metering) effectively is to determine the mean value for two specific subject areas (which will theoretically satisfy both areas) and use it to set the exposure. These might be the lightest and the darkest areas of the subject. Or you can take readings from important light and dark details, realizing that even brighter or darker (though not as important) parts may be undefined in the picture. Adjusting this mean value on the EOS-1N is easy. Measure the exposure, store the result (using the AE lock button) and measure a second time. Both results are represented by two arrows on the exposure level scale on the right side of the viewfinder. When the quick control dial is rotated, the arrows will move maintaining an equal distance between one another, up or down the exposure level scale. The mean value will be adjusted as soon as the two arrows are equidistant from the correct exposure indicator, the triangle in the center of the scale.

**Hint:** When center-weighted average metering was still available in almost all cameras, the suggestion was frequently made to measure the exposure at the lens' greatest focal length and use this value for shots requiring shorter focal lengths. Of course this advice is still valid today. You should consider it, particularly when working in fine spot metering with a wide-angle telephoto zoom lens, because the wide-angle focal length expands the metering range.

## Exposure Compensation

### When to Use Exposure Compensation

No matter how good a camera's light meter may be, many situations require that the system's recommended exposure be adjusted to some extent.

One such situation is when the subject or scene is very bright, reflecting far more than 18% overall. Two typical examples of this would be a snowy landscape and a bride dressed in white standing in front of a white wall. Because the camera's metering system is set to assume 18% overall reflectance, it will provide an exposure that will be far too dark and appear slightly gray. (You have probably seen winter photographs that are unnaturally gray.) The remedy for this is to add exposure (plus compensation), which makes the scene lighter on film. When photographing subjects that are brighter than 18% reflectance you must *add light* to render them realistically. This sounds backwards to many people. But again, it is simply because the camera is programmed to make everything medium gray, and a white subject is made gray by

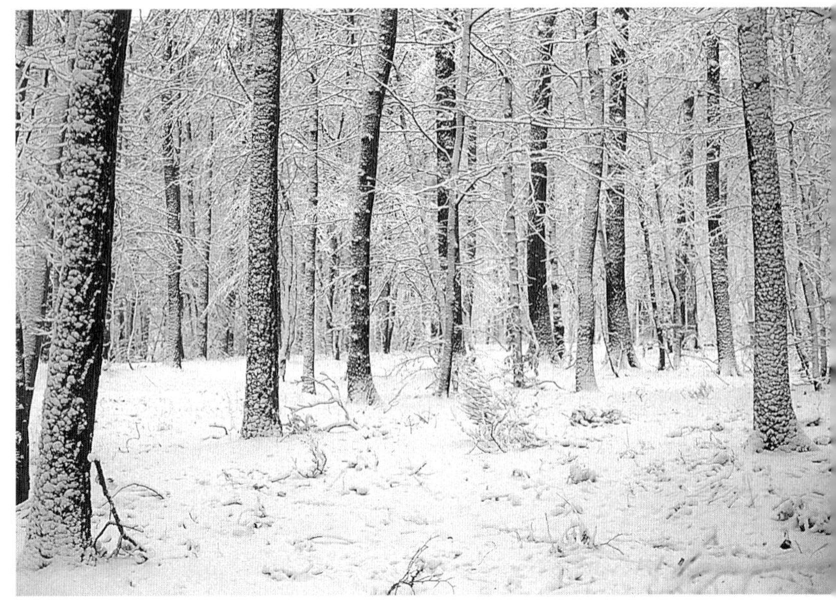

**In a scene like this in which snow predominates, the snow will be rendered as white only with increased exposure (plus compensation). Using the meter's recommendation would make the snow look gray.**

underexposing it. To make it white again, you must add light by *increasing* the exposure. That is the reason for using a plus compensation in this case.

The second situation requiring exposure compensation is when you are shooting a picture in which some parts of the scene are very bright and reflect far more light than the main subject. Examples of this are a scene of a boat on the water in which the sunlight glitters, or a landscape of a brilliant sunset over a mountain range. The bright areas in both of these cases influence the light meter so strongly that the camera will render the main subject darkly, and, in extreme cases, it can end up being a black silhouette without any detail. Again, this calls for a plus correction to add light to the exposure and delineate detail.

The third situation calling for exposure compensation is a subject or scene that is very dark overall and does not reflect much light. A good example would be a black cat on a black velvet cushion. The light meter will produce an exposure value that brings the dark subject up to medium gray, thus overexposing it in the process and producing a "washed out" appearance. In this case you must use less exposure (minus compensation) to make these subjects darker by removing some of the light.

A fourth situation is one in which a large part of the subject or scene reflects much less light than the main subject. An example might be a table-top shot of antique jewelry set on a black velvet background. The meter reading will respond to the predominant, black background and overexpose it making it gray, and all detail in the jewelry will be lost because it is rendered far too light. Again, a minus correction is what is needed to set things right.

If some detail in the subject or scene has about an 18% gray reflectance, no matter what color it actually is, you can use the camera's spot meter to measure exposure. As long as the contrast range of the film is not exceeded in the scene, the photograph should be well exposed. If, instead, you use the spot meter to take a reading and then revert to one of the other metering modes, you can remember the spot meter reading and use it to set exposure compensation for the balance of the photos of the same subject or scene.

In most exposure modes you can use the quick control dial to set the exposure compensation displayed in the viewfinder and on the exposure compensation scale on the lower right of the LCD panel. Or you can manually adjust the ISO rating by pressing the AF mode selector and the metering mode selector while turning the main dial until the desired speed is displayed in the LCD panel. The ISO scale is graduated in 1/3-stop increments (the values will appear in sequence in the LCD panel as the main dial is turned). Increasing the film speed setting is equivalent to setting a minus correction (reducing exposure), while decreasing the film speed setting is equivalent to making a plus correction (increasing exposure). If the + or - 3 stops of compensation displayed on the exposure compensation scale are not enough, you can resort to adjusting the ISO for greater compensation, or even combine the two options. Whenever the ISO value has been set differently from the DX-coded value, the ISO indicator on the LCD panel will flash continually as a reminder that this has been done.

Setting exposure is an acquired skill that is refined with practice. Most photographers develop their own preferred methods of making adjustments in various types of situations. However, even the experienced pro is fooled occasionally, and bracketing exposures can help ensure a higher rate of success. See page 69 for more information on autoexposure bracketing.

### Setting Compensation Factors

Exposure compensation factors can be entered in the range of +/- 3 EV in 1/3-stop increments using Custom Function 6, setting 0 (F-6, 0), which makes aperture and shutter speed changes in 1/3-stop increments. Setting F-6, 1 tells the camera to set aperture and shutter speeds in full-stop increments, and exposure compensation (both flash and ambient light) and autoexposure bracketing values in 1/3-stop increments. You can set all these values to be adjusted in 1/2-stop increments using Custom Function 6, setting 2. Setting exposure compensation affects all metering and exposure modes.

Whether the shutter speed or aperture is adjusted for exposure compensation depends on the autoexposure mode in use. In Aperture-Priority AE and Shutter-Priority AE modes, the manually set value is retained (aperture and shutter speed, respectively), and the other value is adjusted for compensation. In Depth-of-Field AE mode the aperture selected by the automatic system is retained and the shutter speed is adjusted for compensation. In this way the desired zone of focus remains unaffected. Both the shutter speed and aperture change if you are shooting in Program mode.

If you frequently work with fast-action subjects and timing is critical, you will love using the quick control dial to make exposure adjustments quickly. When you meter the scene, the current value will be noted by an arrow pointing to the correct exposure indicator (the triangle) in the center of the exposure compensation scale. If you continue to rotate the dial, the arrow will move up or down the scale, displaying the extent of compensation in 1/3 stops. This method permits you to bracket exposures quickly. (This can also be controlled automatically using continuous advance mode.) The amount of compensation is also displayed on the LCD panel by an indicator that moves along the exposure compensation scale as compensation is set.

Whereas setting compensation with the quick control dial is best for adjusting individual shots, preset exposure compensation is best when exposing an entire series. To do this, first press the exposure compensation button (+/-). You then have 6 seconds to set a compensation value with the main dial. An indicator will move along the exposure compensation scale on the LCD panel, showing the extent of compensation. If you are using the EOS-1N's data back, the Command Back E1, your only option is to use the main dial because this special back does not feature a quick control dial.

## AE Lock

Using AE lock is recommended when the exposure must be set precisely for a specific detail or when a substitute midtone subject is used as the basis for determining the exposure.

But when is it most effective? The EOS-1N's 16-zone evaluative metering is linked to the active focusing point and includes in its metering calculations a certain adjustment for the subject within that focusing area. Exposure is calculated for the main subject because the exposure value is locked automatically when focus is achieved (through pressing the shutter button halfway). Center-weighted average metering evaluates the entire viewfinder image regardless of which focusing point is active. Thus, these metering systems are not particularly suitable for work with AE lock.

***Note:*** Because exposure lock and focus lock are linked when One-Shot AF is used with evaluative metering, Custom Function 4, setting 1 (which separates exposure and focus lock into two separate commands) must not be activated!

AE lock is most useful when used with either partial or spot metering, because the small central metering area of these two systems does not include the distracting surroundings in its readings. In these modes you can set exposure for the main subject or a substitute subject. AE lock is particularly useful when shooting a scene with an extreme range of contrast between the subject and its surroundings.

When using AE lock, it is important that only the part of the subject critical to the picture is used as the basis for the locked-in exposure. In addition, the brightness of this part of the subject should correspond to the standard 18% gray to which the exposure meter has been calibrated. This ensures the proper exposure (provided you are within the film's range of contrast). Should the subject be lighter or darker, it will be improperly reproduced as midtone gray, and the remaining subject details will be proportionally lighter or darker.

A gray card, such as those sold by Kodak, is ideal for substitute subject metering. The gray side of the card reflects 18% of the light striking it. If it is not possible to use the gray side for metering because the light is too dim, the white side of the card (on the reverse) can be used because it reflects more light. Meter readings taken from the white side must be compensated for by opening up 2-1/3 stops (adding exposure) before the picture can be taken.

Because it is not always convenient to hold the AE lock button on the camera with your thumb for prolonged sequences, it probably makes more sense to switch over to Manual exposure mode and set the shutter speed and aperture manually based on the substitute meter reading.

**Hint:** Because a gray card is not always handy, you may wish to calculate the reflectance of your camera bag (which you are more likely to have on hand), giving you an exposure factor you can use in any situation. Meter on a gray card and then meter on your camera bag. Note the difference between these two measurements. Now you can use your camera bag as a substitute subject to meter on in any critical situation, however, do not forget to adjust for the difference between the bag and the gray card!

Another substitute subject always available is the palm of your hand. A palm generally reflects twice the amount of light reflected by an 18% gray card. This means the meter reading from your hand must be corrected by adding one (+) stop.

An interesting feature of AE lock is that it can help you determine the contrast between two subject details. The stored metered value is represented in the viewfinder by an arrow opposite the triangle in the center of the exposure level scale. Now if you pan the camera, the actual metering value will be represented by a second arrow that moves up or down the scale. Depending on the increments selected for adjusting shutter speed and aperture values (using Custom Function 6), the difference between a stored and a measured exposure value is indicated in 1/2, 1/3, or full stops.

The metering mode, AF mode, film advance mode, and Custom Function 4 determine whether or not the AE lock feature is used and, if so, how it is activated. The section on Custom Function 4 provides information regarding the various combinations and how they work with AE lock (see page 117).

***Note:*** When the AE lock is activated by pressing the AE lock button (other options are available through Custom Function 4), the meter reading is locked for 6 seconds. Should you require more than 6 seconds to compose your picture, you must either continue to hold the AE lock button down or press it a second time before the 6 seconds have elapsed.

## Automatic Exposure Bracketing (AEB)

Automatic exposure bracketing (AEB) has long been a proven method of insuring against the uncertainties of exposure metering. The automatic exposure bracketing feature allows you to take three successive shots, with the camera automatically making different exposure adjustments. One exposure corresponds to the exposure meter's reading, the second is just under that reading, and the third is just over that reading. The under- and overexposure values are made in equal increments of 1/3 or 1/2 stops over and under the camera's "correct" meter reading, depending upon how you have configured your camera. See page 118 on how to adjust these increment values using Custom Function 6.

Activate the AEB function by opening the EOS-1N's palm door and pressing the gray battery check button and blue film winding mode selector simultaneously. Three exposure value indicators will appear under the exposure compensation scale on the LCD panel. When the main dial is rotated toward the right (clockwise), the two outer exposure value indicators will move away in equal increments from the central indicator. These, as well as the number appearing in the LCD's AEB value field, indicate the exposure differential between each shot.

You can also select the order in which the different exposures are taken and how the AEB function is activated or deactivated by using Custom Function 9. Settings F-9, 0 and F-9, 1 produce shots following the order underexposure, "correct" exposure, and

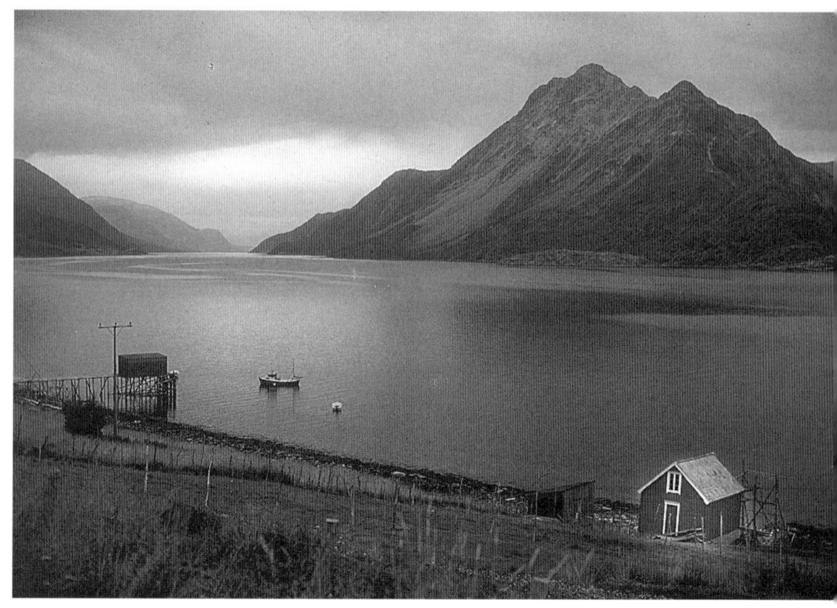

**If you are not sure whether the tranquil mood of the scene would be better portrayed using the metered exposure value or one with slightly more exposure, autoexposure bracketing can help.**

overexposure. Settings F-9, 2 and F-9, 3 result in an order of "correct" exposure, underexposure, and overexposure. Settings F-9, 0 and F-9, 2 enable the AEB function as described above and is disabled when the film is rewound, the lens is changed, or the camera is switched off, among other situations. See page 120 for more information on Custom Function 9.

In settings F-9, 1 and F-9, 3 the AEB function remains active until it is manually deactivated. In these settings, the AEB function can be activated conventionally, as described above, or by pressing the AF mode selector (AF) and shooting mode selector (MODE) on the left upper side of the camera and rotating the main dial to set the AEB increments. To disable the AEB function, press either set of buttons (AF and MODE, or battery check and film winding mode selector) and turn the main dial to reset the exposure differential values on the LCD's exposure compensation scale to "0.0."

Automatic exposure bracketing that makes equivalent adjustments above and below zero ("correct" exposure) is not always optimal for the situation being photographed. For instance, assume that your camera is set to bracket a series at -1, 0, +1. Automatic exposure bracketing can be combined with an exposure compensation factor, correcting the exposure series to -2, -1, 0. A compensation factor can be entered by pressing the exposure compensation button (+/-) and turning the main dial. You will see the amount of exposure compensation move on the LCD's scale. When the shutter button is pressed halfway, the corrected AEB values will be shown. Or you can add exposure compensation an alternate way. Press the exposure compensation button, then the shutter button halfway, and adjust the values by turning the quick control dial. In this case you must watch the exposure level scale in the viewfinder as the three arrows move up or down the scale. Once the center indicator (which represents the starting exposure) has reached the end of the scale, additional compensation is no longer possible. This is because the compensation factor range limit is -3 or +3 stops.

If the starting exposure is at the end of the scale and one of the arrows has disappeared, the third shot of the series will still be taken. However, due to the system's limitations, it is not guaranteed that the shot will be made with the desired exposure bracket. In this situation, chances of success are best if you have set Aperture-Priority mode because the compensation takes place through changing the shutter speed, and the range of available shutter speeds usually offers enough latitude for correction.

When working with automatic exposure bracketing, remember that plus corrections can also be made by lengthening the shutter speed. However, this means that the shot taken with added (+) exposure can be blurred! (In Shutter-Priority mode the correction takes place by changing the aperture; in automatic Program mode, by changing either shutter speed or aperture; and in Depth-of-Field AE mode by changing the shutter speed.)

Whether you work in single-frame advance mode or remove your finger quickly from the release after taking an exposure in continuous advance mode, the blinking "AEB" displayed on the LCD panel and the blinking AEB indicator (*) in the viewfinder point out that the bracketed series has not been completed. As usual, shutter speeds and apertures are indicated in the LCD and

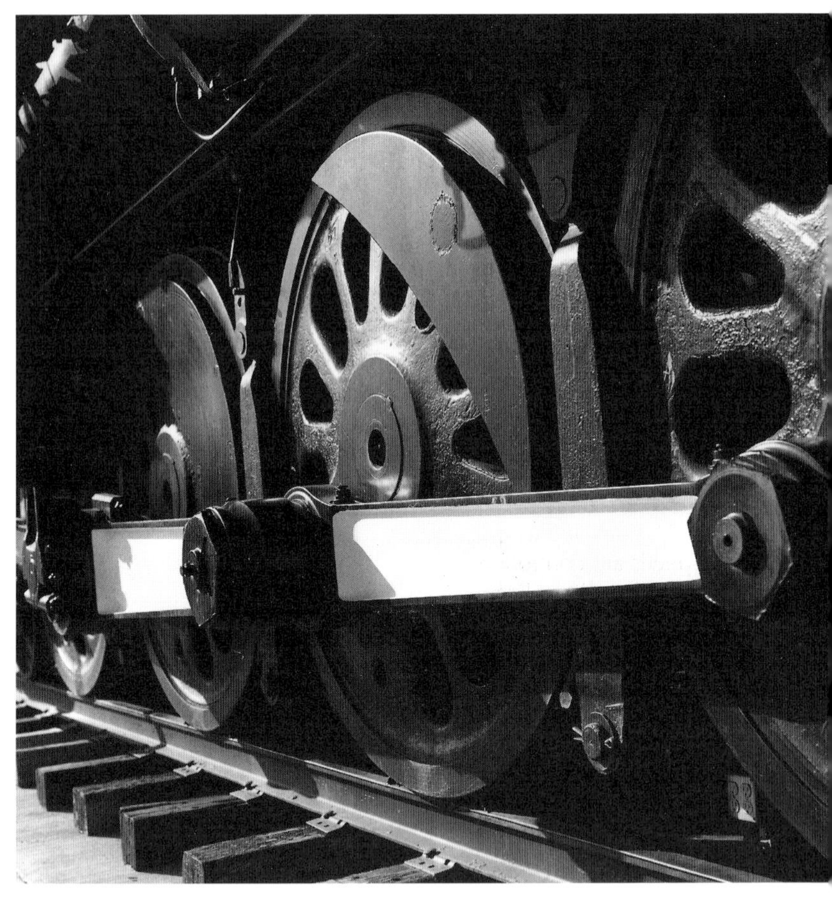

**In extreme lighting conditions, use the autoexposure bracketing feature to ensure that you bring home the best possible photograph. Photo by Paul Comon.**

viewfinder displays for each shot. When you leave your finger on the release in continuous mode, all three shots are taken in succession, yielding interesting results, particularly if the subject is moving.

# Exposure Controls

Together, the camera's aperture and shutter speed control the amount of light that reaches the film. Shutter speed and aperture increments are equivalent, formulated to complement one another so that as one variable is increased by one full stop, the other must be decreased by one full stop to achieve an equivalent exposure. With each full stop, the light transmitted is doubled or cut in half, depending upon the direction you move on the aperture or shutter speed scale.

## The Shutter

The EOS-1N uses an electronic motor to cock the shutter, and its shutter speeds are controlled by the focal plane shutter composed of vertically traveling, lightweight (yet strong) carbon-fiber and duralumin blades. This combination allows the shutter to accelerate incredibly fast, permitting a minimum shutter speed of 1/8000 second and a flash synchronization speed of 1/250 second.

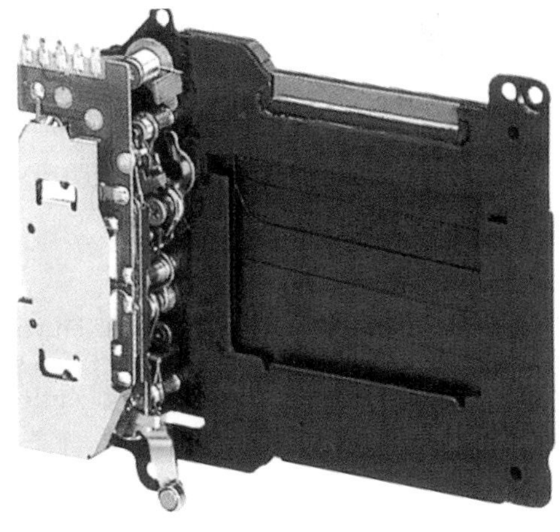

**The strong, yet lightweight blades of the focal plane shutter allow for extremely fast shutter speeds (up to 1/8000 second!).**

## The Lens Diaphragm

Canon EF lenses feature an Electro-Magnetic Diaphragm (EMD), which controls the size of the aperture with extreme accuracy. The maximum apertures of Canon's EF lenses range between f/1 and f/5.6, and the minimum apertures range between f/16 and f/45. Due to the high degree of precision in shutter and aperture control, the exposure meter's accuracy is maintained during exposure. Shutter speed and aperture values are adjusted on the EOS-1N body, hence these lenses have no aperture ring. Adjustments are instead made using the main dial and the quick control dial.

As a rule, the main dial is used for shutter speed adjustments in Shutter-Priority mode and for aperture selection in Aperture-Priority mode. In Manual mode the main dial is used to select the shutter speed, and the quick control dial is used for the aperture. You can also configure your camera to respond to different controls by selecting Custom Functions 5 and 11. See pages 89 and 122 for more information.

Selected shutter speed and aperture values are displayed on the LCD panel and at the base of the viewfinder. The shutter speed is displayed as the reciprocal of the actual time value, i.e., 8000 = 1/8000 second, 0″8 = 0.8 second, and 8″ = 8 seconds.

Shutter speeds and apertures are defined in standard 1/3 stops, however this can be changed with Custom Function 6. Setting F-6, 1 sets the system to full stops, setting F-6, 2 to 1/2 stops. (Setting F-6, 2 also affects the increments used in exposure compensation and automatic exposure bracketing.)

Many photographers feel that negative (print) films have too much latitude to respond to exposure differences of only 1/3 stop. Therefore they prefer to make changes in 1/2-stop increments. However, if you work mostly with transparency (slide) material, we recommend that you stick to 1/3 stops.

## Intelligent Program Autoexposure Mode

Canon's Intelligent Program AE mode ensures that even an absolute beginner can take outstanding pictures with the sophisticated EOS-1N camera. This feature is also useful to professionals because it allows them to concentrate fully on the subject (and their own safety, if shooting in precarious situations). It is also helpful in situations that involve quick action when time is limited.

Press the shooting mode selector and rotate the main dial until the letter "P" (for Program) is displayed on the upper left-hand corner of the LCD panel. In this mode, the EOS-1N sets both the shutter speed and aperture based on the meter reading and the focal length of the lens in use (or the set focal length when a zoom lens is used).

The EOS-1N's Program AE mode follows the general guideline that a camera should not be handheld at shutter speeds slower than the reciprocal of the focal length in use with the slowest speed being 1/60 second for lenses 60mm or shorter. To safeguard against blurry photos, the Program AE mode will set a shutter speed fast enough for handholding the camera, provided there is enough light to do so. Should the photographer wish to change the shutter speed-aperture combination, Program Shift can be applied.

**Program Shift**

Obviously, there will be times that the photographer does not want to simply accept the camera's Program AE mode exposure settings. If that is the case, Program Shift can be applied by rotating the main dial. This adjusts the shutter speed-aperture combination without changing the exposure value. For example, the photographer may want to put the camera on a tripod and use a very slow shutter speed; the camera will then set the equivalent aperture automatically. What will change is the manner in which motion is portrayed and the extent of the depth of field. That is, the shutter speed and aperture combination will shift while maintaining consistent exposure.

It is Program Shift that makes the automatic Program mode so attractive. It gives the photographer control over shutter speed or aperture values while maintaining an equivalent exposure for the given film speed and subject brightness. Whenever you want to create a special effect, such as setting selective focus on a flower, freezing motion, etc., use Program Shift and choose the appropriate aperture or shutter speed. Thanks to the information displayed in the EOS-1N's viewfinder, you will always know exactly what the camera is doing.

Should Program mode not be able to set an appropriate shutter speed-aperture combination, you will be clearly warned of the

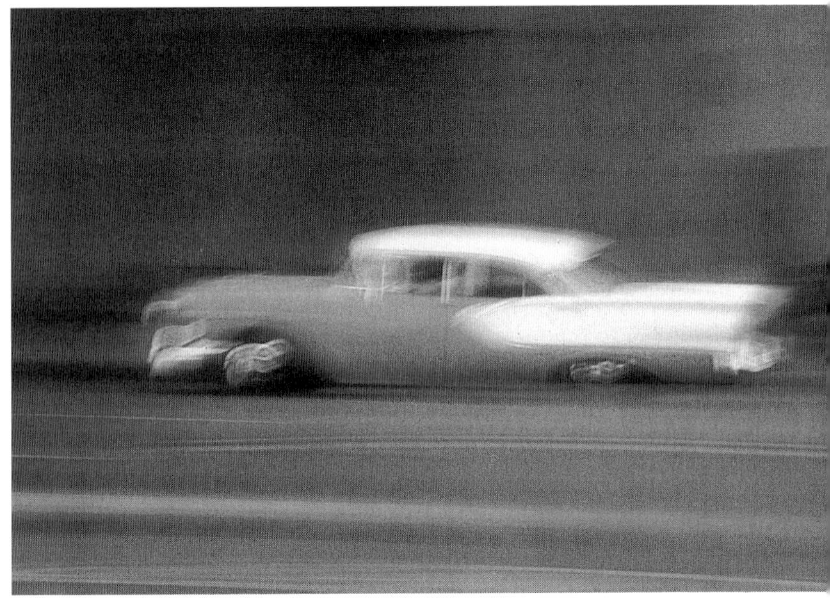

**When Program AE mode is set but motion blur is desired, Program Shift permits you to switch to a slower shutter speed quickly and easily.**

risk of erroneous exposure. If the conditions will result in overexposure, "8000" and the lens' smallest aperture value will blink on the viewfinder's LCD and on the main LCD panel; in addition, you will see an upward-pointing arrow above the exposure level scale in the viewfinder. If the conditions will result in underexposure, "30" and the largest aperture value of the lens will blink in the viewfinder and on the LCD, and a downward-pointing arrow will light below the viewfinder's exposure level scale.

The EOS-1N's Program mode is particularly useful with the EOS-1N's 16-zone evaluative metering and automatic focusing point selection. With these settings, the autofocus system will recognize the closest subject detail with lightning speed and adjust itself accordingly. The exposure meter will base the exposure on this subject detail while also comparing the luminance of the surroundings. Differences in brightness in the 16 metering zones allow the camera to recognize a variety of different lighting situations and

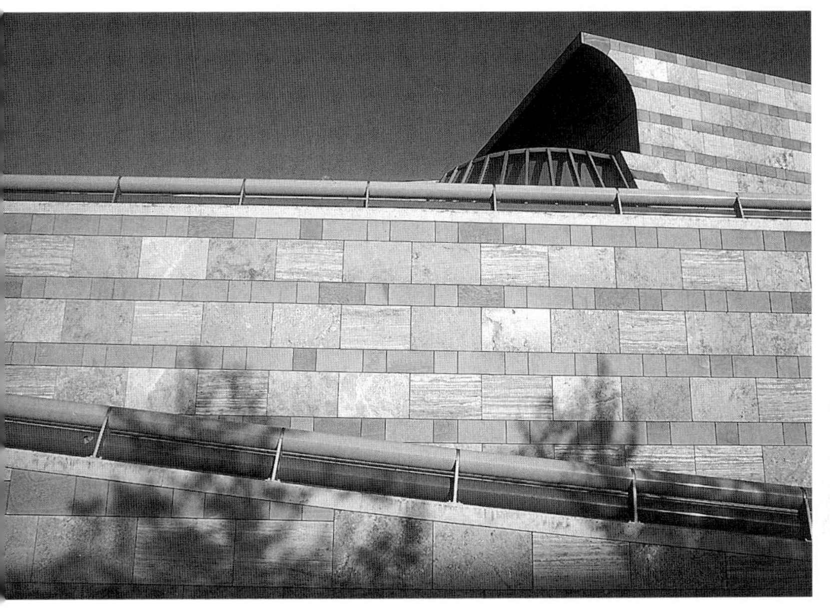

**Program AE mode is great for subjects in which controlling depth of field or the rendition of motion is unimportant.**

compensate for them if necessary. Program AE mode immediately converts the measured information into an appropriate shutter speed-aperture combination, taking into consideration the focal length of the lens in use.

Therefore, for general photography, when your photos do not require a specific shutter speed or aperture and the lighting is fairly even in contrast, Program AE mode is a great choice for exposure control.

## Aperture-Priority Autoexposure Mode

Aperture-Priority AE mode is the appropriate choice for shooting quickly while maintaining control over depth of field. Press the shooting mode selector (MODE) and rotate the main dial until "Av" is displayed in the upper left-hand corner of the LCD panel.

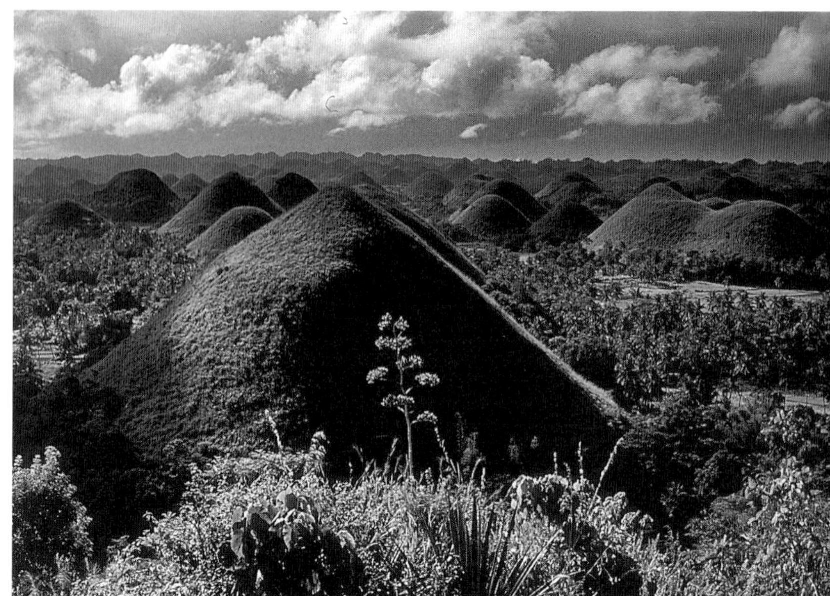

**Use Aperture-Priority AE mode when controlling depth of field is important in achieving the desired effect.**

"Av" stands for "Aperture Value." In this mode the aperture is normally selected in 1/3-stop increments by rotating the main dial. This increment can be changed to 1/2 or full stops with Custom Function 6.

The aperture range that is available is determined by the lens in use. Most Canon lenses have a range of seven stops for which the EOS-1N will automatically choose a correct corresponding shutter speed from 1/8000 second to 30 seconds.

Should the Aperture-Priority system find that an appropriate shutter speed is not available for the existing conditions, a clear warning will be given. Impending overexposure is indicated by a blinking "8000" on the LCD panel and an upward-pointing arrow that lights up above the exposure level scale in the viewfinder. Anticipated underexposure is indicated by a blinking "30" on the LCD panel and a downward-pointing arrow that lights up below the viewfinder's exposure level scale.

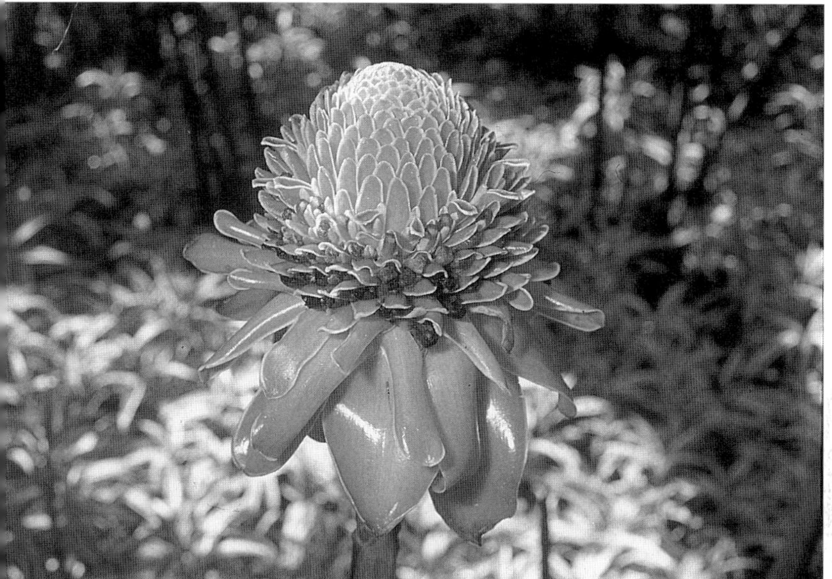

**For this picture, selecting a large aperture in Aperture-Priority AE mode resulted in narrow depth of field and a sufficiently fast shutter speed to prevent recording the effects of camera shake.**

Select Aperture-Priority mode when you require a specific depth of field to capture your subject in focus. Small aperture openings result in large depth of field, which is appropriate for general scenic shots. Large apertures result in a narrow depth of field, which isolates the main subject against a blurred foreground or background.

**Aperture Pre-Selection**

Pre-selecting an aperture that provides plenty of depth of field can sometimes allow you to dispense with the entire focusing procedure. This is the "snapshot setting" (hyperfocal distance) that was frequently used by photographers in the manual focus days but has almost been lost in the flurry of AF technology. To take advantage of the snapshot setting you will need a lens with a depth-of-field scale, such as any fixed focal length lens from Canon's EF line. The EF 28mm f/2.8 lens is used in this example. Its depth-of-field scale includes three apertures, f/5.6, f/11, and f/16. Each of these three apertures is associated with two appropriately identified marks—one to the left and one to the right of the focusing index. If you are holding the camera in the shooting position and looking down at the lens, the left mark represents the closest distance to which depth of field will extend for the aperture opposite it on the lens barrel; the right mark represents the farthest distance reached by the depth-of-field zone for the aperture opposite it on the scale. You can then read the depth-of-field range for each of the three apertures directly off the lens' distance scale.

Now switch the lens from automatic to manual focus. Rotate the lens' focusing ring until the desired depth of field is indicated by the distance scale and check which of the three apertures should be set in order to achieve this zone of sharp focus. Then check to see that there is an equivalent shutter speed for correct exposure with the required aperture. Also take care to note if the shutter speed is fast enough to handhold the camera (at least 1/60 second) or if a camera support is needed. Once this is done, it is easy to take fast, candid shots. You do not even have to bring the camera up to your eye. Point your EOS-1N in the desired direction and shoot.

### Using Aperture to Control Depth of Field

The focal length, shooting distance (i.e., the scale of reproduction), and the aperture determine the depth of field in a photo. Controlling depth of field is one technique a photographer can use to determine how a subject is portrayed. Every detail in a photograph can be rendered sharply in order to place the subject within an environment, or a subject can be isolated against an intentionally blurred background to give it prominence.

***Large vs. small apertures:*** Provided the focal length and shooting distance remain the same, a picture taken with a small aperture will exhibit a large degree of depth of field, whereas a picture taken with a large aperture will exhibit narrow (small) depth of field.

***Long vs. short focal lengths:*** If the focal length is changed while the aperture and the shooting distance remain the same, short focal lengths will provide greater depth of field, and long focal lengths provide narrower depth of field.

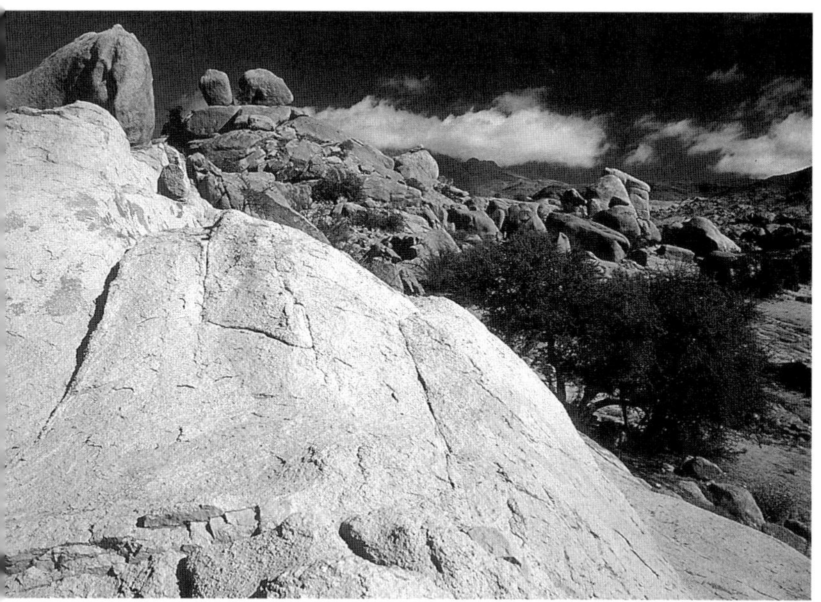

**When landscapes are shot with a wide-angle lens, selecting a small aperture to extend the range of focus (depth of field) is recommended.**

***Near vs. distant subjects:*** If the aperture and focal length remain unchanged, depth of field will increase as the camera-to-subject distance increases.

You will find that knowing these correlations will be quite helpful when you want to use depth of field to its best advantage while composing images with your EOS-1N. True, the camera's Depth-of-Field AE mode makes determining the exact depth of field easy, and it even makes the required computations for you, but sometimes it cannot cope with a certain situation. In those instances it is helpful to know what might have caused the problem and how to solve it. See page 85 for more information on Depth-of-Field AE mode.

A narrow (shallow) depth of field can be used to offset subject details against a blurred background (this is called selective focus). This is particularly appropriate for portraits; however other

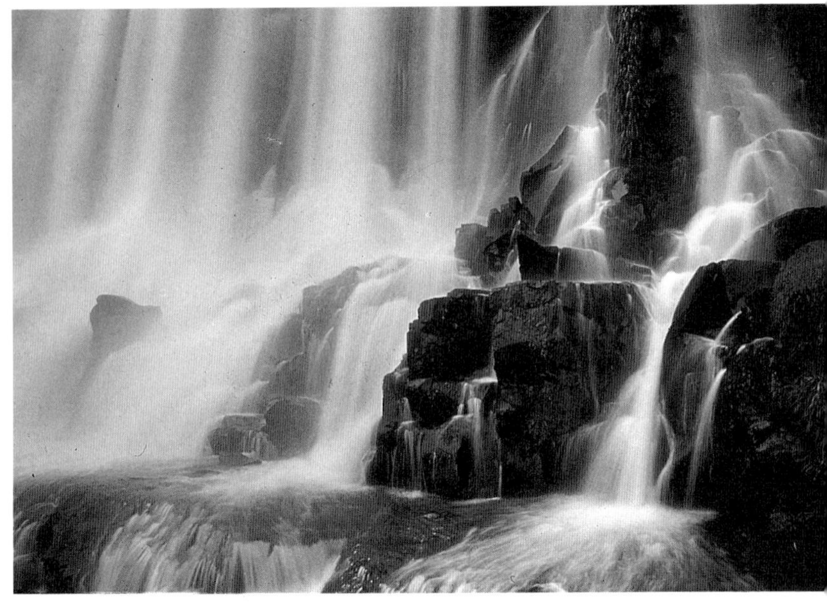

**Select Shutter-Priority AE mode whenever you want to convey the impression of motion.**

subjects, such as flower blossoms, benefit from appearing sharp against a blurred background. This technique is also used often by sports and wildlife photographers.

Extensive depth of field is most desirable for photos such as group shots, landscapes, architectural and interior photography, and product shots. Generally, these types of photos should be in focus throughout the entire depth of the scene.

## Shutter-Priority Autoexposure Mode

Shutter-Priority AE mode is the best automatic exposure mode for sports and action shots, especially when long telephoto lenses and/or continuous film advance are used. Shutter speeds of at least 1/250 second must be used with the motor drive for shooting picture sequences at its highest speed of approximately 3 fps (without the Power Booster attached).

To use Shutter-Priority mode, press the shooting mode selector (MODE) and rotate the main dial until "Tv" (which stands for "Time Value") appears on the LCD panel. The EOS-1N features a shutter speed range extending from 1/8000 second to a full 30 seconds. The main dial is used to select shutter speeds. In basic default mode (Custom Function 6, setting 0) shutter speeds can be set in 1/3-stop increments. These can be changed to full stops (using Custom Function 6, setting 1) or 1/2 stops (using Custom Function 6, setting 2).

The camera will warn you of impending overexposure or underexposure if there is not a small or large enough aperture to produce a proper exposure with the selected shutter speed. The lens' highest f/number will blink on the LCD panel and on the viewfinder display, and an upward-pointing arrow will appear above the viewfinder's exposure level scale. Likewise, the risk of underexposure is indicated by the lowest f/number blinking on the LCD and a downward-pointing arrow appearing below the viewfinder's exposure level scale.

**Hint:** If it is too dark to set shutter speeds fast enough to prevent camera shake, use a monopod, or better yet, a tripod. If a tripod is not handy, as is often the case, set your camera on top of something. Benches, backs of chairs, railings, fences, door frames, or any stable, sturdy surface make good substitute "tripods."

### Using Shutter Speed to Control Motion

With the appropriate shutter speed, you can create motion blur in a picture or you can capture and freeze action.

Long exposure times can portray motion effectively by creating motion blur. The shutter speed must be relatively slow, depending on the rate of the subject's motion and the desired blur effect. A race car whizzing by the camera will result in motion blur at a shutter speed of 1/250 second. The cascading water of a mountain brook will be blurred with a shutter speed of 1/8 second. To render pedestrians slowly promenading in streets at dusk as shadowy silhouettes, shutter speeds of one second or longer must be selected. Slow shutter speeds usually require the use of a camera support to prevent a blurred image resulting from camera shake. If the desired shutter speed cannot be set without overexposure—even though the aperture is closed all the way down—use

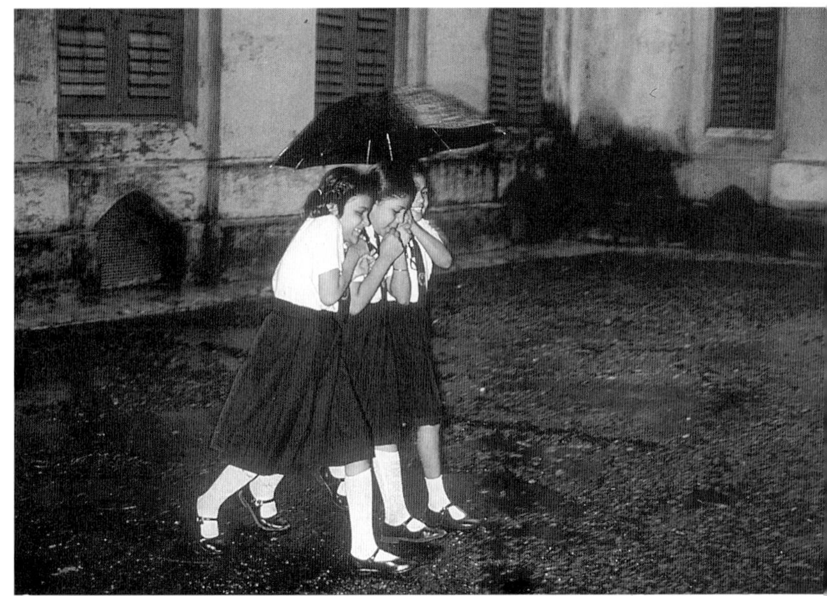

**Shutter-Priority AE mode was used to select a fast shutter speed to freeze the motion of these girls running to escape the rain.**

slower film or add a neutral density filter (ND 2x reduces the light by one stop, ND 4x by two stops).

If motion blur is not desirable, then relatively fast shutter speeds are required. To obtain a sharp picture of a person walking, choose 1/60 or 1/125 second; sharp pictures of runners, animals in motion, or moving vehicles can be taken at 1/500 or 1/1000 second. Race cars require shutter speeds of 1/1000 or 1/2000 second, and 1/8000 second will give you a (fairly) sharp picture of the spinning blades of a helicopter.

It is also possible to capture sharp images of a subject in motion while conveying motion by blurring the background using a slow shutter speed. The trick is to pan the camera following the subject's motion. To achieve this, it is best to mount your EOS-1N on a tripod with a pan head and select a shutter speed of 1/8 second or slower, depending on the subject's speed. After firing the shutter, follow the subject with the camera. Panning creates a picture with an acceptably sharp subject against a blurred background. Plan on taking quite a few practice shots until you get the hang of this. This technique is even easier with the EOS-1N RS camera. It comes with a non-moving (or fixed) reflex mirror, so there is no blackout during the exposure and you can see your subject in the viewfinder while panning. As you pan, you can keep your eye on the subject!

## Depth-of-Field Autoexposure Mode

For more accurate control over the depth of field in a photograph, the EOS-1N offers Depth-of-Field AE mode. It allows the photographer to actively select the closest and farthest points within the photo that will be in apparent focus. This selection is linked to the active focusing point, so the camera needs to be set for the appropriate focusing point for the situation at hand. If the camera is set for automatic focusing point selection, measurements will be calculated through the central focusing point. To focus on the closest object in the desired depth of field range, one of the off-center focusing points may need to be selected manually.

Activate the Depth-of-Field autoexposure mode by pressing the shooting mode selector (MODE) while turning the main dial until "DEP" is displayed on the LCD panel. To set the desired depth-of-field range, first aim the focusing point at an object located at the closest distance in the desired depth-of-field area and lightly press the shutter button. Take your finger off the shutter button and repeat this procedure for the farthest point that should be in focus within the desired depth-of-field range. Both measurements will be acknowledged below the viewfinder and on the LCD panel by the displays "dEP 1" and "dEP 2." Now you can compose your picture. When you press the shutter button a third time, the EOS-1N will compute the appropriate aperture for the desired depth of field and the complementary shutter speed. Focus will also be set automatically, based on the two distances selected and the focal length of the lens in use. The focusing point will be chosen by the camera with approximately one-third of the range of focus in front of the focusing point and two-thirds of the range of focus falling behind the focusing point.

***Note:*** Selection of the closest and farthest focusing distance readings can also be made in reverse order.

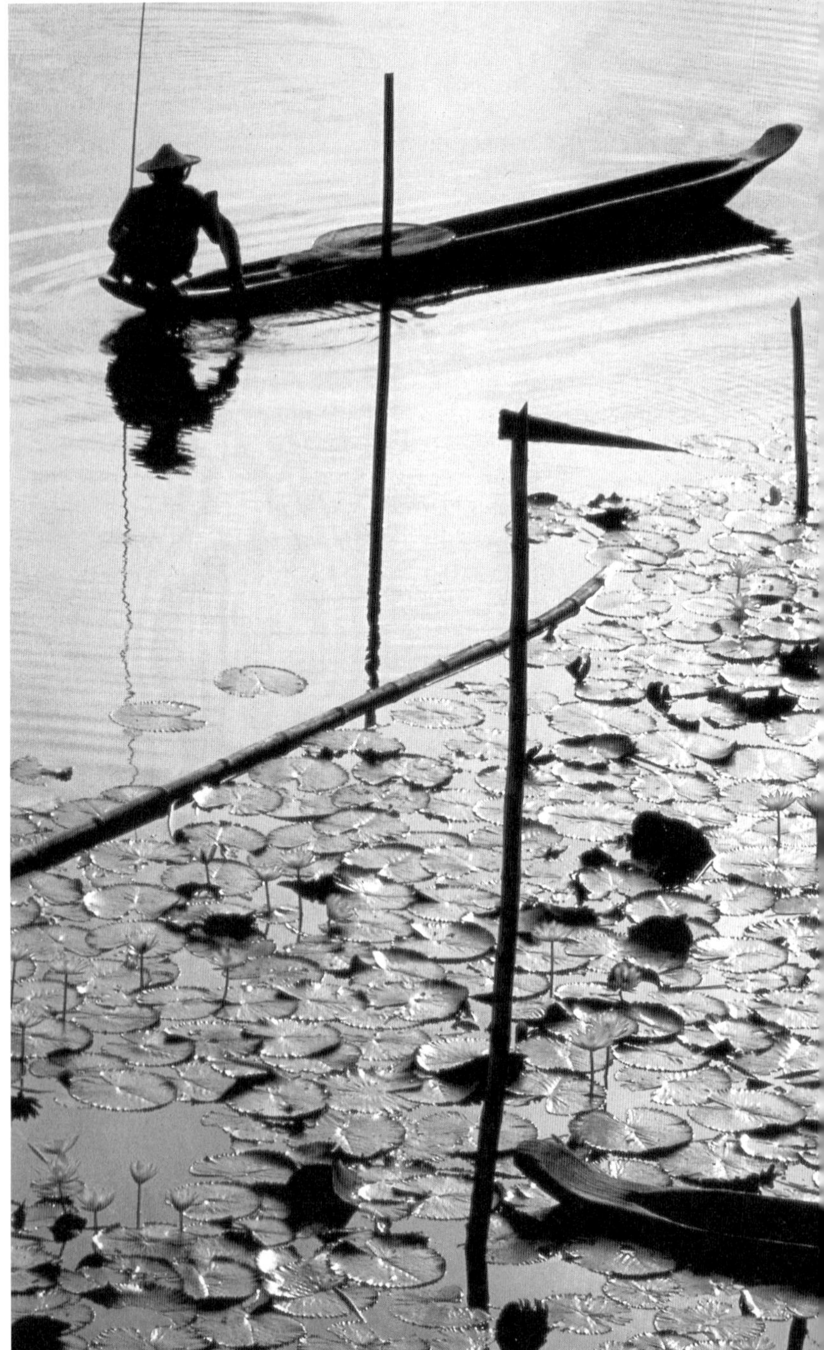

The aperture required to achieve the desired depth of field is the basis for determining the exposure setting in Depth-of-Field mode in the same way that the user-selected aperture is in Aperture-Priority mode. However, in Depth-of-Field mode it is based on the range of apparent focus.

If the situation changes after you have made one or both distance limit readings, you can cancel them by pressing any of the four mode selector buttons (focusing point, shooting mode, AF mode, or metering mode). The camera will, however, remain in Depth-of-Field mode, ready for you to take another reading.

Of course, there might be times when the desired depth of field is not possible with the lens in use. Your EOS-1N will not be able to set the required aperture because it is not available on the lens you are using. In this case you will be warned by the aperture value blinking in the viewfinder and on the LCD panel. If the correct aperture can be set but a corresponding shutter speed is not available, "8000" and the smallest lens aperture value will blink to warn of potential overexposure, while "30" and the largest aperture value will blink to warn of potential underexposure. If this happens, the desired depth of field might be impossible to achieve with the given lens, film, and lighting conditions.

Working with Depth-of-Field AE mode requires slightly more time than working in Aperture-Priority mode, however the results are more precise. Very large zones of sharp focus require attention because the resulting small aperture usually requires shooting with a long shutter speed. In these situations, a tripod should be used.

Depth-of-Field AE mode can be used with zoom lenses, however this can be problematic. If the focal length is changed after the aperture has been set, your EOS-1N will try to adjust the aperture accordingly, and success is not always guaranteed. Also, when taking pictures using flash, the Depth-of-Field AE feature is ineffective. The resultant photo will approximate one taken in Program AE mode. In these situations, we suggest you switch to Program AE for more accurate results.

**Depth-of-Field AE mode permits you to select the exact range of focus.**

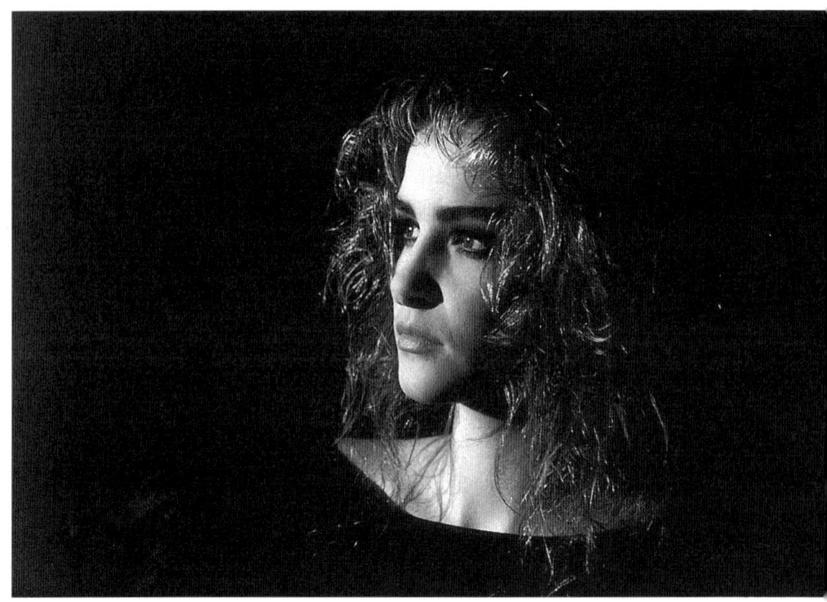

**Manual mode is recommended when precise control of exposure is needed in unusual lighting situations or for studio flash work.**

## Manual Exposure Mode

Setting the camera's shutter speed and aperture manually is slower and requires more of the photographer's attention than using an automatic exposure mode. Nevertheless, there are situations when photographers prefer to shoot in Manual mode.

In order to manually set the shutter speed and aperture, first activate the quick control dial by turning the quick control dial switch to "I." Then press the shooting mode selector (MODE) and rotate the main dial until "M" is displayed in the upper left-hand corner of the LCD panel. It will also appear on the left of the viewfinder display.

Change the shutter speed and/or aperture settings until the arrow on the exposure level scale is opposite the correct exposure indicator (a triangle in the center of the scale). While it is also possible to modify the exposure of any automatic system by entering exposure compensation factors, setting shutter speed and aperture manually is important in situations such as studio shots where the exposure is determined with a handheld exposure meter or a flash exposure meter. The shutter speed and aperture combination determined with the handheld exposure meter is then input manually into the camera. To expose the photograph more than is indicated by the camera's meter (plus exposure compensation), the exposure level indicator must be located above the correct exposure indicator; for intentional underexposure (minus exposure compensation) it must be located at a point below the correct exposure indicator.

Furthermore, Manual exposure mode can be useful when working in continuous advance mode because the exposure remains the same from frame to frame. For example, when shooting a series of a subject that is moving in front of a background that has sections of varying brightness, Manual mode ensures that the subject will have consistent exposure as long as the lighting on it remains the same, regardless of the background's variation.

**Customizing Manual Mode**

In the EOS-1N's default setting for Manual mode, the shutter speed is set with the main dial and the aperture is set with the quick control dial (or by pressing the exposure compensation button [+/-] and turning the main dial). The focusing point is set by pressing the focusing point selector and turning the main dial.

These default control settings can be set to your specific needs by using Custom Functions 5 and 11. With Custom Function 5, setting 0, (and Custom Function 11, setting 0) the shutter speed is selected by turning the main dial. (This is the default setting.) Now, if you activate Custom Function 11, setting 1, the aperture is selected by either using the quick control dial or by pressing the focusing point selector and turning the main dial. Selecting a focusing point manually is not possible. However, if you activate setting F-11, 2, the aperture must be set by activating the focusing point selector and turning the main dial. The focusing point can be selected manually by using the quick control dial.

By selecting Custom Function 5, setting 1, the aperture is set using the main dial. By adding Custom Function 11, setting 0, the shutter speed can be set either by using the quick control dial or by pressing the exposure compensation (+/-) button and turning the main dial, while the focusing point can still be selected manually by pressing the focusing point selector and turning the main dial. Setting F-11, 1 allows you to select the shutter speed either with the quick control dial or by pressing the focusing point selector and turning the main dial. However the focusing point cannot be set manually. Finally, if Custom Function 5, setting 1 is combined with Custom Function 11, setting 2, you can change the shutter speed by pressing the focusing point selector and turning the main dial. The focusing point can then be set manually using the quick control dial.

When shooting static subjects, for instance product shots, we recommend using a combination of settings F-5, 0 and F-11, 0 because the shutter speed and aperture can be set rapidly and reliably.

For series of shots of subjects in motion, using the combination of settings F-5, 1 and F-11, 2 is recommended. The shutter speed is fixed (unless you change it by holding the focusing point selector in while turning the main dial) in order to freeze or blur the subject's motion, as desired. Adjustments to exposure can be made quickly using the main dial to change the aperture, and the focusing point can be shifted quickly with the quick control dial to adapt to the subject's movements.

## Bulb Mode

The Bulb or "B" setting allows exposure times ranging from a few minutes to several hours. Some say it is called "Bulb" because of the rubber bulb that was squeezed to activate the shutter with air pressure when photography was in its infancy. Others say that it represents flash bulbs, because early cameras did not have synchronized shutters for automatic operation with flash bulbs.

To set Bulb on the EOS-1N, press the shooting mode selector and rotate the main dial until "buLb" is displayed on the LCD panel. Exposure time is determined by the length of time the shutter release button or the Remote Switch 60T3 (which is plugged into the remote control socket on the right side of the camera) is engaged.

The LCD monitor's frame counter will count in one-second increments an exposure time of up to 30 seconds. As soon as

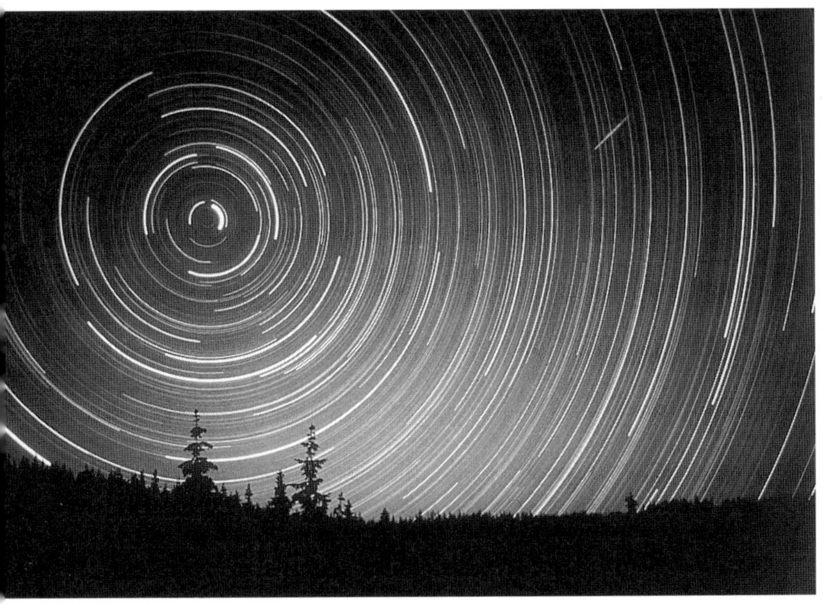

**This star track photo was created using the Bulb mode, a stable tripod, and an exposure that lasted several hours.**

those 30 seconds have been counted down, a battery check bar composed of four short bars (----) will be displayed in the LCD. The LCD will display a new battery check bar as each 30-second countdown elapses. Long time exposures of up to 120 seconds can be controlled reliably by watching these bars and the LCD's 30-second display. For longer exposure times, use the second hand of your watch. Unfortunately, the EOS-1N's LCD panel display is difficult to read in the dark because the LCD illuminator light goes out as soon as exposure starts (are you listening Canon engineers?).

In Bulb you can set the aperture with the main dial or the quick control dial, the latter being used only when you have *not* selected Custom Function 11, setting 2. Of course the shutter speed is determined by how long the shutter button is pressed!

Because the EOS-1N is capable of timing shutter speeds only as long as 30 seconds, the Bulb setting is needed only in very low-light situations. Use a hand-held meter, which can calculate very long exposure times, or set the camera to Shutter-Priority AE mode and set the shutter speed to 30 seconds. Note the aperture that the camera suggests and set the camera to Bulb. Now close down the aperture stop by stop (which will increase depth of field) and increase the exposure time accordingly (stop by stop) until you reach the exposure you need to achieve the desired effect (for instance, shooting star trails will take a longer exposure than shooting the strip in Las Vegas).

Unfortunately, the film adds another variable. Due to reciprocity failure (Schwarzschild effect), doubling very slow shutter speeds (longer than 1/15 second) does not in turn double the effect of light on the film (the exposure). Instead, exposure is increased by less than one stop each time the exposure time is doubled. This means that in order to double the exposure, you need to increase the shutter speed by more than 2x and/or open up the aperture. Refer to the reciprocity failure charts (sometimes labeled "Exposure and Development Adjustments for Long and Short Exposures") included in most film packaging for likely exposure compensation adjustments. This still does not guarantee that you will end up with a good picture. We suggest that you bracket your exposures to increase your chances. Also, color shifts may occur with films subjected to extended exposure times.

There are many subjects that invite long exposure times! Take advantage of the Bulb setting for exposing subjects that determine their own exposure time by virtue of their limited duration, such as car headlights and taillights, fireworks, or lightning during a thunderstorm. Each one of these situations requires the use of a sturdy tripod. Set up your EOS-1N so that the lens (wide-angle lenses are recommended) will capture the environment in which these illuminated subjects are most likely to appear. For exposures of moving cars this would mean aiming the lens at the road (or at an expressway, viewed from a bridge); for fireworks, the sky over a fairground; and for exposures of lightning, the darkest cloud. Use an aperture of f/11 to capture fireworks with an ISO 100 film and an aperture of f/8 with an ISO 50 film, for instance. Using an ISO 100 film, an aperture of f/8 is preferred for lightning and an aperture of f/5.6 or f/8 is recommended for photographing moving cars. In order to be certain of capturing a successful photo, you should take several shots at different aperture settings. Activate the shutter release as soon as something occurs within the lens' angle of view. Stop exposure after a number of cars have passed

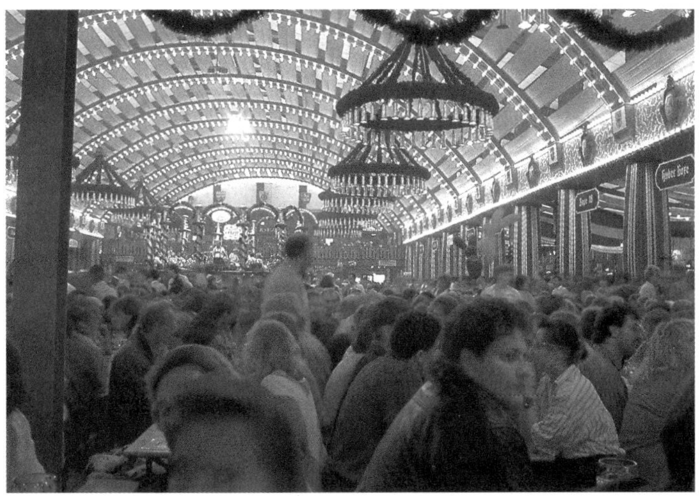

**When photographing indoors under limited lighting conditions, be sure to use a tripod or rest the camera on a stable surface in order to minimize the effects of camera shake. Photo by Bob Shell.**

through the picture, a number of lightning bolts have cracked across the sky, or several fireworks have exploded.

***Caution:*** *When taking pictures of lightning, please remember that no picture is worth risking death! And, although photos of lightning through bare tree branches can be beautiful, do not be tempted to stand under a tree during an electrical storm! Caution should also be used when photographing traffic. Be sure that you are positioned safely and wearing light and/or reflective clothing.*

The Bulb setting can also produce interesting effects with flash. Determine the aperture to use by using the following formula: Guide Number ÷ Flash-to-Subject Distance = Aperture. Open the shutter and illuminate the subject by firing the flash. To expose a large subject, such as a darkened room, fire the flash several times pointing it in different directions. Try not to let the flashes overlap, and be sure to let the flash unit recycle after each firing. Since the results are somewhat unpredictable, it is worthwhile to take numerous shots.

## Multiple Exposures

Only those who have used older cameras will remember the trick of making multiple exposures by playing with the rewind release button, the rewind release crank, and the film advance lever! Those who remember this and are now switching to a modern camera will find real joy in the simple and elegant solutions offered by the EOS-1N (as well as by other EOS models).

To achieve multiple exposures with this camera, press the shooting mode selector (MODE) and metering mode selector simultaneously. Two overlapping rectangles (the symbol for multiple exposures) will appear on the LCD panel. When this symbol is displayed, the frame counter window disappears. Instead a "1" will be displayed. Rotate the main dial clockwise (right) to set the number of exposures you want to make (up to nine). This number will be displayed in the frame counter window. If you select too many exposures, turn the main dial counterclockwise (left) to backtrack. Selecting "1" will cancel multiple exposure mode. If you want to make more than nine exposures on one frame, it can be done! Simply reset the multiple exposure counter *before* the last frame in the sequence has been shot. This can be done an infinite number of times, and, in theory, any number of exposures can be made on one frame of film. The film will not advance until the set number of exposures has been taken. Then the film will automatically advance to the next frame and multiple exposure mode will be canceled.

Multiple exposure mode can create two fundamentally different effects. One is to partially or completely overlap several images. The other is to expose several subjects next to each other in front of a dark background. When shooting overlapping subjects, the film frame is exposed once, twice, three times, or more. To prevent overexposure, minus corrections are required. As a rule of thumb, double exposures require a -1-stop correction, triple exposures a -1-1/2-stop correction, and quadruple exposures a -2-stop correction. However, an easier method is to multiply the number of desired exposures by the film's ISO rating and adjust the camera's ISO setting to that number.

Subjects that do not overlap and are shot before a dark or black background are each exposed as if they were normal exposures. However, in order to keep the background really dark, a correction of -1/3 stop can be helpful. A frequently used subject of this type is the moon, which can be shot so that its many images float over the landscape at night. When taking this kind of picture, please remember that it is daylight in the visible region of the moon and your exposure must be set accordingly. In order to prevent the moon from becoming a bare, white spot, it should be exposed for 1/125 second at f/16 (ISO 100). (With a clear sky 1/250 second may be enough. In high humidity, 1/60 second may be a better choice, because humidity absorbs light. A series of test exposures is highly recommended.)

To return to single-frame film advance before all multiple exposures have been made, press the shooting mode selector and metering mode selector simultaneously and rotate the main dial until the field displaying the number of multiple frames on the LCD is blank. Once you let go of the buttons, the frame counter window will reappear. Do not forget to reset the exposure compensation to "0" and the film speed back to its correct value! A look through the film window on the back of the camera should display the film speed in use.

## Depth-of-Field Preview

Taking advantage of depth of field is an important creative tool in photography. Aperture-Priority mode, the lens' depth-of-field scale, and Depth-of-Field AE mode help in determining depth of field. But what effect does it really have on the picture?

The EOS-1N's depth-of-field preview button permits you to view the scene through the actual set aperture. The EOS-1N can stop down the aperture at any time to the value that it is set to have at the time of exposure. This allows you to accurately evaluate the picture's depth of field. (The viewfinder normally displays the scene at the camera's widest setting for brightest viewing and then closes down to the set aperture when the shutter is released.)

Press the depth-of-field preview button, which projects from the right side of the camera near the lens mount. As soon as the aperture has closed down, you can actually see through the viewfinder which subject details are within the depth of field range and if there is a noticeable lack of sharpness.

Even though the EOS-1N's viewfinder is designed to be bright, problems arise in evaluating the extent of the depth of field when aperture values of f/8 or smaller are set. Darkening of the image in the viewfinder is caused by the reduction of light passing through the smaller aperture and by the fact that the viewfinder image is not very large.

Once you press the depth-of-field preview button, exposure is metered and—depending on the exposure mode you have selected—the respective shutter speed-aperture combination is set. By turning the quick control dial you can open or close the lens aperture (you can hear it opening and closing down!) and see the resultant effect on the image's depth of field. The exposure value is stored in memory until you let go of the depth-of-field preview button. Also, the shutter cannot be released until you let go of the depth-of-field preview button.

## Self-Timer and Mirror Lock-Up

A self-timer is not just designed for photographers who want to make self-portraits or include themselves in group shots. A self-timer can also be used to prevent image blur, especially when the camera features mirror lock-up.

The EOS-1N's self-timer is activated by pressing the blue film winding mode selector (DRIVE) behind the palm door and rotating the main dial until a clock symbol with a "10" or a "2" appears in the frame counter field, framed in blue on the LCD panel. This indicates that an exposure delay of 10 or 2 seconds (respectively) has been set. Self-timer countdown will begin when the shutter button is triggered and it is indicated by the blinking LED on the front of the EOS-1N (the self-timer indicator). During the final 2 seconds of the 10-second countdown the blinking will accelerate noticeably. Focus and exposure will be set and locked when the shutter release is triggered.

Ten seconds should be enough for anyone to trigger the release and run in front of the camera to get into the picture. Two seconds are obviously not enough; however they are enough to allow vibrations caused by triggering the shutter release to subside. This is a

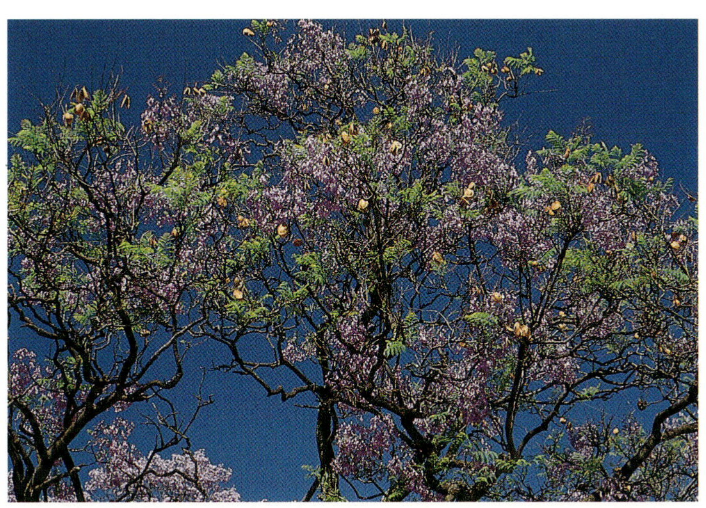

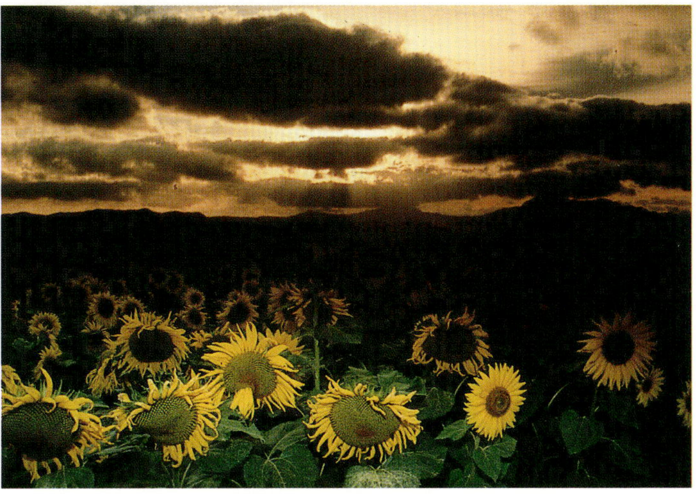

The EOS-1N's quick control dial was used to make a slight minus exposure correction, which enriched the colors, allowing the flowers and leaves to stand out strongly against the sky.

The approaching clouds were made even more threatening by using a Cokin® neutral density filter, and the sunflowers were illuminated by flash. The combination created a surreal effect.

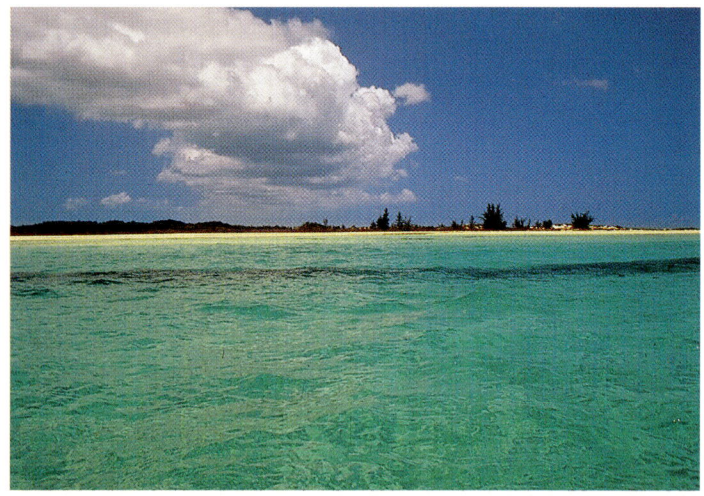

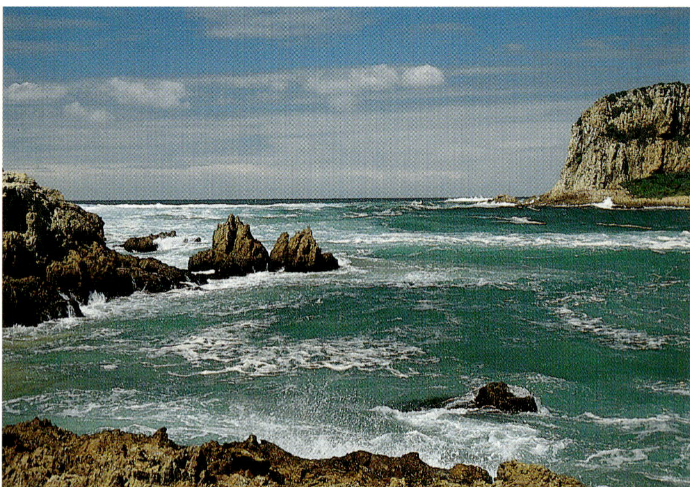

A polarizing filter enhanced this image in three ways. It intensified the color of the sky, increased the contrast in the clouds, and eliminated the reflections in the water, making the ocean appear to be crystal clear.

A wide-angle lens allowed the photographer to include the shoreline at the bottom and to either side of the photo. His composition conveys a sense of space by leading the viewer's eye through the image, following the path of the water.

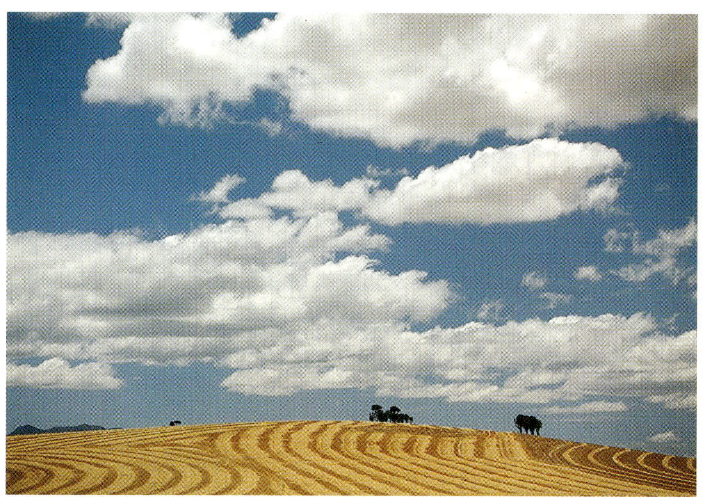

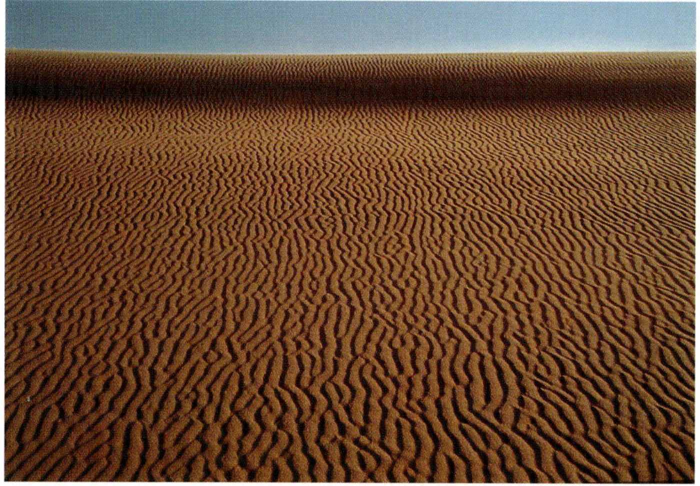

The position of the horizon line is extremely important when photographing landscapes. More dynamic compositions can be achieved if the picture does not appear to be divided in half. Placing the horizon low gives the sky prominence, emphasizing the vast, open space of this South African landscape (above). The very high horizon line in the bottom photo imparts a similar sense of vastness by accentuating the pattern of the desert sand instead.

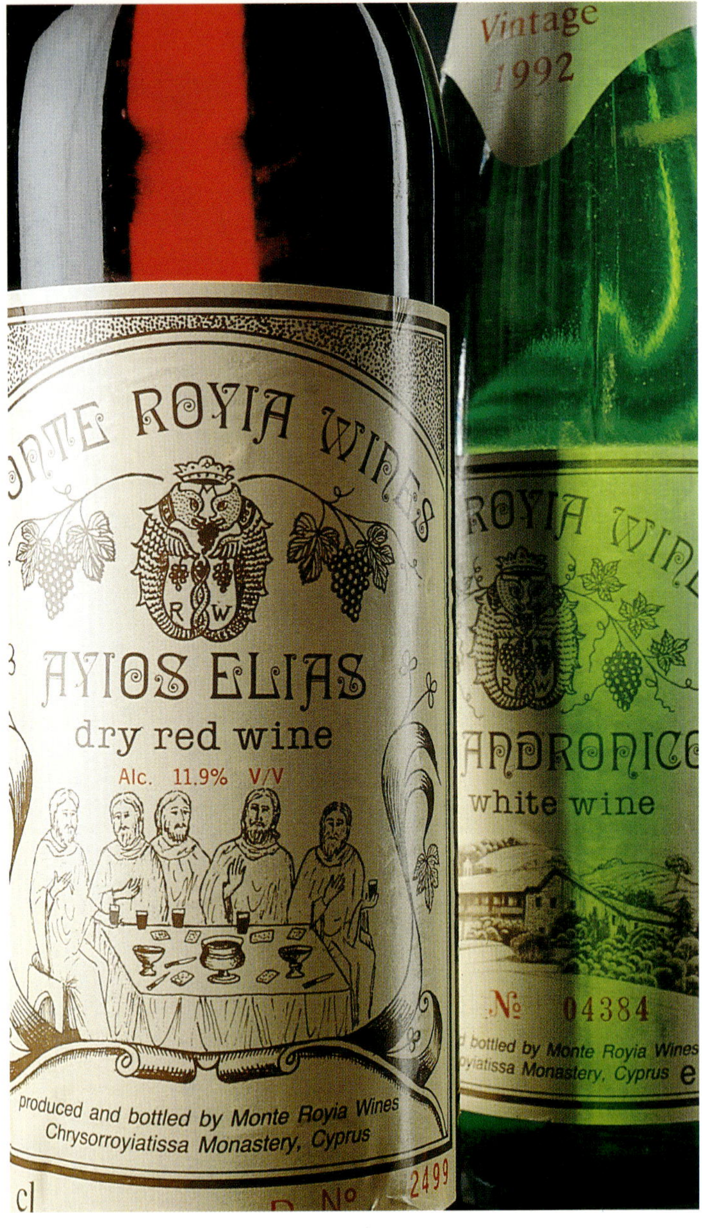


**Precise camera placement allows you to avoid distortion when linear composition is important. Front- and backlighting work together to enhance the colors of the bottles.**

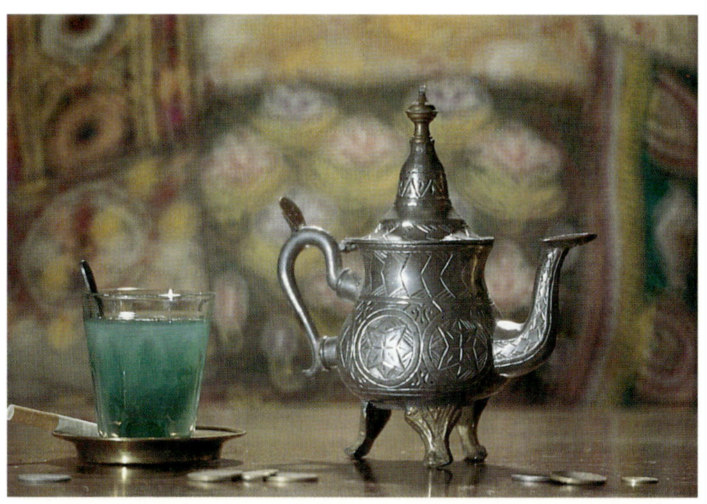

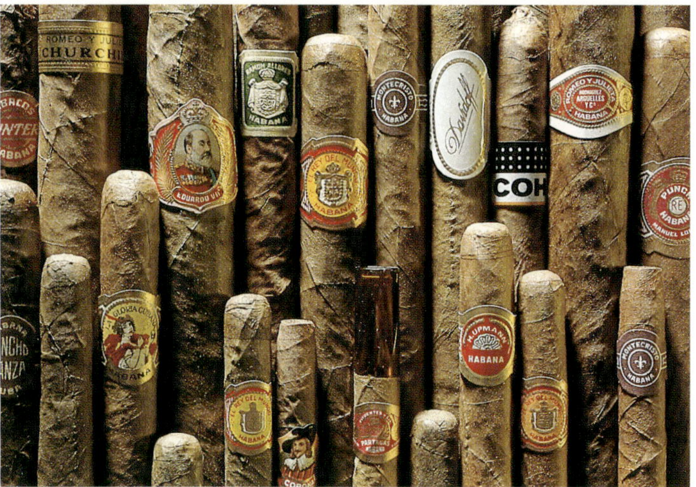


You can make beautiful still lifes with everyday items. By setting a wide aperture on a short telephoto lens, the strongly patterned fabric in the background was reduced to a soft blur.

A zoom lens with a short minimum focusing distance allowed the photographer to come in close enough to make the labels of these Cuban cigars legible.

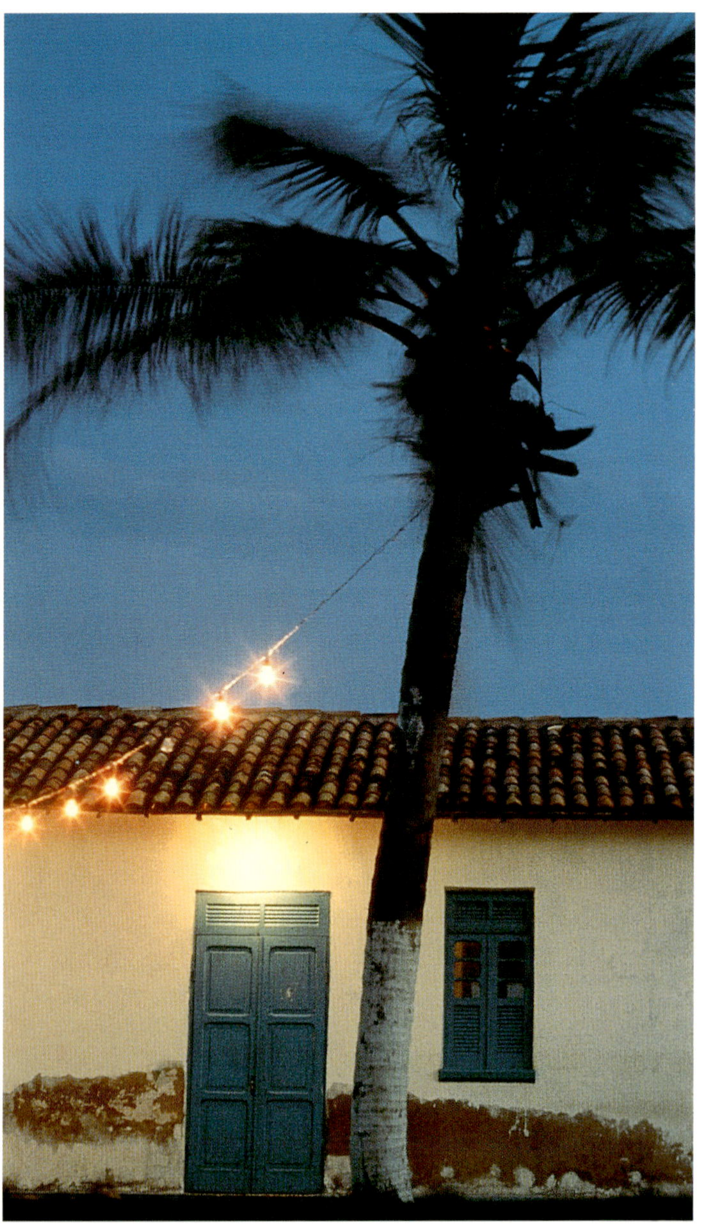

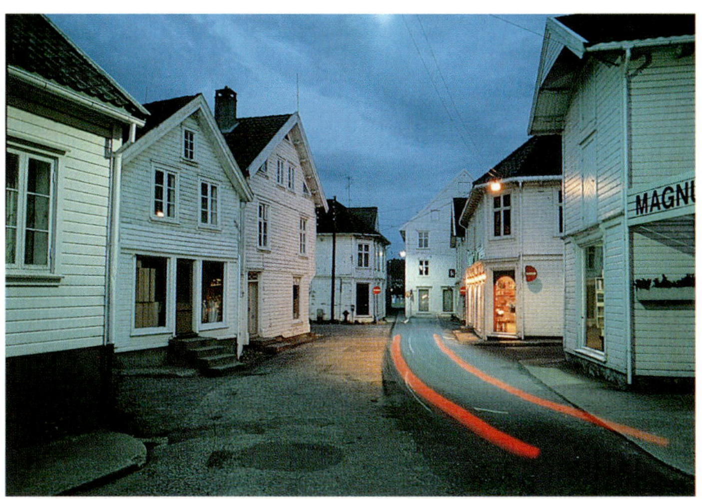

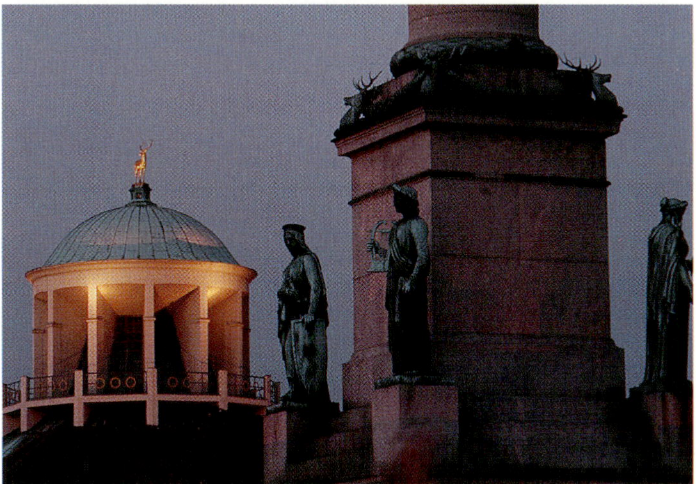

Photos taken at dusk have a particular allure. Using a handheld light meter is a good idea. Or spot meter, which will allow you to exclude direct sources of light from the reading. Evening shots are best taken with a stable tripod, which allows long exposures to be made without risking the effects of camera shake. A little patience is necessary with long exposures, though, because light from unexpected sources can leave its trace in the photo. And, when night falls and artificial light replaces natural sunlight even partially, an unanticipated color cast (often green) can result.

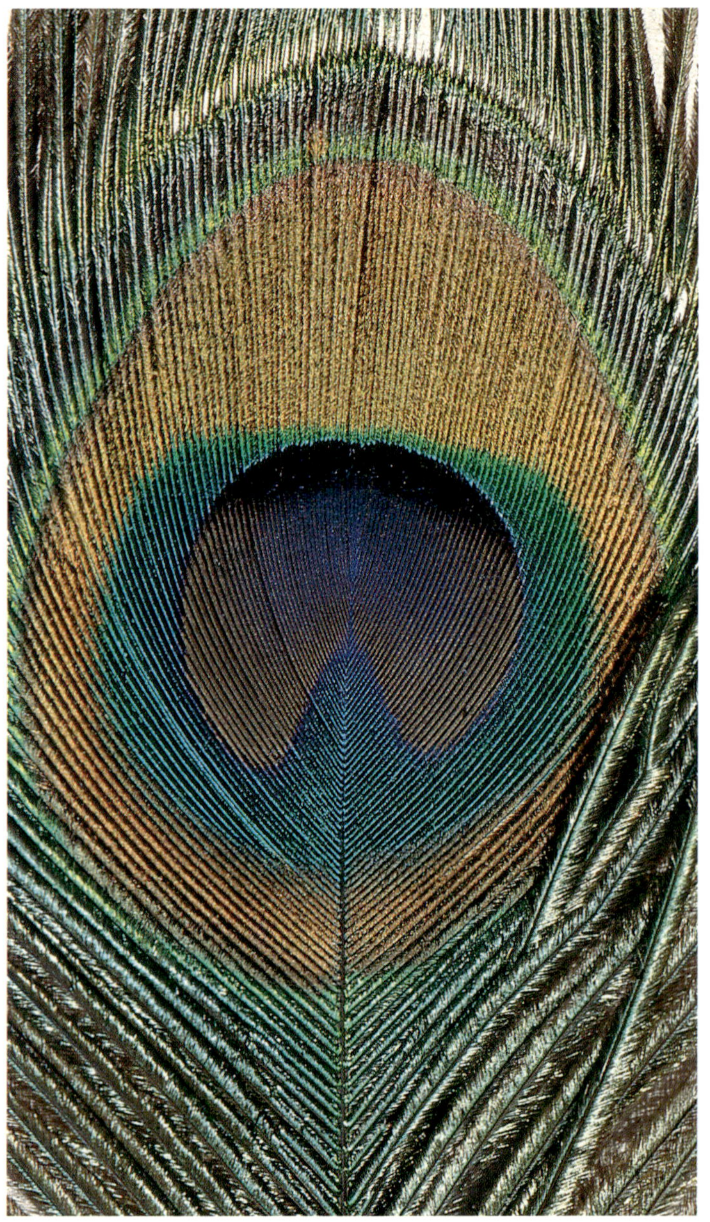

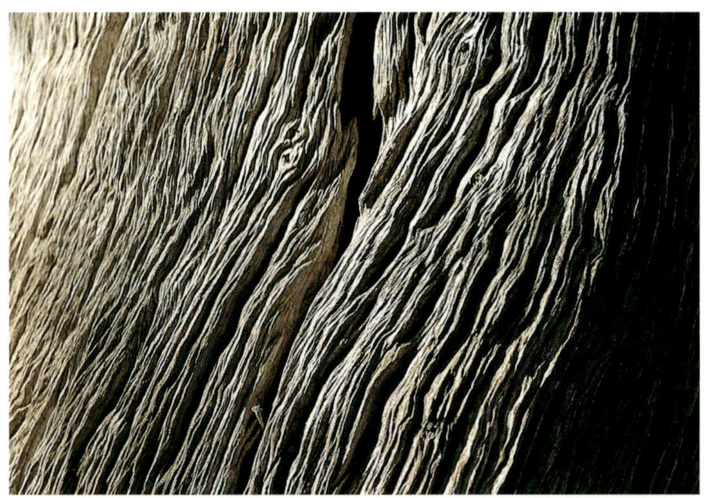

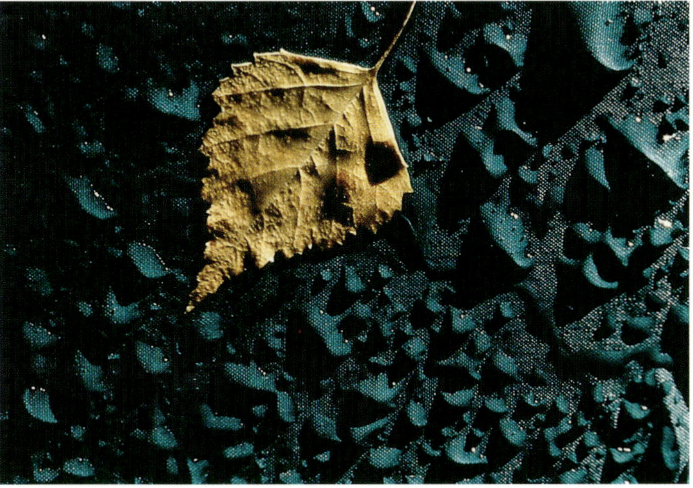

Macro lenses are excellent for taking detailed pictures of delicate patterns. Lighting is very important in macro photography. Side lighting works well to emphasize the three-dimensional quality of the pattern. When shooting a relatively light subject with a dark background, use a gray card to assure an accurate exposure. If you are lighting the subject with tungsten light, use an 80A (blue) filter with daylight film to neutralize the yellow cast.

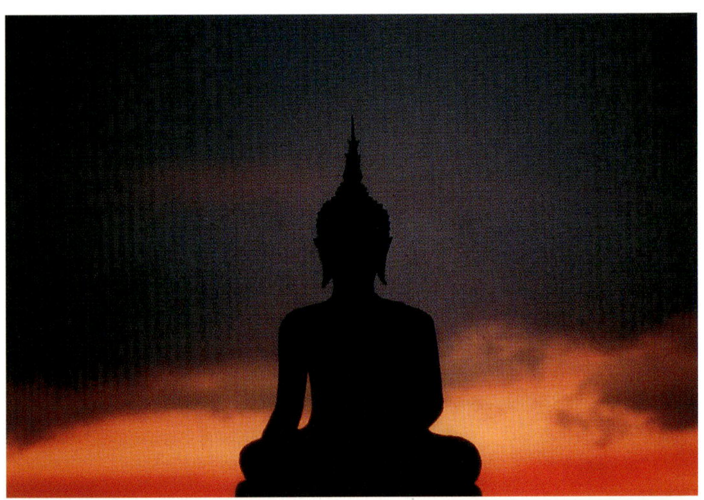

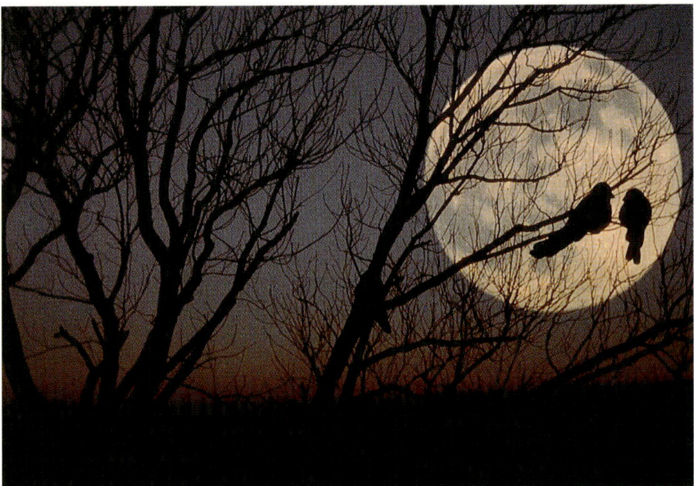

Meter on the bright background, and use a slight minus exposure compensation to achieve a darkly silhouetted subject. And, if the chance arises, you can create a strong composition by taking a double exposure. The above photo was made by first taking an exposure of the birds and the trees. Then the moon was exposed on the same frame using a focal length of 800mm. Exposure compensation was unnecessary because of the darkness of the sky.

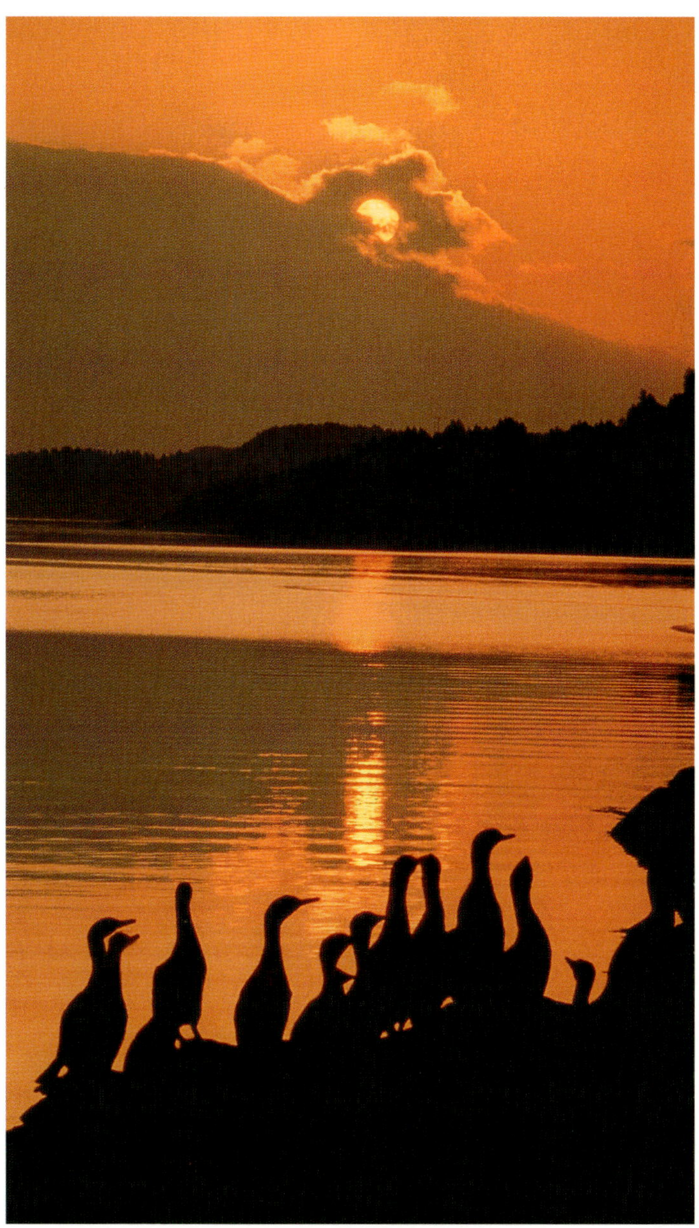

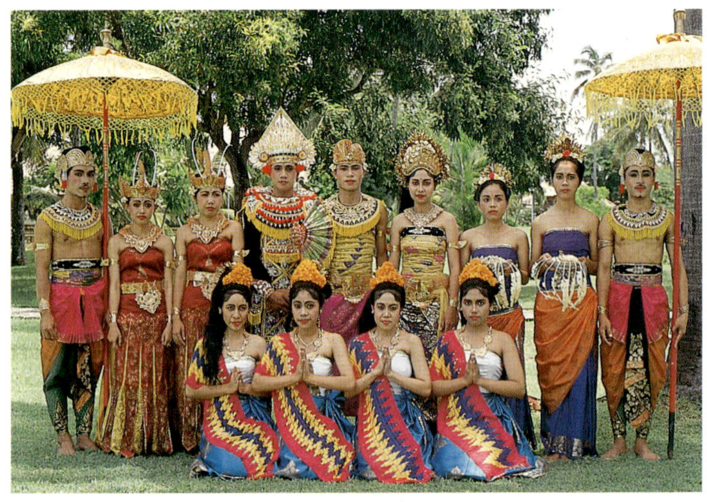

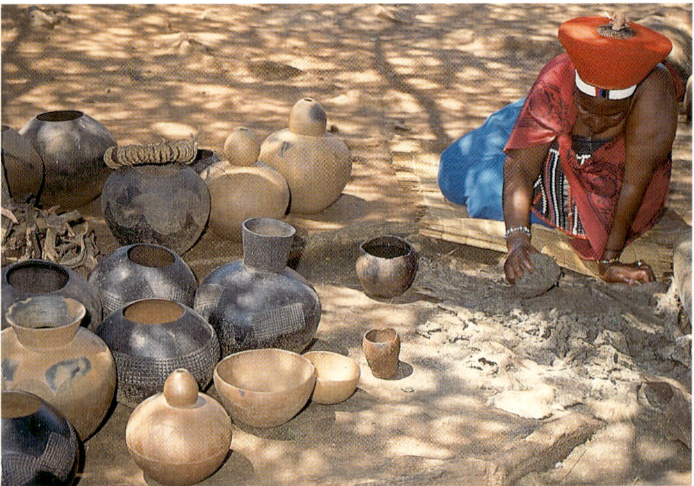

A moderate wide-angle is the lens of choice for group photos. If you use a lens with a focal length that is too short, the people toward the edges of the photo will be distorted.

Patience is invaluable when taking pictures of people in their everyday routine. Ideally your subject should not pay any attention to the camera, but should attend to her own activities. A zoom lens made it possible for the photographer to quickly compose and shoot this photo.

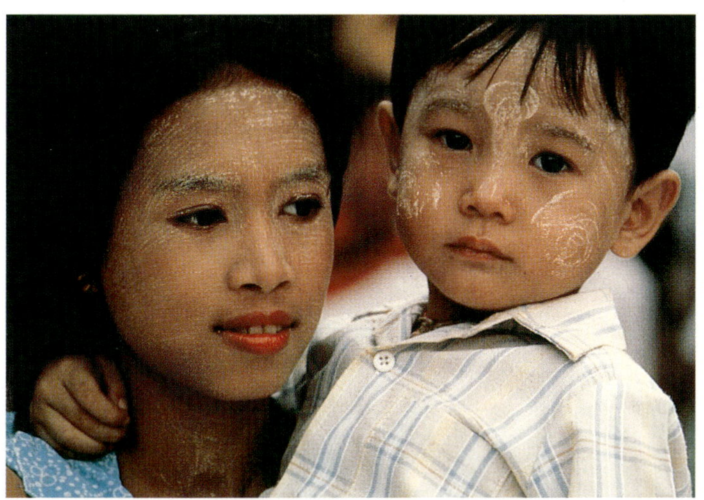

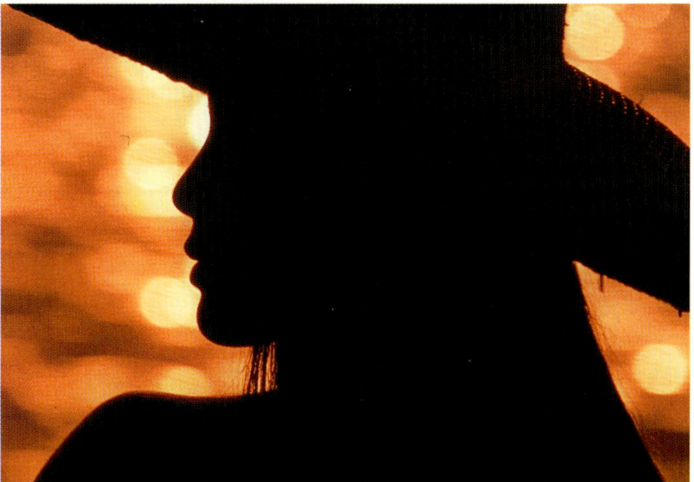

Try to communicate with your subjects before taking portraits of them, even if it means communicating with your hands and facial expressions to get your point across! By doing so, you eliminate the risk of offending your subject and increase the chance of getting a better shot.

A telephoto zoom can be used to take effective portraits. You can move in close with the lens to tighten up framing without altering the perspective (i.e., the position of the points of light in the background of this photo).

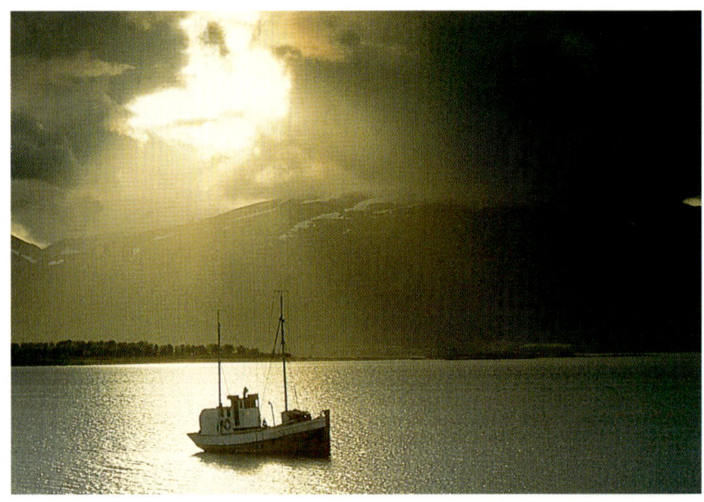

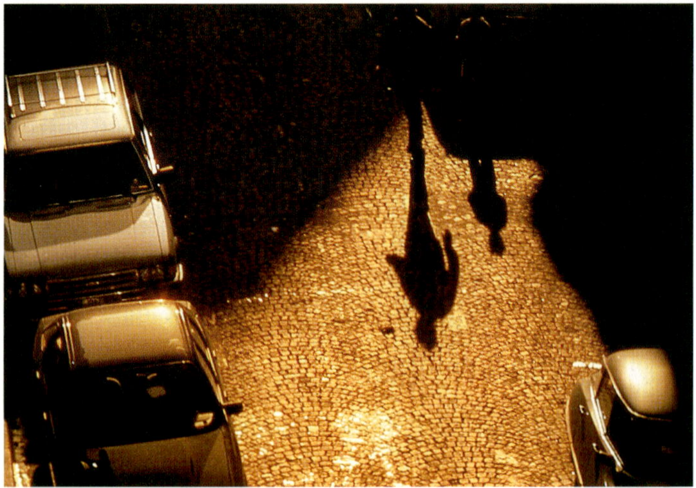

**Backlighting offers a rich source of material for fascinating pictures. The area that you choose to meter determines the amount of detail that will be recorded.**

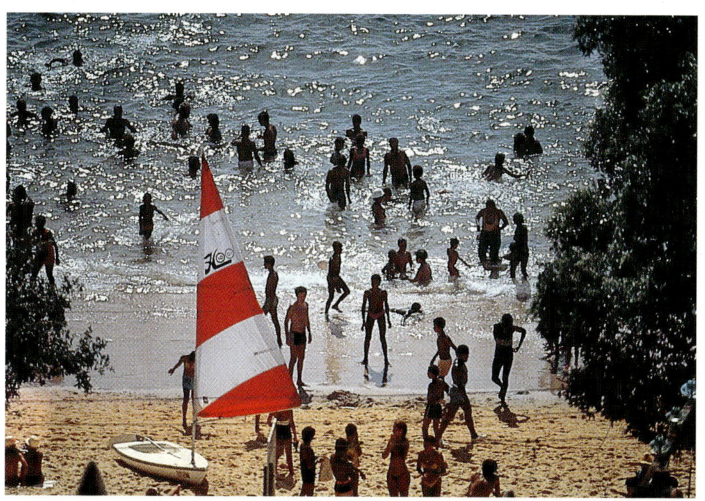

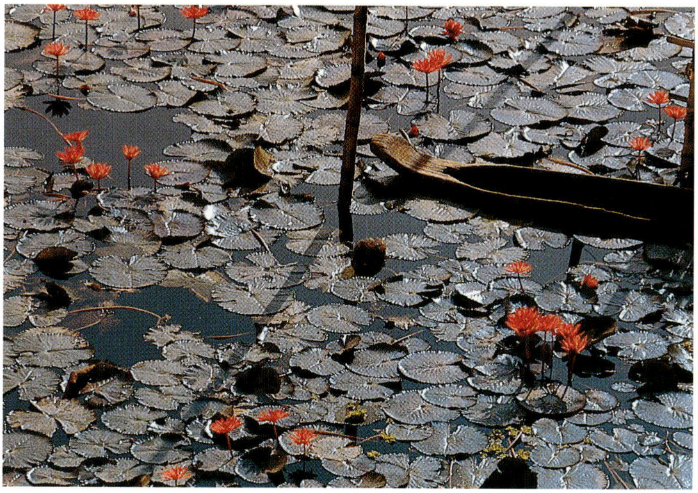

Backlighting doesn't necessarily come from one source. Many small points of light, like reflections on the ocean's surface, can fool the meter. AEB is an excellent feature for ensuring that you will have an exposure that will produce the mood you want to convey.

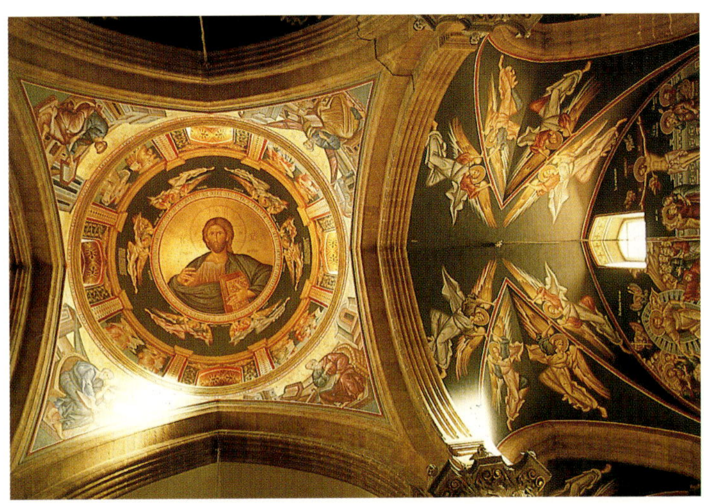

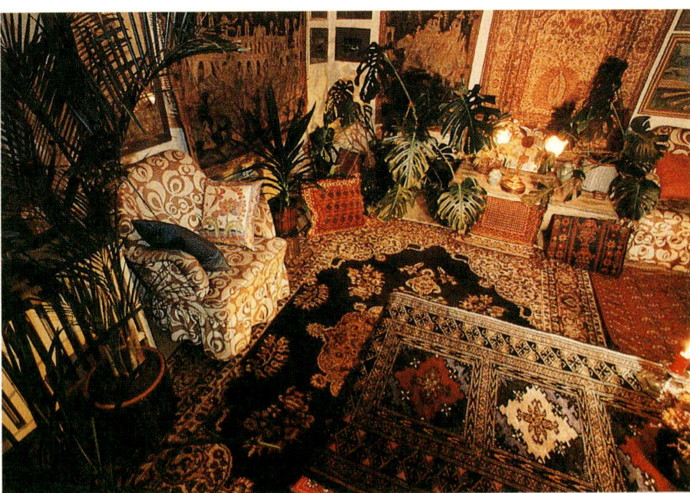

For taking pictures of subjects overhead (like a chapel ceiling), it is best to nest your camera in of a soft, malleable cradle like a sweater or jacket, and put it on the floor, pointing upwards. A small bubble-level is also helpful to ensure that the camera is positioned correctly.

Using daylight film to shoot interiors illuminated by tungsten light often creates a desirable, warm, yellowish hue. To create a noticeably cooler effect, you can add an 80A filter.

handy feature when taking close-up, telephoto, or super-telephoto shots and a cable release is not available.

For group shots that include the photographer, make sure the shutter button is triggered with enough delay to allow him or her to get into the picture. In this type of situation the eye is often not at the eyepiece when the release is triggered and the light can enter into the viewfinder from the back and thus alter the metering reading. To prevent this, you should close the eyepiece. Move the eyepiece shutter lever (located to the right, above the eyepiece) clockwise. The eyepiece shutter is also useful when exposures are taken with an intervalometer or when shooting with a tripod and a cable release.

Although the two-second delay eliminates vibrations caused by the shutter release, the impact of the mirror lifting up just before the shutter fires—no matter how well the camera's mirror movement has been dampened—can still result in minor camera shake. To prevent this, the EOS-1N's mirror can be flipped up before the actual picture is taken.

First, select Custom Function 12, setting 1. When the shutter button is pressed the first time, the mirror will flip up and be held there for 30 seconds. When the shutter release button is pressed a second time, the picture will be taken. If you wait too long before pressing the release button the second time, the mirror will flip down again.

In order to eliminate any risk of vibrations, the mirror-up feature can be combined with the self-timer feature. Now you can press the release button just once. The mirror will flip up, and two to ten seconds later the exposure will be taken. Also, enlarging an object in a photograph (when using a telephoto or a macro lens, for instance) magnifies the problem of camera shake. In these situations, using the mirror lock-up feature is recommended to help ensure a clear photo.

When the mirror is up, light can fall directly onto the shutter. Canon cautions that direct sunlight can damage the shutter. Therefore, use the mirror lock-up feature only when it is absolutely necessary, and be careful to prevent sunlight from shining directly into the lens because it will act as a magnifying glass. Unfortunately, it is not possible to use the mirror lock-up feature in continuous advance mode. Ideally, this would dampen the background noise and would be a useful feature—but Canon didn't design it that way, and that's just the way it goes.

# Custom Functions

There is no camera that will accommodate every photographer's specific needs, preferences, or assignments. Canon's EOS-1N with its Custom Functions comes very close to this ideal though.

The EOS-1N features 14 Custom Functions offering a total of 35 different settings, some of which can be combined to offer additional options. It is easy to program the EOS-1N for one's individualized needs, though sometimes it might be difficult to remember everything one has programmed! Therefore, if you think that your camera should be responding differently than it is, first check the Custom Function settings.

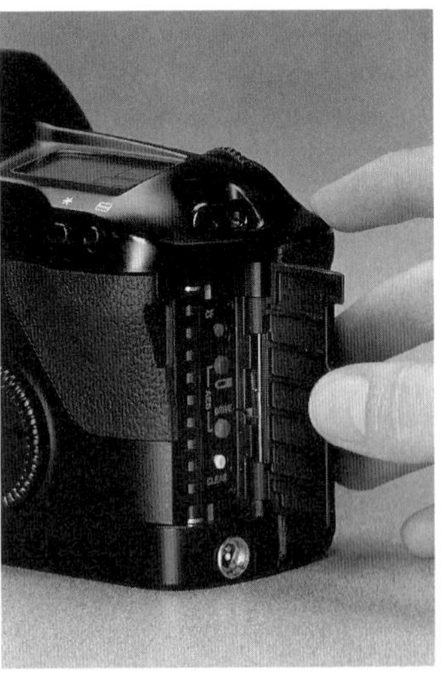

**Use the buttons behind the palm door to select (CF) or clear (CLEAR) a Custom Function, check battery status, select a film advance mode (DRIVE), and use the autoexposure bracketing feature (AEB).**

You can obtain an overview of the Custom Functions that are active by pressing the Custom Function set button (labeled "CF") behind the camera's palm door. Look at the exposure compensation scale on the LCD panel. If there are no large, black, rectangular dots under the scale, no Custom Functions are set. Any large, rectangular dots displayed under the scale indicate the Custom

Functions that are enabled. Each number and small, round dot on the scale represents a Custom Function number. For example: -3=Custom Function 1, -2=Custom Function 4, 0=Custom Function 10, etc. An alternative method, which the authors prefer, is to press the CF button and turn the main dial. By doing this, an "F" followed by the Custom Function number will be displayed at the top of the LCD panel and the setting (0, 1, 2, or 3) will be displayed below it. You can rapidly scroll through the Custom Functions by turning the main dial and push the CF button to see what setting you have selected for each.

To make or change a setting, use the main dial to select the appropriate Custom Function number and then press the CF button until the correct setting number is indicated on the LCD panel. Press the shutter button halfway to input the setting. This will also restore the standard LCD panel display.

To reset any Custom Function to its default setting (0), select the appropriate Custom Function number and then press the CF button until "0" is displayed below the Custom Function number. Should you want to erase all of the Custom Function settings at once, press the CF button and then press the white CLEAR button. The camera's default settings will then be active.

What follows is a brief overview of options available for you to modify your EOS-1N's operation with your preferences.

## Custom Function 1: Film Rewind

**F-1, 0:** High-speed film rewind begins automatically when you have reached the end of a roll of film.

**F-1, 1:** High-speed film rewind must be started manually by pressing the film rewind button.

**F-1, 2:** Silent rewind (at a slower speed) begins automatically at the end of a roll of film.

**F-1, 3:** Silent rewind (at a slower speed) must be started manually by pressing the film rewind button.

## Custom Function 2: Film Leader

**F-2, 0:** When the film is rewound, the film leader is pulled entirely into the cassette.

**F-2, 1:** After rewinding is complete, the film leader is left protruding from the cassette.

Setting F-2, 0 is useful as a standard setting because it prevents film from accidentally being loaded a second time, thus ruining all the pictures in the roll. F-2, 1 is useful if you have access to a darkroom and do not wish to break open the film cassette, or if you wish to expose a portion of the film and shoot the rest at a later time. If you do this, use a permanent marker to write on the film leader how many frames have been shot. When you reload the film, set the camera for Manual exposure mode, put the lens cap on, and press the shutter button to advance the film one or two frames past the number that have been exposed, just to be sure that you don't inadvertently make a double exposure. If you are doing this with slide film and are having a photo lab develop and mount your transparencies, be sure to alert the lab that frame spacing may vary so your frames aren't chopped in half by the automated machine! Setting F-2, 1 is also useful when shooting Polaroid instant-process 35mm film, since it saves you the trouble of "fishing" for the film leader with a leader retriever.

## Custom Function 3: Film Speed

**F-3, 0:** Each time a film cassette is loaded, the ISO film speed rating is read by the camera's automatic DX sensors. This is useful for those who use a variety of films and may forget to manually reset the speed.

**F-3, 1:** Film speed is set manually (the DX rating is ignored by the system). The setting is retained when the next roll is loaded. This Custom Function setting helps those who are familiar with particular films and like to use ISO settings that are different from the films' standard speeds in order to achieve a particular effect (such as increasing color saturation).

## Custom Function 4: Autofocus and AE Lock

**F-4, 0:** Automatic focus is activated by pressing the shutter button partway down. Pressing the AE lock button (*) locks exposure values.

**F-4, 1:** Automatic focus is activated by pressing the AE lock button (*). Exposure locks when the shutter button is pressed partway down.

**F-4, 2:** Automatic focus is activated by pressing the shutter button partway down. Focus is locked by pressing the AE lock button (*). It is not possible to lock exposure values in this setting.

The Custom Function 4 settings allow you to customize your camera to lock exposure and focus separately or together, depending on the AF mode (One-Shot or AI Servo) and film winding mode (single-frame or continuous advance) selected.

## Custom Function 5: Manual Exposure Mode

**F-5, 0:** In Manual exposure mode the shutter speed is selected with the main dial, and the aperture is selected by turning the quick control dial or by pressing the exposure compensation button (+/-) and turning the main dial.

**F-5, 1:** In Manual exposure mode the shutter speed is selected with the quick control dial or by pressing the exposure compensation button (+/-) and turning the main dial, and the aperture is set with the main dial.

The choice depends entirely on your preference. See Custom Function 11 for further options for configuring shutter speed and aperture controls.

## Custom Function 6: Exposure Value Increments

**F-6, 0:** Shutter speed, aperture, exposure compensation, flash exposure compensation, and autoexposure bracketing (AEB) values are set in 1/3-stop increments.

**F-6, 1:** Shutter speed and aperture values are adjusted in full stops. Exposure compensation, flash exposure compensation, and AEB values are set in 1/3-stop increments.

**F-6, 2:** Shutter speed, aperture, exposure compensation, flash exposure compensation, and AEB values are adjusted in 1/2-stop increments.

We recommend Custom Function 6, setting 0 (F-6, 0) for shooting with slide film and setting F-6, 2 for shooting with negative (print) film. Custom Function 6, setting 1 is valuable when you are using the EOS-1N in conjunction with an EOS-1 or with other EOS model cameras and you want to coordinate the increment values. The EOS-1 offers only 1/3- and full-stop increments, and other EOS models are set in 1/2-stop increments.

## Custom Function 7: Manual Focus

Custom Function 7 is applicable only when using USM (Ultrasonic Motor) lenses featuring electronic manual focus. At the time of publication appropriate lenses are:

EF 50mm f/1.0L USM
EF 85mm f/1.2L USM
EF 200mm f/1.8L USM
EF 300mm f/2.8L USM
EF 400mm f/2.8L USM
EF 500mm f/4.5L USM
EF 600mm f/4.0L USM
EF 1200mm f/5.6L USM
EF 28-80mm f/2.8-4.0L USM

**F-7, 0:** Automatic focus can be adjusted manually even when the lens' AF/M switch is set to "AF."

**F-7, 1:** Focus can be changed manually only when the lens' AF/M switch is set to "M." When the switch is set to "AF," manual focus is disabled.

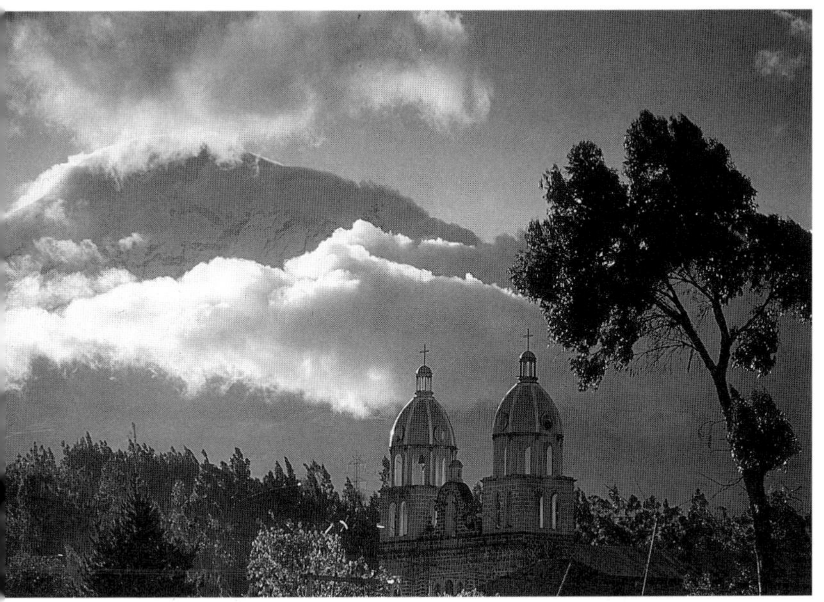

**Center-weighted average metering (Custom Function 8, setting 1) and a little additional exposure compensation made the sky appear to glow over the church bell towers.**

## Custom Function 8: 16-Zone Evaluative Metering

**F-8, 0:** The camera offers 16-zone evaluative metering.

**F-8, 1:** 16-zone evaluative metering is replaced by center-weighted average metering. (The LCD panel will still display the evaluative metering symbol.)

F-8, 1 is recommended for photographers who are experienced with center-weighted average metering and want more control over which position of the scene is evaluated by the camera's meter.

## Custom Function 9: Autoexposure Bracketing

**F-9, 0:** Automatic exposure bracketing (AEB) is set to take three shots in the sequence: underexposure, correct (metered) exposure, overexposure. AEB is enabled by simultaneously pressing the AEB buttons (the gray battery check button and the blue film winding mode selector) behind the palm door. AEB is automatically disabled when the film is rewound, the lens is changed, Bulb exposure mode is set, the flash is charged, the CLEAR button is pressed, or the camera is switched off ("L").

**F-9, 1:** AEB is set to take three shots in the sequence: underexposure, correct exposure, overexposure. This Custom Function setting allows AEB to be enabled either by pressing the two AEB buttons as described above, or by pressing the AF mode selector ("AF") and shooting mode selector ("MODE") buttons simultaneously and rotating the main dial until the appropriate f/stop increment appears on the LCD. AEB must be disabled manually by pressing the CLEAR button, setting the shooting mode to Bulb, or by pressing the AEB buttons simultaneously and then turning the main dial until the bracketing amount is set to "0" on the LCD's exposure compensation scale.

**F-9, 2:** AEB is set to take three shots in the sequence: correct exposure, underexposure, overexposure. This function is enabled by pressing the AEB buttons behind the palm door. This function is disabled automatically when the film is rewound, Bulb exposure mode is set, the lens is changed, the flash is charged, the CLEAR button is pressed, or the camera is switched off ("L").

**F-9, 3:** AEB is set to take three shots in the sequence: correct exposure, underexposure, overexposure. This feature can be enabled and disabled in the same way as the F-9, 1 setting (see above).

The sequence of shots made in settings F-9, 0 and F-9, 1 appears to be most logical, however which sequence you choose is entirely a matter of preference. If you intend to publish or display your pictures, we recommend selecting F-9, 1 with 1/3-stop increments and using the AEB feature as often as possible.

Remember, bracketing increment values can be changed to 1/2- or 1/3-stop increments by setting Custom Function 6.

## Custom Function 10: Focusing Point Illumination

**F-10, 0:** In One-Shot autofocus mode the active focusing point glows red in the viewfinder.

**F-10, 1:** The active focusing point *does not* glow red in either autofocus mode.

F-10, 1 is useful when shooting in a dark environment and the red focusing point interferes with your ability to evaluate the viewfinder image.

## Custom Function 11: Focusing Point Selection

**F-11, 0:** The focusing point is selected by pressing the focusing point selector and rotating the main dial.

**F-11, 1:** The focusing point is selected by pressing the exposure compensation button (+/-) and rotating the main dial.

**F-11, 2:** The focusing point is selected by pressing the exposure compensation button (+/-) and rotating the main dial or by turning the quick control dial. If you use the quick control dial, there will be no focusing point indication on the LCD panel, however the selected focusing point will light up red in the viewfinder.

A setting of F-11, 2 is recommended when you are tracking a moving subject. Or, you could use the EOS-1N's automatic focusing point selection feature instead in this situation.

**Combining Custom Functions 5 and 11**

Shutter speed and aperture settings are altered as follows when Custom Functions 5 and 11 are combined:

**F-11, 0 with F-5, 0:** Shutter speed is set by turning the main dial. Aperture is set either by turning the quick control dial or by pressing the exposure compensation dial and turning the main dial.

**F-11, 0 with F-5, 1:** Aperture is set by turning the main dial. Shutter speed is set either by turning the quick control dial or pressing the exposure compensation button and turning the main dial.

**F-11, 1 with F-5, 0:** Shutter speed is set by turning the main dial. Aperture is set by using the quick control dial or by pressing the focusing point selector and turning the main dial.

**F-11, 1 with F-5, 1:** Aperture is set by turning the main dial. Shutter speed is set by using the quick control dial or by pressing the focusing point selector and turning the main dial.

**F-11, 2 with F-5, 0:** Shutter speed is set by turning the main dial. Aperture is set by pressing the focusing point selector and turning the main dial.

**F-11, 2 with F-5, 1:** Aperture is set by turning the main dial. Shutter speed is set by pressing the focusing point selector and turning the main dial.

## Custom Function 12: Mirror Lock-Up

**F-12, 0:** The reflex mirror flips up immediately prior to exposure.

**F-12, 1:** The reflex mirror flips up when the shutter button is pressed. Exposure is initiated by pressing the shutter button a second time. (When the self-timer is activated, it is sufficient to press the shutter button once. Exposure is triggered after the self-timer has completed its cycle.)

It is recommended that you set F-12, 1 when working with slow shutter speeds, long telephoto lenses, macro lenses, or a bellows.

## Custom Function 13: Linking Spot Metering to a Focusing Point

**F-13, 0:** Fine spot metering takes place in the center of the image frame.

**F-13, 1:** Spot metering is linked to the manually selected focusing point. If automatic focusing point selection is active, spot metering is linked to the center focusing point.

F-13, 1 should be chosen whenever a focusing point other than the one in the center has been selected. Exposure values are calculated for the subject falling within the selected focusing point.

## Custom Function 14: Flash Output

**F-14, 0:** Flash unit performance is reduced in bright ambient light in order to prevent overexposure.

**F-14, 1:** Flash unit performance will not be reduced even in bright ambient light. This prevents underexposing backlit subjects when flash is used. This setting should be approached carefully because backlit shots with too much fill flash have a slightly artificial quality. Taking a second photograph with -1/3-stop flash exposure compensation (set manually) is recommended.

# Canon EF Lenses

Those buying an EOS-1N are probably basing their decision on two major factors. One, of course, is the professional features and reliability of the camera body. The other factor, no doubt, is the top-quality, professional-level lenses produced by Canon. Many photographers truly believe that Canon EF lenses are the best currently available for any SLR camera system.

Canon offers a wide range of lenses suitable for any application, many of which are exemplary in design and engineering. A few, such as Canon's Tilt-Shift lenses, are unique in their class, with features not offered by any other 35mm SLR camera or lens manufacturer.

Canon's line of EF lenses includes those that suit routine and specialized photographic situations. Expensive lenses are available, as are some that are more affordably priced. There are many different types of zoom lenses, fixed focal length lenses, and, should you need a high-speed lens for work in low light, you will be able to find one to suit that need as well.

Canon manufactures more affordable lenses in commonly used focal lengths intended for the general consumer. While anything but low quality, these consumer lenses do not perform to as high specifications as other EF lenses (which, are heavier, bigger, and more expensive). While they may not meet the rigorous demands

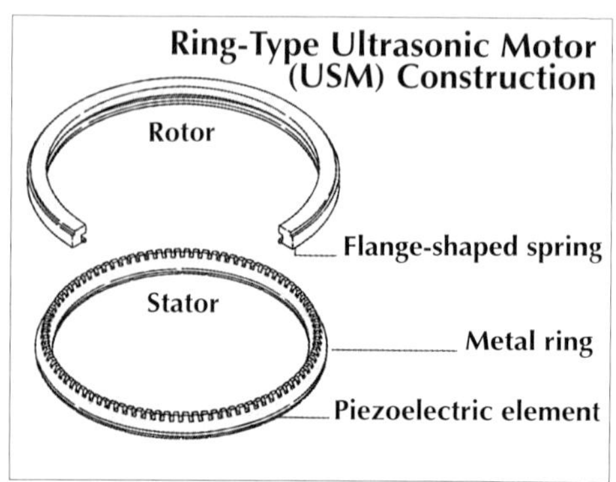


**The two central components of Canon's ultrasonic focusing motor.**

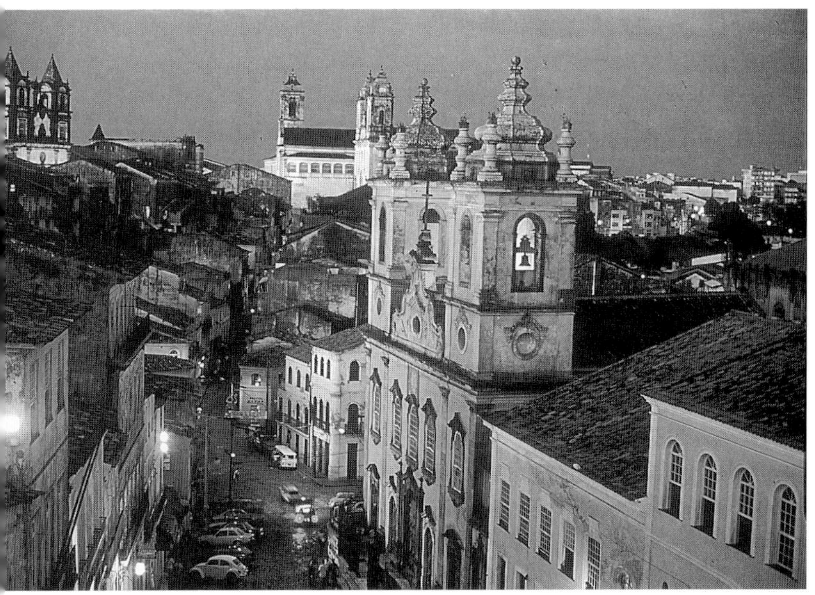

**From extreme wide-angle (used above) to super-telephoto lenses, Canon's product line offers the right lens for any situation.**

of a full-time professional photographer, these lenses (such as the EF 50mm f/1.8 II or the zoom EF 35-80mm f/4-5.6 and the EF 80-200mm f/4.5-5.6) produce excellent results and are compact, lightweight, and reasonably priced.

There are also a few specialized lenses that are usually out of the question for the average amateur photographer and are rarely purchased by the professional—they are usually rented for a job. This is largely due to their high cost and/or limited, specialized applications. Some examples are the high-speed telephoto giants, such as the Canon EF 400mm f/2.8L USM, EF 600mm f/4L USM, or the 1200mm model, which costs as much as a luxury car. These lenses offer maximum performance when the aperture is wide open. Another highly specialized lens with limited application in the Canon EF line is their extreme fish-eye, the EF 15mm f/2.8 Fish-eye.

All Canon EF lenses are multicoated. This means that several extremely thin layers of vaporous coating have been deposited on the lens' surface. Canon's exclusive Super Spectra Coating reduces the reflectance and increases the lens' ability to transmit light. Surfaces treated in this manner are less subject to flare, thereby improving image contrast.

***Note:*** An L (which stands for Luxus or Luxury) in a lens' name indicates that special glass types and designs were used in manufacturing the lens. These can include aspherical elements or lens elements made of fluorite and Ultra-Low Dispersion (UD) glass, which are different from standard optics in that they have a special index of refraction. If "USM" appears in the lens name, it indicates that an ultrasonic motor is used for focusing. These ultrasonic motors are particularly small and especially quiet.

## Aperture and Lens Speed

A lens' aperture value indicates the relationship between its effective aperture and its focal length. The term "maximum aperture" is the largest diaphragm opening that can be set on a particular lens. The size of the maximum aperture determines what is commonly referred to as the "speed" of the lens, and lenses with large maximum apertures are considered "fast." For those who work frequently in low light, high-speed (large aperture) lenses can make a huge difference because they can often allow you to use a fast enough shutter speed to still make a handheld shot in poor lighting conditions. However, there are many considerations and tradeoffs in designing (and buying!) such a lens, including price, weight, size, and speed.

### Canon's Ultra-Fast Lenses

Canon engineers have designed a few EF lenses that are exceptionally high speed, challenging the limits of what is possible in lens design.

These "speed demons" are large, heavy, and expensive. In the fall of 1994, when the EOS-1N was introduced, the EF 50mm f/1.0L USM lens had a suggested list price of more than $2,632, and the EF 300mm f/2.8 L USM, $10,640. The 1200mm, however, is unrivaled with a suggested list price $85,526. Lenses in these price categories are generally purchased by the government, large

| Lens | Diameter | Weight |
|---|---|---|
| EF 50mm f/1.0L USM | 91.5 mm | 985 g (2.2 lb.) |
| EF 85mm f/1.2L USM | 91.5 mm | 1,025 g (2.3 lb.) |
| EF 200mm f/1.8L USM | 130 mm | 3,000 g (6.6 lb.) |
| EF 300mm f/2.8L USM | 125 mm | 2,855 g (6.3 lb.) |
| EF 400mm f/2.8L USM | 167 mm | 6,100 g (13.5 lb.) |
| EF 600 mm f/4.0L USM | 167 mm | 6,000 g (13.2 lb.) |
| EF 1200mm f/5.6 L USM | 228 mm | 16,500 g (36.3 lb.) |

news publications, or agencies that loan them to photographers for special assignments. Sometimes they are also available from large rental houses. But before you begin dreaming of these lenses (and they really are worth dreaming about) you should weigh the pros and cons of a high-speed lens.

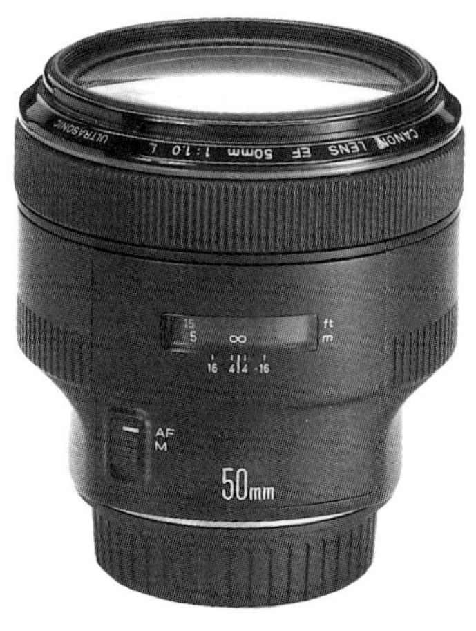


**Canon's EF 50mm f/1.0L USM lens is the fastest lens made for their 35mm SLRs.**

If you usually work under normal lighting conditions there is really no need for you to purchase a high-speed lens. To shoot in daylight, even using fast shutter speeds, does not require a maximum aperture of f/1.0. Even the incredibly bright viewfinder image produced by the lens' large maximum aperture is not really worth the lens' extremely high price.

However, if you frequently work in low-light conditions, such as at dusk or indoors without flash, then high-speed lenses can be extremely useful. The option of being able to open the lens by one additional f/stop allows you to use a shutter speed that is one stop faster, which may make the difference between a poor hand-held shot (which shows the effects of camera shake) and a successful, or at least acceptable, picture.

But do not overlook the fact that extremely fast high-speed lenses also have a disadvantage. With the aperture wide open, depth of field shrinks to a minimum, sometimes to only a few inches. Although this can be useful in isolating a subject, it can mean that parts of the subject are likely to be out of focus.

### High-Speed Lenses

Lenses that are fast but have a maximum aperture that has not been pushed to the maximum limit are often a good compromise. A few examples are:

EF 35mm f/2.0
EF 85mm f/1.8 USM
EF 100mm f/2.0 USM
EF 200mm f/2.8L USM
EF 300mm f/4L USM
EF 20-35mm f/2.8L
EF 80-200mm f/2.8L

These lenses are more portable than the ultra-fast lenses and make more sense in terms of weight and price (even though they are not exactly inexpensive). Used with an ISO 200 speed film (instead of an ISO 100 film), these lenses allow fast shutter speeds similar to ultra-fast lenses without the extreme limitations in depth of field.

### Normal-Speed Lenses

If you always swear by fast (high ISO number) films and often take the time to shoot with a tripod or monopod, you will do just fine with zoom lenses that have maximum apertures of f/4.5 to f/5.6.

The fast and quiet USM zoom lenses allow any zoom setting from the standard wide-angle range to the short telephoto range (for example, the EF 35-135mm f/4.5-5.6 USM). They are suitable for candid and landscape shots, as well as outdoor pictures of individuals and groups.

**Hint:** A few zoom lenses do not feature constant apertures—their maximum and minimum apertures change depending on the focal length in use. The reason for this variable lens speed is that when

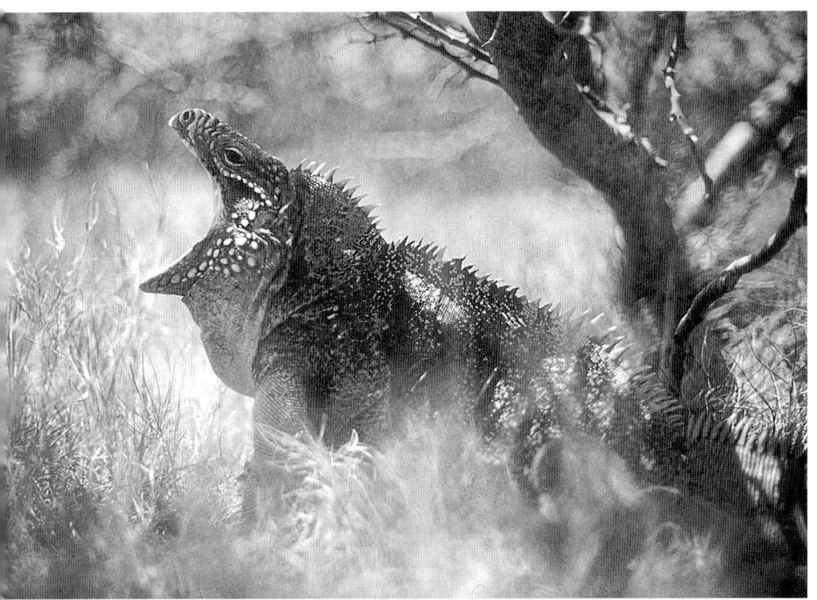

**A high-speed telephoto lens allows you to stand back and take a picture from a safe distance.**

the lens is zoomed to longer focal lengths, the size of the aperture does not increase proportionately. This allows lens designers to create smaller, lighter-weight lenses with greater zoom ranges. However, since the apertures are controlled from the camera body (as they should be) and not by an aperture ring on the lens, only the maximum and minimum apertures will vary. At any other setting you can select a desired aperture with full confidence that it will not change when you zoom the lens to a different focal length. This is one of Canon's technological triumphs, which puts them well ahead of most of their competition.

## The Zoom Lens Debate

While some professional photographers who own a top-of-the-line SLR camera (such as the EOS-1N) do not use zoom lenses, most agree that these lenses offer many advantages. Fixed focal length lenses are generally smaller and lighter weight than zoom lenses. But several will fill a camera bag, making it heavier than a zoom lens covering the same focal lengths would. This is especially true when the zoom lens is a super-zoom like the EF 35-350mm f/3.5-5.6L USM. With this lens alone or with two complementary zoom lenses (the EF 28-70mm f/2.8L USM and the EF 80-200mm f/2.8L, for example), you can handle most photographic situations without carrying the weight of a full range of fixed focal length lenses. Major modifications can be made to your framing without having to change positions and without varying perspective. However, when fixed focal length lenses are used, fine-tuning the image often requires changing the distance between camera and subject (moving closer to have a subject fill the frame, or farther away to include more background). This, of course, creates a different perspective. Perspective is a function of the location of the camera and *not* of the focal length. This is a very important concept to remember.

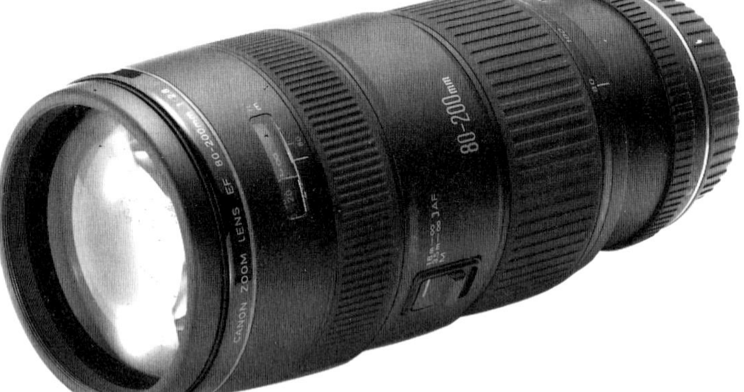


**Canon's EF 80-200mm f/2.8L telephoto-zoom is a practical lens, combining speed, light weight, and a wide range of focal lengths.**

If lens speed is a factor, as a rule fixed focal length lenses are faster (but there are always exceptions). In addition, generally these lenses are slightly superior to zoom lenses in terms of sharpness and contrast.

Even if you are considering lenses with extreme focal lengths, zoom lenses can still be an option. While a fixed focal length is required for shooting at focal lengths of 14mm or 15mm, an ultra wide-angle focal length of 20mm is possible with zoom lenses such as the EF 20-35mm f/2.8L or the EF 20-35mm f/3.5-4.5 USM.

### Vignetting

Vignetting refers to the darkening of an image around its periphery. It most commonly occurs in photos taken with a lens that has a shade attached that is too long for its focal length. A disproportionately long shade prevents light from entering the lens at its rim, resulting in a darkened image edge. This effect is especially common when using wide-angle or zoom lenses.

### Linear Distortion

Linear distortion causes lines that are parallel to the edge of the image frame to bend. The closer these lines are to the edge of the frame, the more extreme the curve. However, lines that pass through the center of the image will remain straight. Outward bending is called "barrel distortion" and tends to occur with wide-angle lenses. The inward bending, or "pincushion distortion," is apparent with extremely long focal lengths. Lower-cost zoom lenses produce particularly noticeable distortion at each end of the focal range, however, somewhere in between (not necessarily in the exact middle of the lens' range) is a zone that produces only slight distortion. A wave-like distortion can sometimes occur with zoom lenses. This kind of distortion, though often less dramatic than barrel or pincushion distortion, can be more annoying to a viewer than a line that simply bows.

## Lenses and Image Composition

No matter how fascinating a modern camera such as the EOS-1N may be, it is basically nothing but a sophisticated light-tight box for film. The camera plays a small role in the artistic merit of the final image. Image composition is defined first and foremost by the photographer, second by the lens, and only third by the camera's features. The first step toward a successful picture is selecting the subject.

As a rule, the subject should appear as large as possible in the picture; unnecessary extras are distracting and often make the

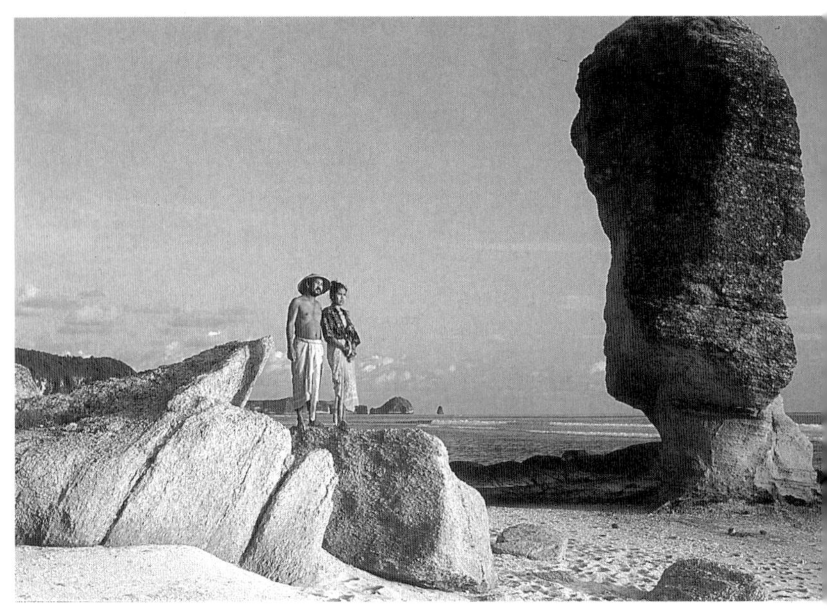

**Wide-angle and telephoto lenses produce different effects. The photo (left) made with a wide-angle lens shows lots of space between the couple and the rock, with a more scenic result. The photo (right), made with a**

picture cluttered and confusing. If extraneous information is to be included, it should serve a purpose such as acting as a size reference to show scale, providing a frame, directing the viewer's eyes toward the main subject, or creating a sense of depth. These scenarios are most easily accomplished with a zoom lens. Zoom lenses allow you to set any focal length within its range steplessly, and hence, offer many angles of view. A slight turn of the zoom ring is often sufficient to remove any distracting elements from the picture.

Another option is to make the subject appear as large as possible in the picture by keeping the same focal length and reducing the shooting distance between you and your subject (by moving in closer). This will alter the perspective, which could change the picture significantly. However, simply moving in laterally to change the distance between the camera and subject is not the

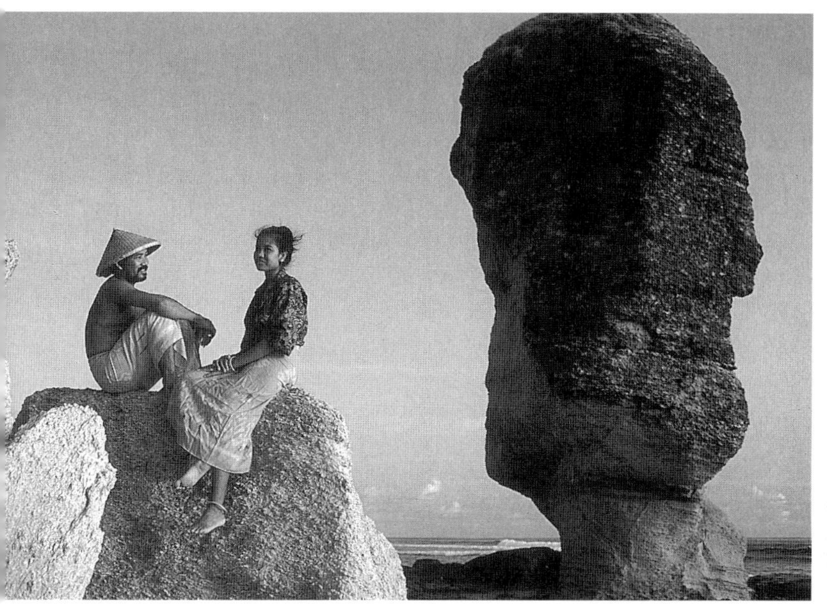

**telephoto lens, compresses the distance, producing a more intimate image. The camera's position was changed between shots, which accounts for the change in perspective.**

only option. It is also possible to remain in the same location and simply squat down or elevate your position in order to achieve a different perspective.

### Composing with Wide-Angle Lenses

Wide-angle lenses allow you to capture the whole subject at short shooting distances. A wide-angle lens also creates converging lines, which convey a sense of depth. Furthermore, when set to a small aperture, wide-angle lenses are capable of capturing everything (close and distant elements) in sharp focus, emphasizing the feeling of depth even more.

We encourage you to take advantage of these characteristics when working with one of Canon's ultra wide-angle EF lenses. Try to include powerful structures (boulders or sculptures, for instance) in the foreground of the picture. This prevents the picture from having a boring foreground, and the distance between the foreground and the main subject will be better defined.

**Composing with Telephoto Lenses**

Using long focal length lenses at longer distances constricts the angle of view and makes objects located at different distances appear to be closer to each other or compressed in the image. A telephoto lens allows you to shoot from a longer distance, which enhances this type of perspective. When used in landscape photography, a telephoto lens compresses elements at different distances within the scene, and distant elements appear disproportionately large. These elements may also take on a bluish cast because the air mass between them and the lens filters out most other colors.

Telephoto lenses are also useful in isolating the main subject. Because the telephoto has less depth of field than a wide-angle lens used at the same aperture and subject distance, the subject not only becomes larger but also stands out from the distracting background elements.

## Fish-Eye Lens

If you think that the sole purpose of the fish-eye lens is to get as much as possible into the picture, you do not know enough about this unusual lens. Fish-eye lenses are fascinating, having properties that can be put to excellent use toward making artistic and creative images.

If you are searching among Canon's autofocus lenses for a successor to the FE 7.5mm f/5.6, you will be disappointed. No circular fish-eye lens has been developed yet for the EOS camera series. However, Canon does offer the EF 15mm f/2.8 full-frame fish-eye. (This is not, however, the EF lens with the shortest focal length—remember, it is not the focal length, but the image reproduction that makes a lens a fish-eye!)

With the exception of straight lines that pass directly through the center of the image, the 15mm lens bends everything in the frame outward (barrel distortion), in the typical fish-eye manner. This atypical type of projection is related to the lens' extremely wide angle of view. A full 180° angle of view is achieved across the diagonal (141° 54′ across the horizontal and 91° 73′ across

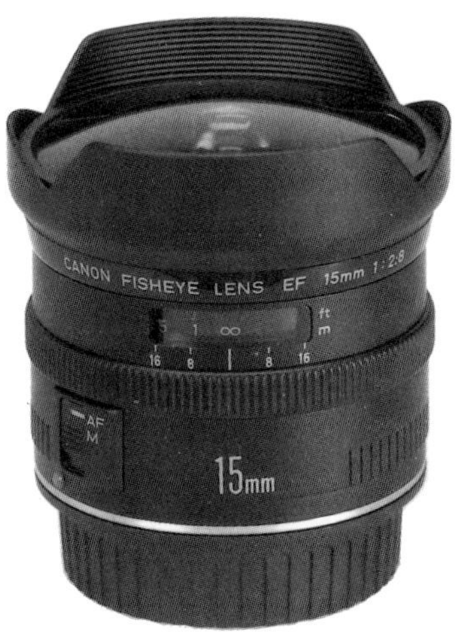


**The EF 15mm f/2.8 is a full-size fish-eye with an angle of view of 180°.**

the vertical). In addition, the 15mm lens features enormous depth of field that captures everything between a few inches in front of the lens and infinity—even with a mid-range aperture. These characteristics make the EF 15mm f/2.8 lens naturally predisposed to take pictures that need to include as much information as possible. This lens will really prove its value when used to photograph inside confined rooms, down narrow alleyways, in warehouses, and even open landscapes.

Still, it is frequently overlooked that the EF 15mm f/2.8 focuses as close as 8 inches (20.3 cm) and can thus be used in the close-up range. Dramatic perspectives can be achieved by using a very small camera-to-subject distance and taking advantage of the lens' large angle of view that exaggerates the converging line effect. However, when this type of picture is taken, remember to pay careful attention to the background and foreground. Watch to ensure that the wide angle of view and the extensive depth of field have not inadvertently included distracting and unimportant details. This is a situation in which the EOS-1N's incredibly bright viewfinder becomes an important tool, as it provides you with an extremely clear view of the scene. It is also a smart idea for you to check the foreground without looking through the viewfinder. The large angle of view reduces things a great deal, making it difficult to spot small problems through the viewfinder. Later, when the picture is enlarged, for example projected on a screen 5 or 6 feet (1.5 or 2 meters) wide, they will magically reappear, larger than life!

The type of subject being photographed and the camera's location determine to what extent the bent lines are exaggerated. If the subject has many lines that are parallel to the image edges, a circular effect will result. Placing the horizon in the upper edge of the frame makes it curve downwards at either edge, while placing the horizon near the bottom of the frame makes it curve it upward like a bowl. The photographer can exaggerate this effect by tilting the camera. If the picture contains many diagonal or irregular lines, the typical fish-eye effect can be greatly subdued, retaining the impression of vast space.

**Hint:** This lens' large angle of view will influence the EOS-1N's exposure metering system. Although the camera's evaluative metering system is very good, if the bright sun is in the picture itself, however small, poor exposures can result. Take a meter reading without the sun in the frame, recompose the image, and then take your picture.

## Ultra Wide-Angle Lenses

The Canon EF series includes four lenses that make up their impressive line of ultra wide-angle lenses. This quartet includes two fixed focal length lenses, the EF 14mm f/2.8L USM and EF 20mm f/2.8 USM. It also includes two zoom lenses, the EF 20-35mm f/2.8L and EF 20-35mm f/3.5-4.5 USM, which have the identical focal length range but are different in terms of speed, design, and price.

These lenses (the zooms included, when set accordingly) feature extremely large angles of view. The 14mm lens covers a 114° angle of view and the 20mm lens, 94°. These lenses have highly corrected optics, which have eliminated the barrel distortion characteristic of fish-eye lenses. Both the 14mm and the 20mm lenses exhibit practically none of the "converging verticals" phenomenon. However the two zoom lenses will produce some linear distortion when critical shots (such as architectural structures) are taken.

There are many fun and interesting ways to use ultra wide-angle lenses, and you should take time to explore them all! Large objects

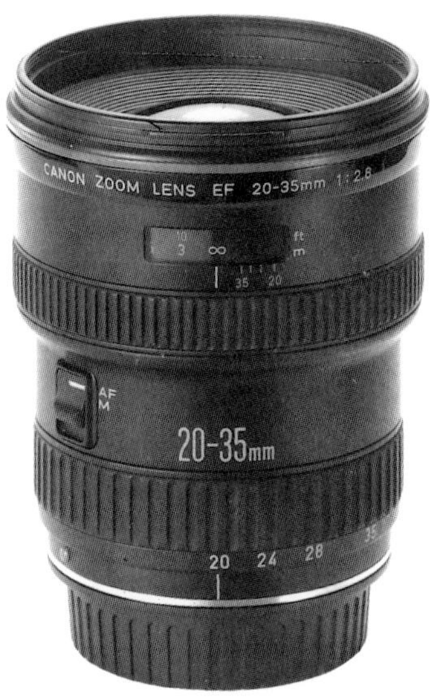


**The EF 20-35mm f/2.8L zoom includes super wide-angle focal lengths as part of its range.**

can be captured in their entirety from short distances. This space-creating characteristic is perfect for pictures taken in confined locations (such as rooms or narrow alleyways). But don't forget that the short shooting distance will result in an exaggerated wide-angle perspective. This means that objects in the foreground will appear inordinately large and the feeling of depth will be exaggerated. If ultra wide-angle lenses are used to shoot large spaces (such as landscapes, meeting rooms, or market squares), the impression of depth can be created very effectively. However, while an ultra wide-angle lens can tend to create space, in doing so it reduces the apparent size of objects in the distance. This effect diminishes details located far away from the camera, making them considerably less impressive in the picture than they are in reality.

Take care when shooting with ultra wide-angle lenses. They can frequently capture extraneous objects such as litter, your camera bag, the leg of a tripod, the camera strap, your foot, etc. Also, even a tidy foreground can be unappealing if it dominates the picture. In order to prevent this, shoot from a higher location while holding the camera perpendicular to the ground. This will result in the picture including less of the foreground, and linear distortion will be minimized. You could also kneel down and hold the camera tilted slightly upwards, taking creative advantage of the

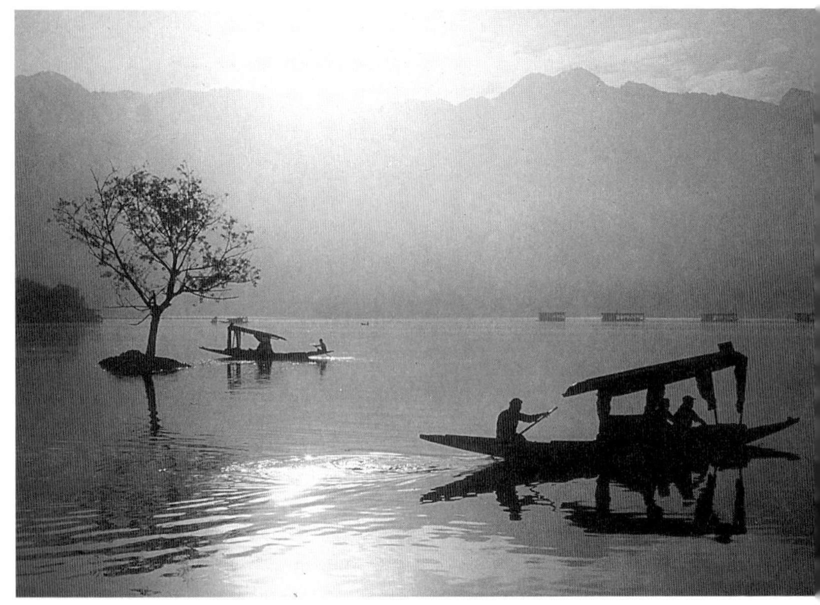

**Wide-angle lenses allow you to include both the main subject and its environment in a photograph. Here, the boat is not isolated, but placed in the context of the river, island, and surrounding mountains.**

resulting converging lines. Another possibility is to wait until the foreground has filled up. You might find that the serendipitous arrival of groups of tourists, roller-skating children, or wildly colorful buses can be extremely useful.

**Hint:** Try using a tripod to bring some life to a static foreground. Mount your EOS-1N on the tripod and select the longest shutter speed possible. People and vehicles moving in the foreground will be blurred while your actual subject will be captured sharp as a tack!

## Wide-Angle Lenses

While fish-eye or ultra wide-angle lenses are appropriate for photographers who have developed a certain visual sense, one or two conventional wide-angle lenses—or a zoom lens that includes a wide-angle focal length in its range—belong in just about any camera bag.

Canon's EF lens system has ten zoom lenses that include wide-angle focal lengths, however it currently offers only three fixed focal length wide-angles. The greatest choice lies in those that include the 35mm focal length. The ten zoom lenses span a range from the EF 20-35mm f/2.8L through the EF 35-350mm f/3.5-5.6L USM. (Incidentally, these two lenses complement one another very well, and if you acquire the high-speed EF 50mm f/1.4 USM as well, you will have an excellent all-around lens selection.) Canon also makes the fast and compact EF 35mm f/2.0 lens, which unfortunately does not feature a USM drive.

The 35mm lens is often considered to be the "other" standard or normal lens. It is ideal for shooting a large variety of subjects including architecture, journalism, group shots, nudes, and landscapes. With an angle of view of 63°, it offers a fairly normal perspective in which subject details are still relatively well defined.

In the 28mm range Canon offers the small, lightweight EF 28mm f/2.8 and five zoom lenses ranging from the two 20-35mm lenses to the EF 28-105mm f/3.5-4.5 USM. In practical applications, many consider a 28mm lens to be very similar to a 35mm lens. Both lenses tend to exaggerate perspective. When shooting pictures of buildings with the camera pointed upwards, the building will appear to lean unnaturally. And when taking photos of people, you must be careful to place adequate distance between you

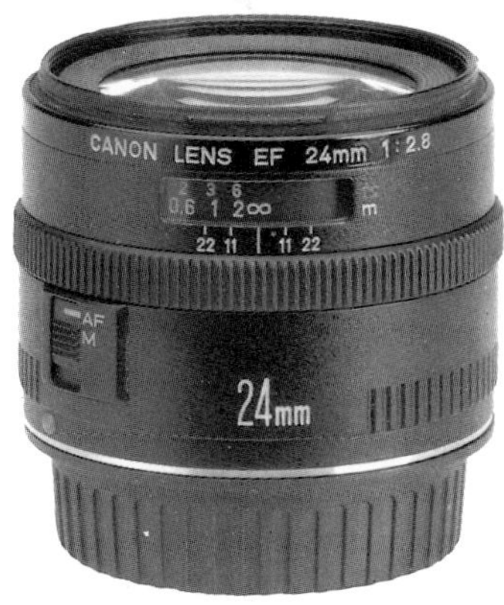


**The small, lightweight EF 24mm f/2.8 hedges the border between being a wide-angle or a super wide-angle lens.**

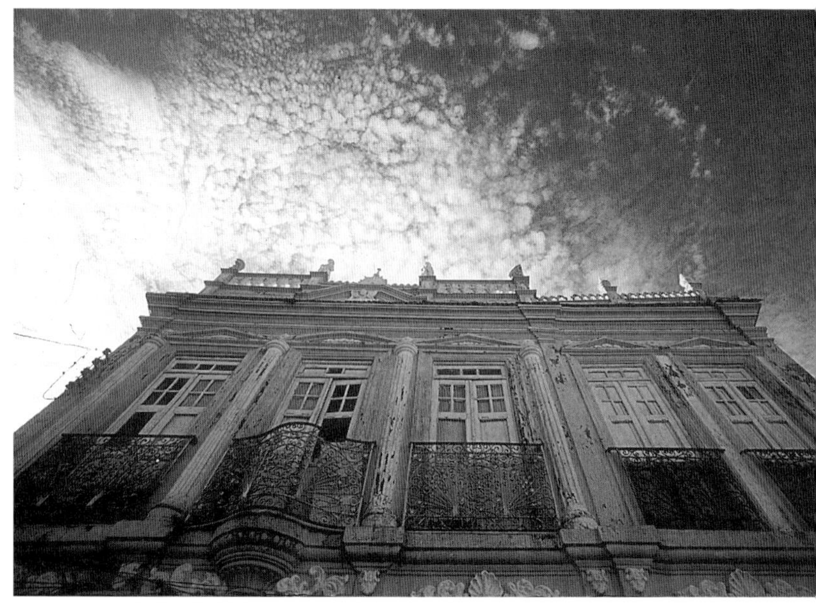

**If you get too close to a building and point the camera upward, you can expect the vertical lines to converge, making the building appear to tilt back.**

and the subject. A person shot from too close a distance and placed too near the image's edge will take on a disproportionate and unflattering shape—not a kind way to photograph one's friends or relatives!

The small and lightweight EF 24mm f/2.8 completes Canon's wide-angle lens line. Of course, the two 20-35mm ultra wide-angle zoom lenses include this focal length as well. A 24mm lens is great for taking photographs of landscapes, architecture (from a high vantage point, if possible), room interiors, narrow alleyways, or large plazas. The 24mm lens has an angle of view of 84°, creating a noticeable wide-angle effect. The apparent "distortion" of the wide-angle effect is minimized the farther you are from your subject, but this can be used to your advantage. As you shorten the focusing distance between you and your subject, the foreground details will appear to dominate the image, and the illusion of depth will become more and more exaggerated.

***Note:*** The convergence of parallel lines is a phenomenon that always seems to be attributed to wide-angle lenses. In fact, this phenomenon is a function of the camera's position, not the lens. If the film and subject planes are parallel, parallel lines will not converge with either a wide-angle or a telephoto lens. However, if the film plane is not parallel to the subject plane, parallel lines will converge in the distance. Pictures of railroad tracks or roadsides show this effect, as they are seldom taken with the film and subject on parallel planes. Shots of architectural structures will exhibit converging verticals, particularly when the structures are shot from a close distance and the camera is tilted upward. Because this effect is most noticeable with wide-angle lenses, they are unfairly credited with causing the distortion. However, if you ever have the opportunity to take pictures in the skyscraper canyons of New York, Chicago, or Hong Kong, take a telephoto shot of a skyscraper in its entirety from its top floor to the street. You'll find that this picture, too, will have converging verticals!

## Standard (Normal) Lenses

With 35mm cameras, lenses having a focal length of 50mm are considered to be standard or "normal" lenses. In addition to the previously mentioned EF 50mm f/1.0L USM, Canon offers two (more affordable) standard fixed focal length lenses, the EF 50mm f/1.4 USM and the EF 50mm f/1.8 II. The f/1.4 lens features an extra 1/3 stop over the f/1.8, which is nice, but not earthshaking. The feature that really makes professional photographers choose the f/1.4 lens is its quiet and fast Ultrasonic motor. If a fast lens is what you're after, the EF 50mm f/1.0L USM would be an even better choice, but it is bulky and expensive!

There are also eight zoom lenses that incorporate the 50mm focal length. They range from the EF 28-70mm f/2.8L USM to the 35-350mm f/3.5-5.6L USM super-zoom, which has a 10x zoom range.

Do not underestimate the 50mm focal length. It is a general-purpose focal length that is ideal for many subjects. The 50mm focal length creates an angle of view that corresponds approximately to the angle of view seen by the human eye and therefore produces pictures that appear very natural or "normal" (hence,

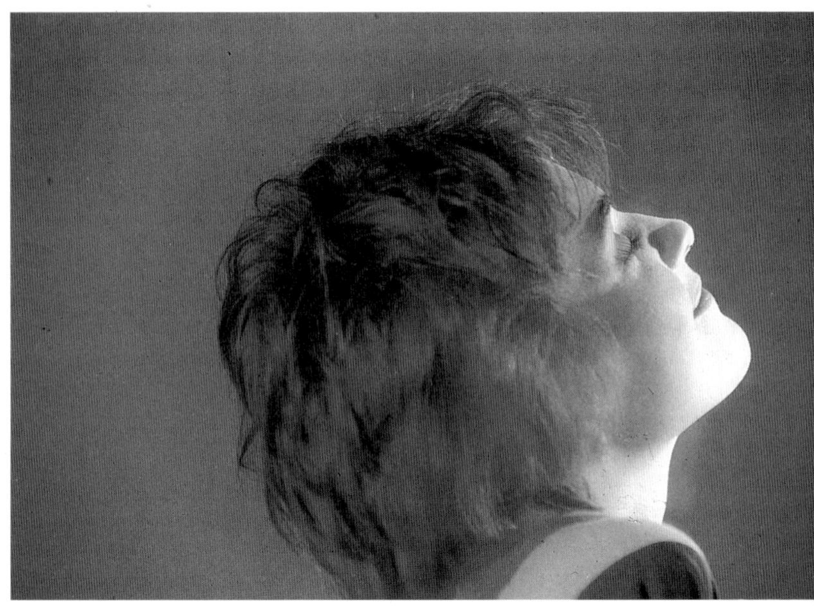

**Medium telephoto lenses are suitable for taking portraits from a comfortable distance, without getting intrusively close to your model.**

the name). (Remember, though, that a view seen with both eyes involves a much larger angle of view—which comes closer to a 35mm or even 28mm format!)

As a rule, it makes sense to include a 50mm fixed focal length lens in your lens selection. We recommend it first of all because the EF 50mm f/1.8 II is relatively inexpensive (and is often available in a dealer's "used" case for even less). This makes it an excellent choice for use in high-risk shooting situations. Another reason is because these normal lenses are all relatively fast compared to most zooms that include 50mm in their range. The EF 50mm f/1.4 USM is two stops faster than the fastest zoom lenses in Canon's EF series and three to five stops faster than the average zoom lens. This means that it would still be possible to take hand-held shots with available light in situations that would require a tripod or flash if a zoom lens were mounted. And if the situation requires flash, the higher speed lens allows greater flash range.

## Medium Telephoto Lenses

Like the normal lenses (50mm) and the 35mm and 28mm wide-angle lenses, the fixed focal length medium telephotos are being replaced increasingly by short zoom lenses. However it would be a pity if these lenses were replaced completely, because a powerful medium telephoto lens is indeed a real treasure.

With the exception of the 20-35mm ultra wide-angle zoom lenses and the 28-70mm f/2.8L USM lens, every zoom lens in Canon's EF series offers at least one medium telephoto focal length. (Although some photographers consider the longest focal length of the 28-70mm lens to be telephoto.)

In addition, there are six fixed focal length lenses within the 85mm to 135mm range, of which three are considered specialty lenses: the EF 100mm f/2.8 Macro, EF 135mm f/2.8 with Soft Focus, and TS-E 90mm f/2.8 Tilt-Shift. The remaining three fixed focal length lenses, in particular the EF 85mm f/1.8 USM and the EF 100mm f/2.0 USM, are highly recommended, especially to EOS-1N owners, while the extremely fast EF 85mm f/1.2L USM, a dream lens, is recommended for those who specialize in taking pictures under poor lighting conditions and are not deterred by the lens' significant expense.

Angles of view of 28°30′ for the two 85mm lenses and 24° for the 100mm lens allow you to photograph people from medium

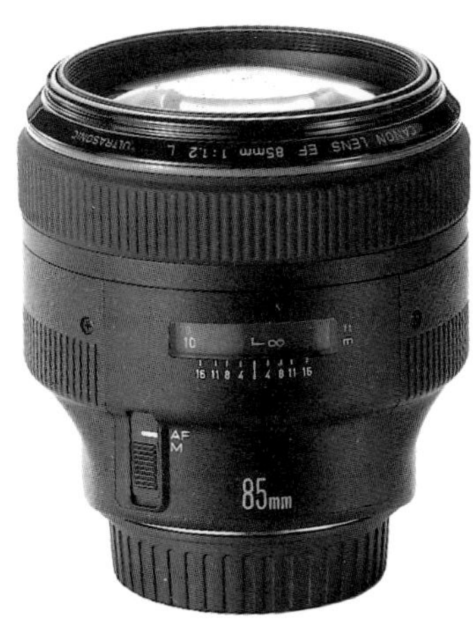


**An extremely fast, medium telephoto lens, the EF 85mm f/1.2L USM is great for taking pictures with available light.**

distances (approximately 4 to 10 feet, or 1 to 3 meters) with a pleasing perspective, while the maximum aperture can be used to keep the depth of field narrow. These characteristics have earned medium telephoto lenses the reputation of being portrait lenses, and frequently they are called just that, but medium telephotos offer a lot more. On one hand, 85mm or 100mm lenses can be used up close to isolate a small detail of a large subject, and on the other hand, subjects (especially people) can fill the frame without the photographer getting uncomfortably close.

***Note:*** Depth of field is a function of the scale of reproduction (determined by distance and focal length) and the aperture. If an EF 85mm or 100mm lens is used with the aperture wide open, the depth of field will become very narrow. The main subject will be in focus, isolated from the out-of-focus background. In this case, out-of-focus does not mean that the background will become a homogenous blur.

Furthermore, the fact that you are always viewing the subject through the viewfinder at the widest aperture means the depth of field always appears narrow. However, this narrow depth of field will actually be reproduced only if you actively select the largest aperture using either Aperture-Priority AE or Manual exposure mode. In all other automatic modes, the metering system is programmed to select a smaller aperture, creating a greater depth of field than is visible through the viewfinder. In order to determine what will or will not be within the depth of field, use the camera's depth-of-field preview button.

## Telephoto Lenses

Tasks most frequently tackled by telephoto lenses involve bridging large distances—bringing distant subjects closer into view. But however true this may be, telephoto lenses are much more versatile than that.

**Telephoto lenses enable you to move in on subjects that are quite far away. These pictures were taken from the same location with a 28mm wide-angle lens (top) and a 200mm telephoto (bottom). (Note the Empire State Building in both pictures.)** ➪

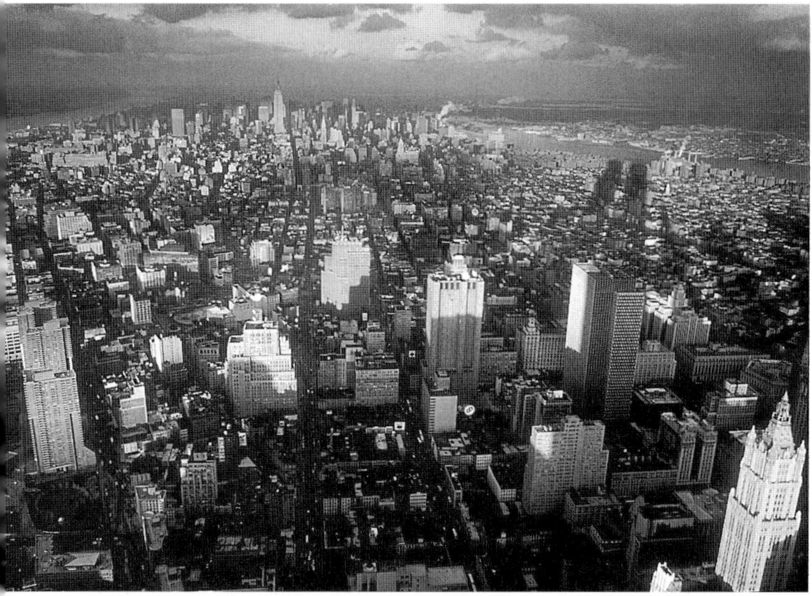

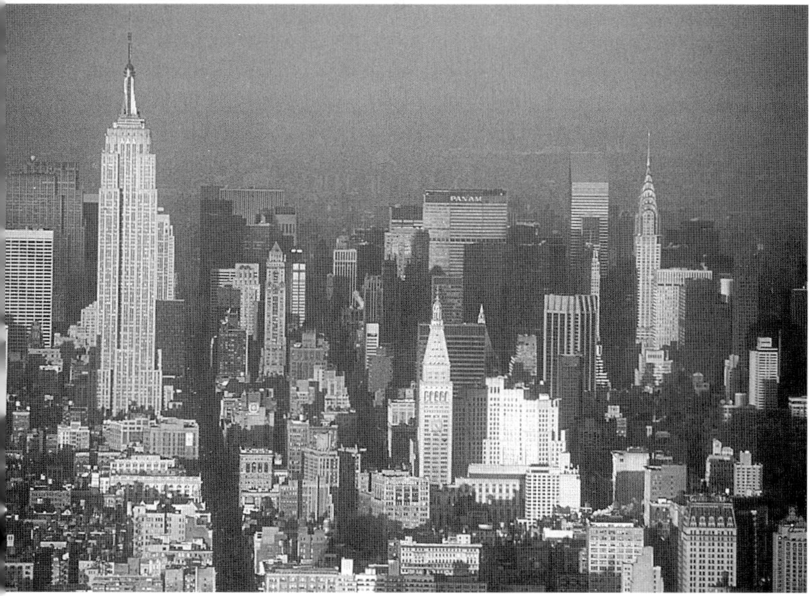

Canon's selection of fixed focal length telephoto lenses in the EF product line is impressive—not so much in number (there are only four in Canon's line of 200mm and 300mm lenses)—but in their specifications. The EF 200mm f/1.8L USM lens is incredibly fast and can be directly compared to the EF 50mm f/1.0L USM and the EF 85mm f/1.2L USM. The EF 300mm f/2.8L USM comes close to this group in speed. Both lenses are essential for sports and action photographers, photojournalists, fashion photographers, and (with some limitations) wildlife photographers. These subjects require a lens that can cover large distances (with a long focal length), be used in poor lighting (with a large aperture), isolate subjects by selective focusing, and capture fast action without blur. Other photographers simply dream about such lenses. Whether that dream can be fulfilled, of course, depends on one's wallet and physical stamina! These fabulous lenses are heavy, and one should consider carefully whether they are worth lugging around while on a family vacation.

Considering their focal length, the other two telephotos, the EF 200mm f/2.8L USM and the EF 300mm f/4.0L USM, are also quite fast. Although these two lenses are not exactly inexpensive, light-weight, or graceful, and although they meet professional photographers' needs, they are highly recommended to any amateur who desires high imaging quality in the telephoto range.

In addition to these four fixed focal length lenses there are seven zoom lenses that feature telephoto focal lengths between 200mm and 300mm. Of particular interest, of course, is the EF 35-350mm f/3.5-5.6L USM zoom lens—the only 10x zoom that exists for 35mm cameras. With a maximum aperture of f/5.6 and maximum focal length of 350mm, this lens is only one stop slower than the fixed focal length EF 300mm f/4.0L USM! You will be ready for any situation if you own this lens, the EF 20-35mm f/2.8L for the wide-angle range, and the EF 50mm f/1.4 USM lens for extra speed.

If speed is a prerequisite for a telephoto or a telephoto zoom lens, by all means consider purchasing the EF 80-200mm f/2.8L. It is an excellent lens.

**A telephoto lens is typically used when you want to isolate a detail and compress space, resulting in a photo of graphic interest.** ⇨

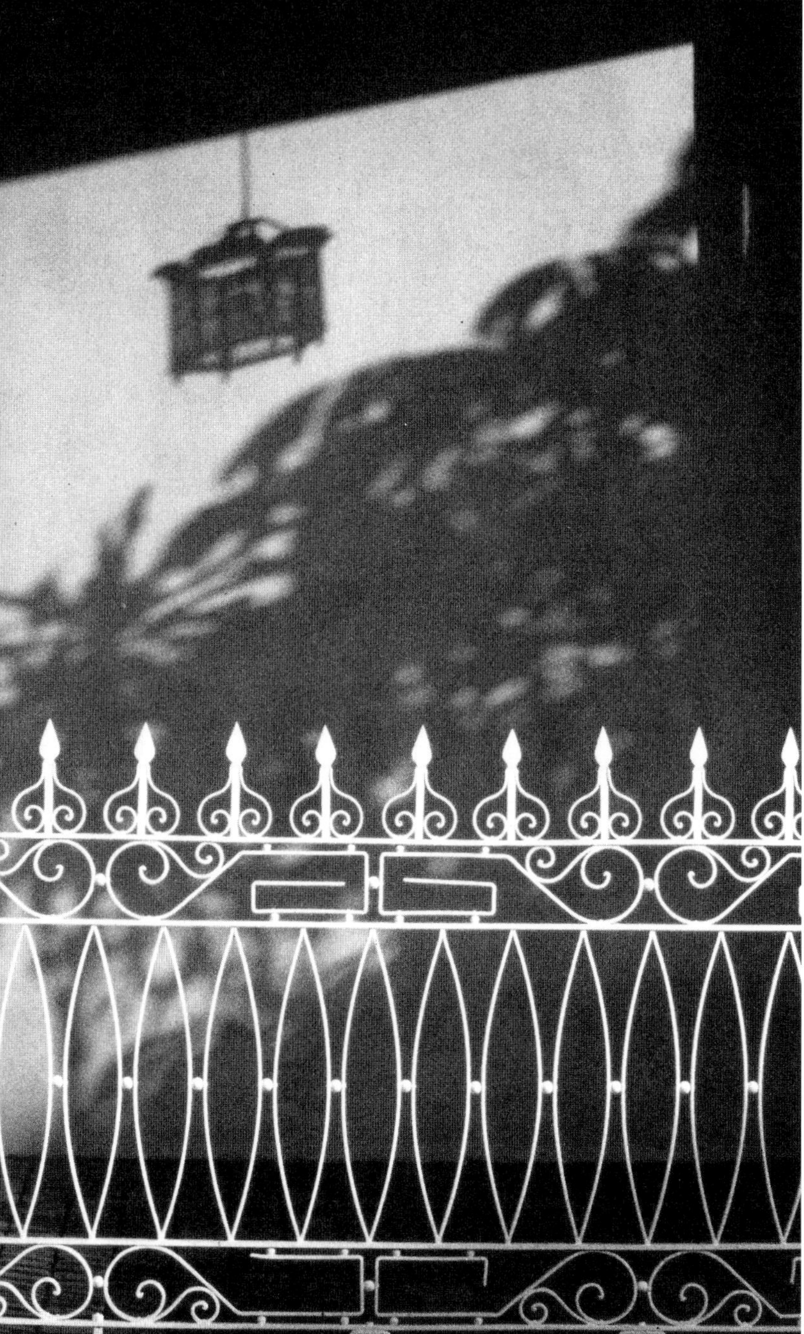

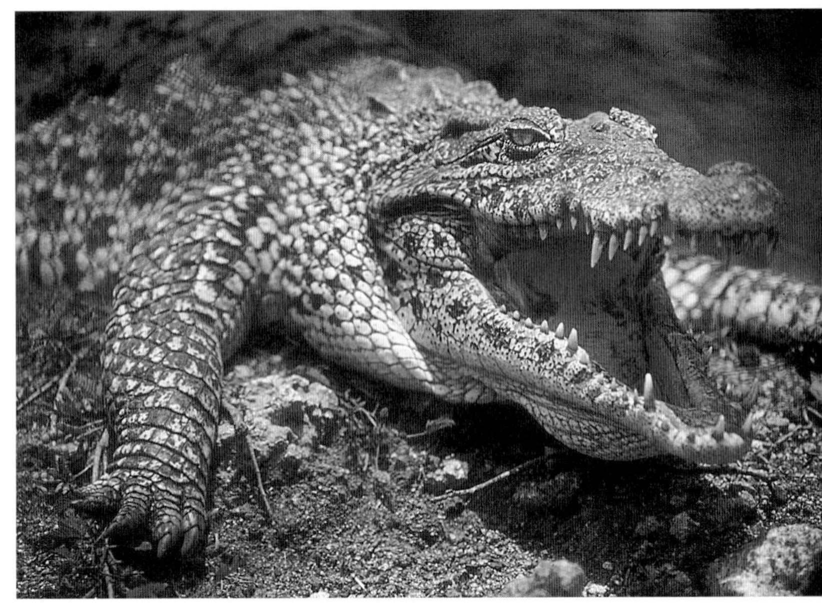

**Taking this photo with a telephoto lens ensured a safe distance, and the wide-open aperture helped reduce the effects of camera shake. The combination of lens and aperture guaranteed a narrow depth of field.**

The five other zoom lenses feature rather average speeds, some of which change when zooming. These are the EF 70-210mm f/3.5-4.5 USM, the EF 75-300mm f/4.0-5.6 USM, the EF 100-300mm f/4.5-5.6 USM, the EF 100-300mm f/5.6L, and the EF 80-200mm f/4.5-5.6 USM lenses, the latter having a plastic bayonet mount designed mainly for use with the EOS Rebel cameras.

Telephoto lenses do not need to be limited only to long-distance shots. You can use focal lengths between 200mm and 300mm to compose very creative images. To achieve a narrow depth of field in order to isolate subjects from a blurred background, you do not need a maximum aperture of f/2.8. At a distance of 30 feet (10 m) and with an aperture of f/5.6, a 300mm lens will still provide a depth of field of approximately 16 inches (40 cm)! A lens with a narrow angle of view can lift a subject out of its environment and be reproduced full size—even at short shooting distances. At a focal length of 300mm, the EF 100-300mm f/5.6L lens features a maximum reproduction ratio of 1:4!

## Super Telephoto Lenses

Canon's "white giants," the EF super telephotos with the pale gray barrels, will always catch your eye. They are most often spotted at sporting events, but also wildlife and action photographers swear by them.

Actually only one of the four super telephoto lenses is of interest to the amateur photographer—the EF 400mm f/5.6L USM. It is not too heavy and costs less than the EOS-1N body. This lens, with an angle of view of 6°10′, is particularly suitable for action and wildlife photography and, with the use of a standard ISO 200 film and good lighting, still allows handheld shots at 1/500 second (though the authors do recommend the use of a monopod).

If f/5.6 is not adequate as a maximum aperture, there is still the EF 400mm f/2.8L USM, however it weighs approximately 13.5 pounds (6.1 kg), has a diameter of approximately 6.8 inches (167 mm), and has a five-figure price. This is also true of the EF 500mm f/4.5L USM and of the EF 600mm f/4.0L USM lenses, to a greater degree. Compared with the cost of the fifth super telephoto in the bunch, approximately $85,000 for the EF 1200mm f/5.6L USM, the cost of the other super telephotos certainly makes them more appealing.

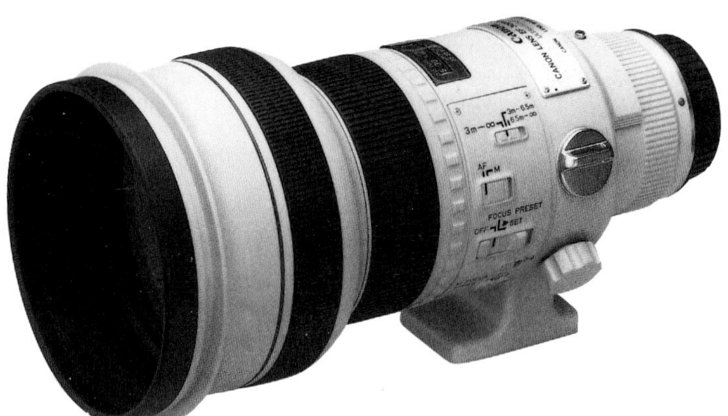


**Though bulky, Canon's EF 400mm f/2.8L USM lens is excellent for sports, modeling, and wildlife photography.**

And speaking of price, in classifying a lens as being "expensive" or "inexpensive," we prefer to think of Canon's super telephoto lenses (and of course the other EF lenses) as being "priceworthy," because they are certainly worth each and every penny.

What are the best uses for these long lenses? Sports and more sports, reporting or action requiring a safe distance (whether it be the safety of the subject or the photographer), and wildlife photography. Their advantages are: excellent imaging performance (the EF 400mm f/2.8L USM and EF 500mm f/4.5L are apochromatic) and a large maximum aperture for shooting in poor lighting situations. The narrow depth of field resulting from these lenses' large maximum aperture and long focal length is acceptable for these applications, though not a substantial consideration. It is more important that they produce precise focus with the EOS-1N. The 400mm f/2.8L USM lens allows the cross-type focusing sensor to be linked with the central metering area.

If the 1200mm f/5.6L lens is too heavy for you, you can create the same focal length by using the EF 2x Extender with your 600mm lens. The maximum aperture of this combination is f/8.0—one full stop slower than the 1200mm giant.

The compressed effect (flattened perspective) that is characteristic of telephoto pictures is particularly noticeable with these lenses, and it should be used to enhance the image's impact. The hills of Tuscany, divided by wide valleys, will be reproduced on

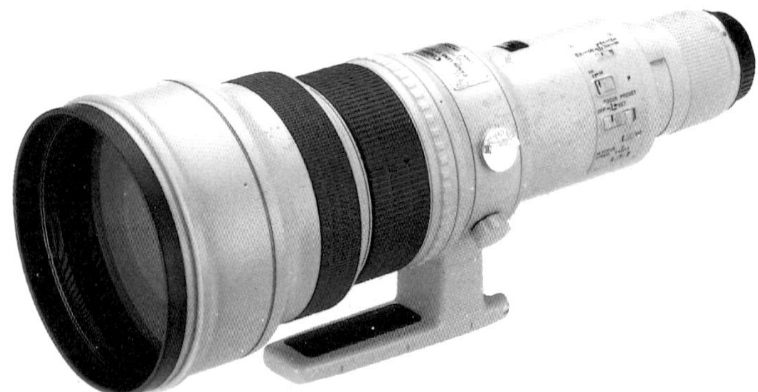

**Canon's fast telephotos and super telephotos are specially designed with a light-colored enamel finish to prevent focus from shifting when working under intense heat.**

top of one another, and the runners in the New York City marathon will become an almost homogeneous mass, even though individuals actually keep a safe distance from each other.

### Telephoto and Super Telephoto Special Features

Canon has provided special features that benefit issues of quality as well as handling specifically for their telephoto and super telephoto lenses.

***Pale gray finish:*** The pale gray enamel finish of most of Canon's EF telephoto lenses prevents them from overheating when placed in direct sunlight, which could result in a shift of focus. (Canon probably finds that the high visibility of these light-colored lenses at sporting events is beneficial, too!)

***Tripod mount:*** Even a sturdily built camera like the EOS-1N does not have a bayonet mount that can handle the weight of a super telephoto lens when attached to a tripod. The camera's base and bayonet mount would both be damaged if they had to support the lens' weight. Damage to the bayonet mount would be particularly disastrous, since the lens support and the film plane would no longer be parallel, making it impossible to focus. For this reason, all Canon super telephoto lenses have rotating tripod mounts.

***Filter drawers:*** If a lens' front element is too large for standard screw-in filters, a filter drawer is built into the rear of the lens. The filter drawer can be loaded with smaller screw-in, snap-on, or gelatin filters. If a lens comes with a filter in the drawer, this means that one must be used (whether it be that filter or another one that is compatible) because a filter has been included in the lens' optical formula.

***Focusing speed control:*** The EOS-1N's autofocus system is very fast, even too fast in some situations. Therefore, the 300mm f/2.8L USM lens allows you to focus manually at your choice of three speeds. This makes focusing easier under low-light and/or low-contrast conditions.

***Focus pre-set:*** A feature for pre-setting and storing (indicated by a beep) distance values, focus pre-set is particularly useful to sports

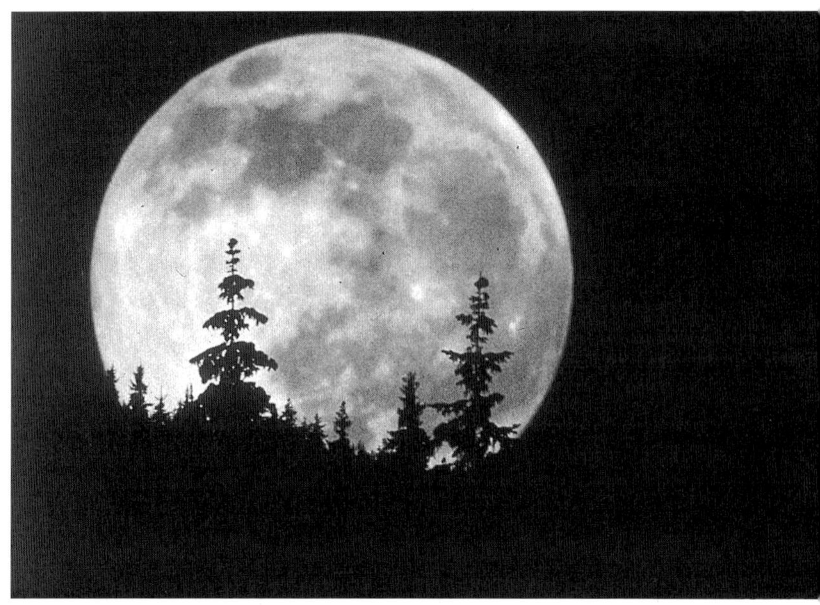

**This composite photograph was made by combining a negative of the moon (taken with a super telephoto lens and enlarged) with negatives of the tree tops in silhouette.**

photographers. For example, a marathon runner's arrival at the finish line can be captured by storing the distance between the camera and the finish line. Then, as you are shooting the crowd or the race and you suddenly see a runner approaching the finish line, you can retrieve the appropriate distance setting with lightning speed (indicated by two beeps, which can be disabled). The focus will be correct even if the runner does not pass through one of the AF metering areas.

***Adjustable focusing ranges:*** In order to prevent the lens from "hunting" through the entire range of focusing distances from close-up to infinity, two or three shorter setting ranges, depending on the lens model, can be pre-selected.

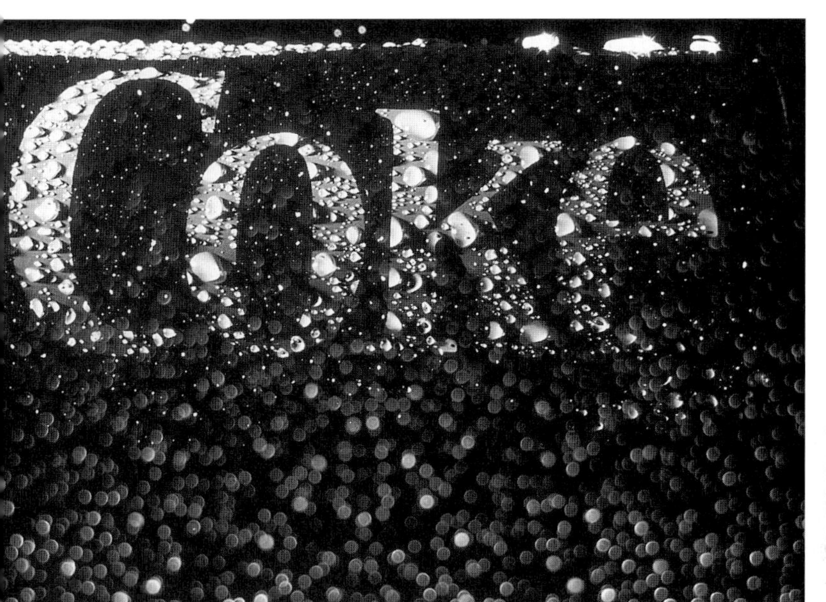


**For taking extreme close-ups, macro lenses are your best choice. They can reveal a whole new world.**

## Macro Lenses

The close-up or macro range has always intrigued photographers. With Canon's macro lenses, which have reproduction ratios of up to 1:1, it is possible to make the invisible visible.

Considering both focal length and speed, the EF 50mm f/2.5 Compact Macro lens can easily be used as a normal lens. The EF 100mm f/2.8 Macro can be used as a medium telephoto or portrait lens. But in fact, both lenses offer more.

The 50mm lens' closest focusing distance is about 9 inches (23 cm), which is measured (as distances always are) from the film to the subject, not from the front of the lens to the subject. This results in a reproduction ratio of 1:2, or half life-size. With the Life Size Converter EF attached, a reproduction ratio of 1:1 is possible, creating an image area of 24 x 36 mm. Because of the larger scale, focus can no longer be set for infinity once the EF Converter is attached.

**With the EF 100mm f/2.8 Macro lens you can make 1:1 reproductions without any additional accessories.**

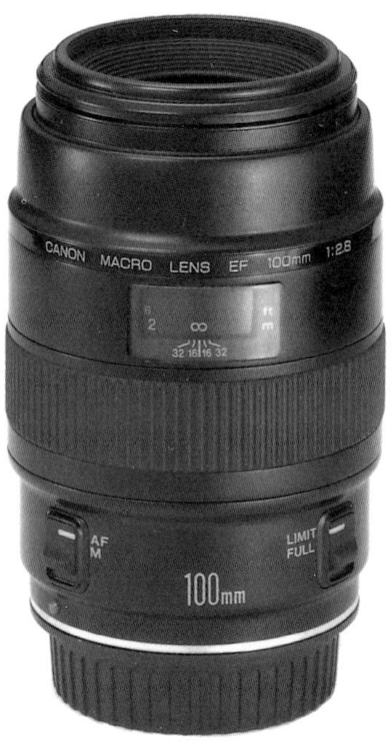


The 100mm Macro is able to shoot at a reproduction ratio of 1:1 without accessories. The close-up limit of this lens is 12.4 inches (31 cm) from the film plane. To prevent the EOS-1N's autofocus system from searching the entire range between 12.4 inches and infinity, the focusing range can be limited to 12.4 to 22.8 inches (31 to 57 cm). This saves time and aggravation when close-ups are taken. In its close-up range this lens has an extremely narrow depth of field, so it is important that the main subject be precisely in focus. Don't forget to take advantage of the depth-of-field button to control the extent and location of focus.

The EOS-1N's central autofocus area's cross-type sensor is active with both lenses, however not with the 50mm Macro if the Life Size Converter is attached, or with the 100mm Macro if the focusing scale is set closer than 1:10. The outer focusing points are particularly useful when taking a picture of an off-center subject. In contrast to cameras that have only one central AF sensor, the EOS-1N does not have to be panned to set and store the focus with its central focusing sensor before such a picture can be taken.

Panning is awkward and impedes precise focus. In the close-up range with narrow depth-of-field and large reproduction ratios, even the slightest camera movement during exposure will have a devastating effect. Therefore, it is best to use a stable tripod or a good copy stand for such close work.

In order to illuminate small subjects effectively (adequate lighting is difficult to achieve when there are short distances between subject and lens) you can use a Macro Ring Lite ML-3. Attach the flash head directly to the front of the lens. Even larger set-ups using several Speedlites with TTL control are possible; however, rather than letting matters become too complex, it may be advisable to reach for a smaller flash unit and a modeling light. This is the only way to evaluate the effect of light and shadows before a picture is taken.

**Hint:** Outdoor shots of flower blossoms, plants, and insects are frequently difficult to achieve because even the slightest gust of wind results in motion blur. A piece of matte board or foam core can be helpful in blocking wind, and it can also be used to reflect light onto the subject.

### Other Macro Options

Canon's EF macro lenses make things easy for the beginner—success is preprogrammed. But there are other ways to take extreme close-ups.

To use other Canon equipment to get in close to small subjects, we recommend that you get ahold of an FD-EOS Macro Lens Mount Converter. This adapter ring fits into the EOS-1N's bayonet mount and, in turn, holds accessories by means of the FD bayonet mount. Of course, autofocus is disabled, but exposure metering is still possible at the selected aperture (stopped-down metering).

The Canon FD Auto Bellows is worth consideration, especially if used in conjunction with 35mm f/2.8 and 20mm f/3.5 Macrophoto lenses. M or FD extension tubes can also be mounted to the FD-EOS Macro Lens Mount Converter and attached to the EOS-1N. It does not make much sense to use FD macro lenses on the EOS-1N if you're serious about close-up photography because the EF macro lenses are much more compatible.

Another option is to use an adapter ring and mount the EOS-1N to a microscope (this requires a Photomicro Unit F adapter).

Since the camera is of secondary importance in photomicrography, this solution is acceptable, even though a much less complex and less expensive camera would be sufficient.

## Soft Focus Lens

The most popular lens attachments are still the so-called soft focus attachments, which are available in great variety. Canon's soft focus lens produces soft, atmospheric pictures without requiring such attachments.

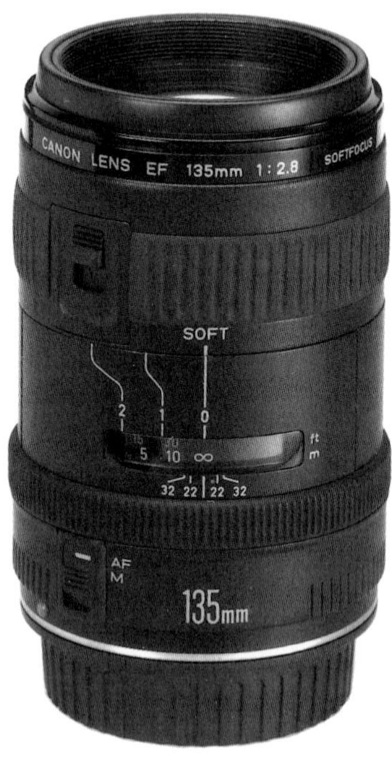


**Canon's EF 135mm f/2.8 Soft Focus lens is a specialty lens that can create soft, romantic photos as well as extremely sharp photos just as Canon's other EF lenses. It is Canon's only 135mm fixed focal length EF lens.**

The EF 135mm f/2.8 lens with Soft Focus has a setting ring not featured on any other EF lens. This ring lets you select whether the lens will produce a sharp image (setting 0) or whether the image will be out of focus in one of two degrees (setting 1 or 2), depending on the setting you select. To achieve this softened effect, an aspherical lens inside the lens assembly is moved along the optical axis. This effect also results in a reduction of contrast.

The effect created can be evaluated quite accurately through the viewfinder and becomes more noticeable at wider apertures. This means that you have one more option (over and above the Soft Focus setting ring) to produce the desired image. For this reason, this lens is best used in Aperture Priority mode.

Incidentally, the EF 135mm f/2.8 Soft Focus is the only 135mm fixed focal length lens in the EF line and can be used quite well as a normal medium-range telephoto lens with a minimum focusing distance of 3.9 feet (1.3 m).

## Tilt-Shift Lenses

Many professional photographers prefer to use large-size studio cameras. Such cameras offer the benefit of making larger pictures and give the photographer greater control. For example, you can more easily take a picture of a mirror without appearing in the picture yourself or shift the focus precisely to where it is needed.

Almost every photographer is familiar with the phenomenon of converging lines. When lines that are actually parallel are photographed, they appear to move closer and closer together as they recede from the camera's position. For example, if a picture is taken down the middle of a road, the shoulders will draw closer to one another as they approach the horizon. This effect can be used to create an impression of depth. However converging verticals can be a nuisance in architectural photography. They are created by taking a picture from a point where the camera must be tilted upward. In the picture the building will appear to be narrower toward the top and lean away from the viewer.

Even pictures of smaller objects can be subject to this phenomenon. If an object (particularly flat artwork) is photographed from above on a table or copy stand without the camera being positioned perfectly perpendicular to the work, the object will "keystone," or be rendered as narrower at one end of the photo than the other.

To circumvent this effect in shots of buildings, you need to align the camera (the film plane) parallel to the front of the building. Wide-angle lenses, however, produce a large foreground in the

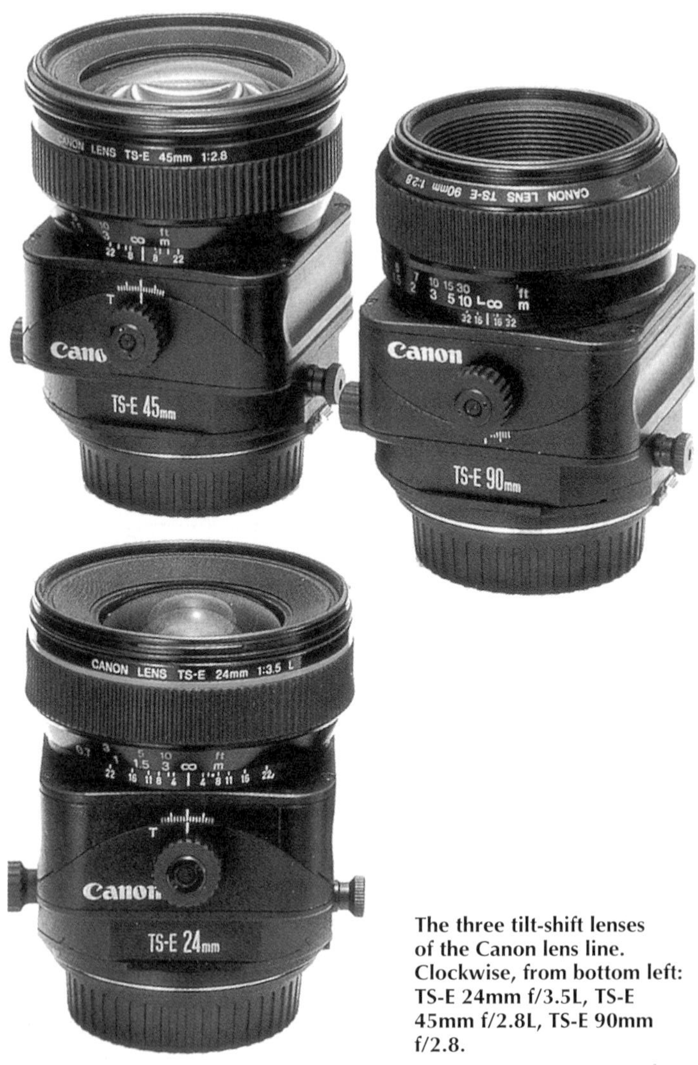


**The three tilt-shift lenses of the Canon lens line. Clockwise, from bottom left: TS-E 24mm f/3.5L, TS-E 45mm f/2.8L, TS-E 90mm f/2.8.**

picture and short telephoto lenses require long shooting distances—which are usually not available. Even in a studio there is not always enough room to move the camera anywhere you would like. And if there is enough room, a change of camera location

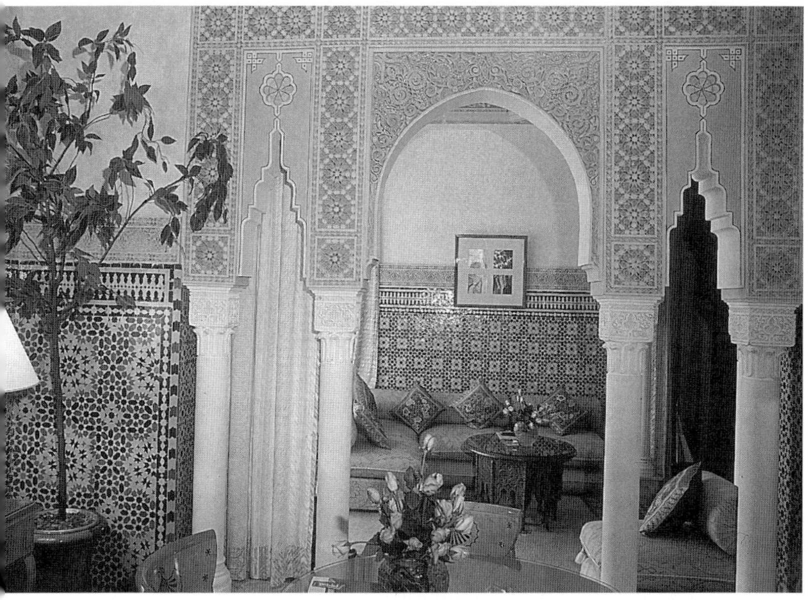

**Tilt-shift lenses eliminate linear distortion by altering the lens' position relative to the camera and subject, making straight lines straight in the photograph. A camera with a conventional lens mounted would most likely be pointed downward at this scene, encouraging linear distortion.**

has to be carefully considered because it inevitably involves a change of perspective.

Shift lenses provide an excellent solution because they can be shifted relative to the film plane axis and provide a larger range of coverage than rigid lenses with the same viewing angle. For example, by moving a shift lens upward and aligning the camera to be parallel with the building, the upper floors will be captured and the foreground will disappear from the picture. By moving the lens laterally relative to the optical axis, it is possible to shoot past an obstacle or shoot into a mirror without capturing yourself or the camera.

When the object plane and the film plane are not parallel, converging lines are not the only problem—sharpness is also at stake. When shooting a flat subject, only the subject plane parallel to the film plane (focal plane) will be in focus. When the subject plane is inclined, only the part of the object that intersects with the focal plane will be in focus. The first step toward bringing a larger part of the inclined subject plane into focus is to reduce the aperture, increasing the depth of field. The plane of sharpness is thus transformed into a zone of sharpness. Although a larger part of the inclined subject plane will be focus, at the same time other details in front of and behind the object plane will also be in focus, which may not be desirable. It also means that a slower shutter speed must be used, and that may not be desirable either. Again, these problems can be solved with a shiftable and, in this case, tiltable lens.

If a tilt lens is pivoted relative to the optical axis, the angle of the focal plane is affected. It is no longer parallel to the film plane, but at an angle relative and, in the ideal case, coincident with the plane of the inclined object. Should this not be adequate, the depth of field can be expanded to meet the range of the inclined focal plane, which is an important aspect of taking photos of three-dimensional objects arranged at an angle. Pivoting the lens will not bring an entire object into focus (especially if it is large) if the front of the object is aligned parallel to the film plane. In this situation the only solution is to reduce the aperture and expand the depth of field.

**Hint:** As a rule the TS-E lens will be tilted so as to make the object plane coincide with the focal plane. This will make the main subject in the object plane be in focus from front to back without requiring the aperture to be reduced. However, tilting also allows you to concentrate the focus on a specific area of the image—in which case the lens must be tilted at an angle opposite that of the object.

The Canon EF series offers three lenses that permit both the shift and the tilt. The TS-E 24mm f/3.5L lens is appropriate whenever large objects must be captured from short distances. This includes architectural and landscape photography, and shots inside large halls can be taken without creating converging verticals. Its extreme close-up limit of 12 inches (0.3 m) makes it a good choice for studio shots in which the tilt feature can be used for exact control of the focal plane. Therefore, this 24mm lens allows you to compose pictures with selective sharpness in situations in which a rigid 24mm lens would require a reduced aperture creating a large depth of field.

The TS-E 45mm f/2.8 is a standard lens that can be focused down to 16 inches (0.4 m). Considering its focal length, this is a good all-around lens that can be used in any situation. It has an advantage over the 24mm lens for architectural shots, in that its smaller angle of view makes it easier for the photographer to concentrate on the main subject.

The TS-E 90mm f/2.8 lens is a real treat that shows off its advantages when used to shoot static objects in the studio. Its narrow angle of view and the related shooting distances provide very natural perspectives, which is particularly important in product photography. In addition, it captures only a small portion of the background environment, which in turn allows the photographer to concentrate on the main subject.

All three lenses can be shifted +/- 11 mm (approx. 1/2 inch) from center and tilted +/- 8° relative to the optical axis. Both movements can be combined, and, in addition, these lenses can be pivoted 90° around the optical axis. This provides the photographer with infinite possibilities in adapting these lenses to a subject and its position in space. This flexibility makes automatic focus impossible, but this should not pose a problem with the kind of work that it is used for. It takes time to fully utilize the features of a TS-E lens, making manual focus a benefit rather than a drawback. A tripod is absolutely required, and adding the type D viewing screen with a grid pattern to your EOS-1N makes it easier to align the camera and lens.

***Note:*** Exposure metering and exposure control are not impaired with these lenses. However, it is very important that the exposure be metered with the lens neither shifted nor tilted, and that shutter speed and aperture be set manually. Readings made with shifted and/or tilted lenses will result in exposure errors due to the lens' altered "geometry."

***Note:*** For more information about Canon's EF lens line, please refer to the *Magic Lantern Guide to Canon Lenses.*

# EOS-1N Flash Photography

Even the fastest lenses and films won't work in total darkness. That is the obvious time for using flash. With a good flash system, a skilled photographer can do a lot more than just bring light into the darkness.

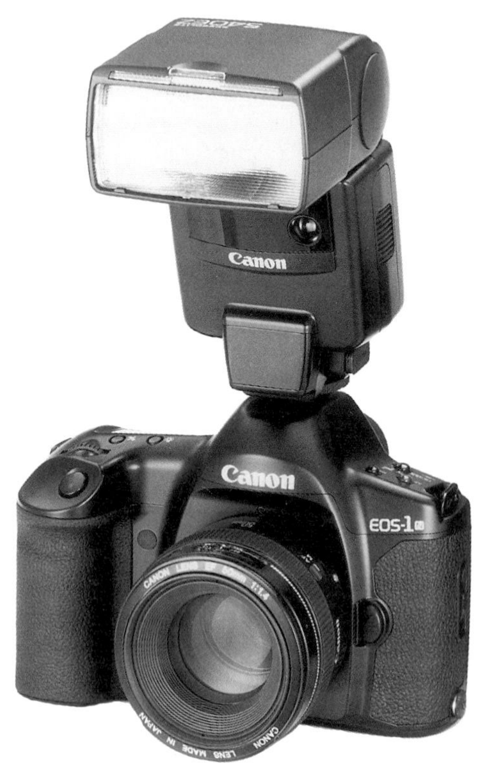


**The Speedlite 540EZ is the flagship of the Speedlite series with a maximum guide number of 177 in feet (54 in meters).**

## Basic Principles

With Canon's sophisticated flash system, anyone can take flash pictures without guesswork or time-consuming computations.

Nevertheless, when using flash for creative photography it is helpful to understand the principles of using flash. Thus, included in this chapter is a brief section on flash fundamentals.

### Guide Number

Guide numbers are used to quantify the relationship between brightness, distance, and film sensitivity and assist in calculating aperture and distance values in practical applications. Guide numbers are usually stated using ISO 100 film as the standard. While these calculations are generally unnecessary with the EOS-1N's dedicated TTL flash equipment, they are useful in situations that require manual adjustments to the flash output.

Guide numbers follow a logarithmic progression comparable to the f/stop scale. (However, a numerically larger guide number means more flash output, while a numerically larger f/stop means less light.) For example, if the distance from the flash to the subject and the guide number corresponding to the film sensitivity are known, the required aperture is easily determined using the formula: aperture = guide number/distance.

***Note:*** In the United States, guide numbers are expressed in feet and are consequently 3.3 times larger than corresponding metric guide numbers.

### Guide Numbers and Zoom Flash Heads

Typically, guide numbers are based on the flash coverage for a standard (50mm) lens. With zoom flash heads such as on the Canon Speedlite 540EZ, the angle of illumination is adjusted to cover the angle of view of different lenses. This is accomplished by changing the position of the flash head's diffuser in relation to the flash tube. By adjusting the zoom head, the flash energy is either concentrated on a smaller angle of illumination, covering a longer distance, or diffused over a larger angle, covering a shorter distance. The guide number will change as the flash unit's angle of illumination is changed. The smaller the angle of illumination (which decreases as the focal length increases), the greater the guide number. The greater the angle of illumination (which increases as the focal length decreases), the smaller the guide number. This explains how a flash unit with a zoom head can have several guide numbers.

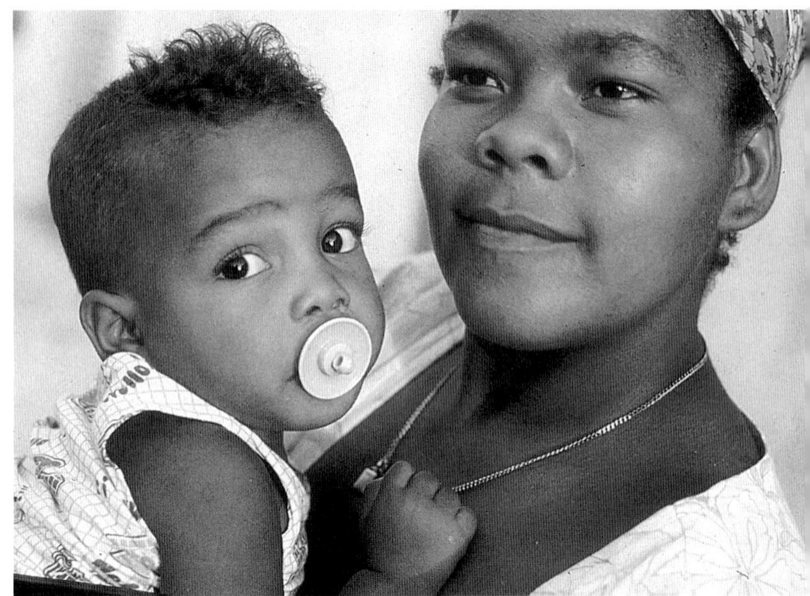

**Although the lighting appears to be natural, fill flash was used in this portrait. If flash output is too great, a picture can have a harsh and artificial appearance.**

### Increased Light and Distance

In flash photography, exposure is determined by the amount of light output by the flash unit, the camera's aperture setting, and the distance between the subject and the flash unit. The subject will receive substantially less light the farther it is located from the source of the light. This is because light emitted by a flash unit is subject to the Inverse Square Law, which states that light from the flash diminishes at a rate inverse to the square of the distance the light has traveled. Therefore, doubling the light output does not double the shooting range, but increases it by slightly less than 1-1/2 times. For example, if the flash provides correct exposure for a subject 10 feet away with the camera's lens set at an aperture of f/5.6, opening the lens one full stop to f/4 to allow twice as much light to pass will provide correct exposure only as far as 14 feet, not 20 feet. Opening the aperture one stop allows the flash to reach only 1.4 times as far.

### Color Temperature

The light from most flash units has a color temperature of 5600°K, which approximates that of daylight. Thus, daylight-balanced film should be used for flash photography. Since it is similar to daylight, flash is an excellent source of light for augmenting ambient light on overcast days or as fill flash to soften harsh sunlight.

### Red-Eye

Red-eye often occurs when using an on-camera flash unit. When the flash and lens share almost the same axis, the light reflects off the blood vessels in the retina, making them visible. When there

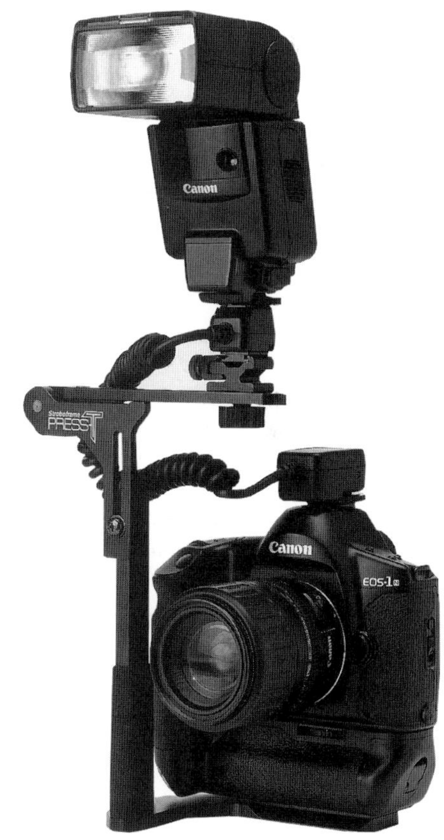


**To reduce the chance of red-eye, separate the lens and flash axes by mounting the flash to the camera with a bracket. Here, Canon's Speedlite 540EZ is attached to the EOS-1N using the Press-T™ bracket made by Stroboframe®.**

is a significant distance between the lens and flash axes, however, this red light is reflected out of the image area. The photographer can handhold the flash off-camera, using a connecting cord to maintain flash synchronization and dedication. Another alternative is to use a flash bracket, such as those manufactured by Stroboframe. These brackets hold the flash high and centered above the camera for better lighting results with no red-eye. Diffusing or bouncing the light from the flash is another technique that can eliminate red-eye, but it also reduces the flash intensity.

### Flash Synchronization

To expose the entire frame of film, the electronic flash must fire when the EOS-1N's focal plane shutter is completely open. This shutter consists of two curtains that move in sequence across the film frame. The first curtain opens, uncovering the film for exposure, and then the second curtain closes, providing a light-tight cover over the film again. Exposure time is changed by varying when the second shutter curtain is released. Thus, the synchronization speed for electronic flash is the highest shutter speed at which the first curtain has completely uncovered the film and the second has not yet begun to close. For the Canon EOS-1N the sync speed is 1/250 second. However, the synchronization speed simply indicates the highest possible shutter speed for a flash exposure. The photographer can always use shutter speeds slower than the sync speed!

With some cameras, if the focal plane shutter is set at a speed higher than the fastest synchronization speed, only a portion of the image area is exposed. The remainder of the film area, which was covered by the shutter curtains during the flash, will be severely underexposed. The EOS-1N automatically prevents this error when used with a Canon system flash unit. It will automatically default to the proper synchronization speed if the photographer tries to set a higher shutter speed.

## Using Flash with the EOS-1N

With the sophistication of the Canon EOS-1N camera and the Speedlite 540EZ flash, getting good results with flash is easy and automatic. Canon has incorporated many advanced features into this new flash system. With the flash unit mounted to the camera's hot shoe or connected with an Off-Camera Shoe Cord 2 and an autoexposure mode set on the camera, well-exposed flash photographs are virtually guaranteed.

The AIM system, which links evaluative metering with the five-point autofocus system, considers the position of the main subject at the time of flash exposure metering, though not as precisely as for ambient light exposures. In flash mode the viewfinder is divided into only three zones, center (the central AF sensor area), right (the two AF sensor areas on the right), and left (the two AF sensor areas on the left).

### A-TTL Flash and Automatic Exposure Modes

When the EOS-1N is used in Program mode, the camera automatically selects a flash synchronization speed between 1/60 and 1/250 second and a lens aperture that is correct for the subject. In daylight or brightly lit indoor situations, the background will always be exposed correctly and the camera will control the fill-flash ratio for optimum results. Indoors or at night, the Speedlite becomes the main source of illumination and the shutter speed will automatically be kept high enough for handheld exposure.

Selecting Aperture-Priority AE mode with flash gives you maximum control over depth of field when it is a concern. The camera will automatically set a shutter speed to provide adequate background exposure, day or night. Outdoors, or in relatively bright indoor lighting, if the selected aperture is unusable, the shutter speed indicators in the camera's viewfinder and external LCD will blink. In that case, just select a smaller aperture and shoot. Indoors or at night, slow shutter speeds are likely, so it is best to use a tripod or pick a different camera exposure mode.

Shooting in Shutter-Priority AE mode with flash lets you select the shutter speed while the camera selects the aperture to give correct background exposure. Fast shutter speeds up to 1/250 second can be used in bright light, while slower speeds down to 30 seconds are more appropriate in dark conditions or for special effects. In low-light situations, the maximum aperture value of the lens may blink in the viewfinder and LCD panel if the selected shutter speed is too fast to produce a good exposure of the background. In this situation, just set a slower shutter speed and shoot, or switch to Manual exposure mode on the camera.

Depth-of-Field AE mode is not well suited to flash exposures.

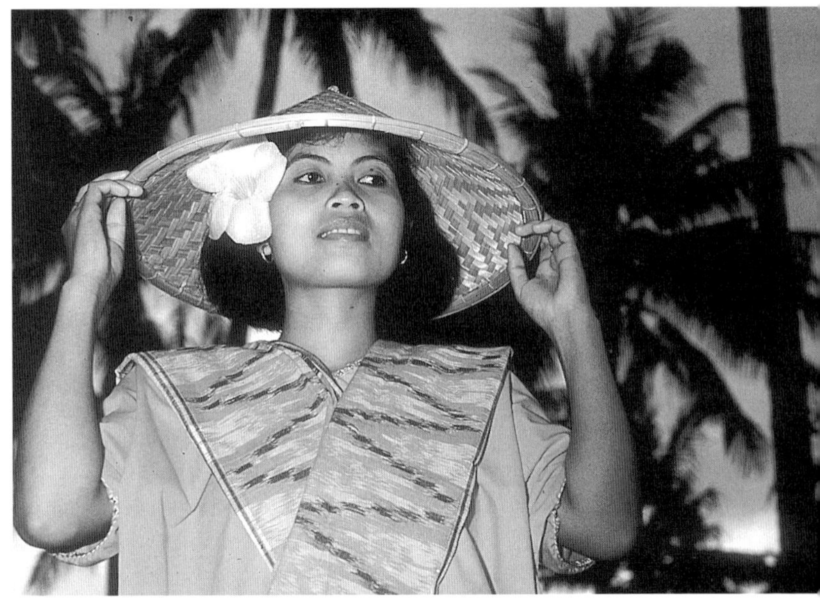

**Even in broad daylight, flash units are quite useful. Flash can equalize contrast and add light to shaded areas.**

### TTL Flash and Manual Mode

Manual exposure mode lets you control both the shutter speed and aperture. (Speeds faster than 1/250 second, however, will not be accepted.) This option is important in low-light situations when you want to combine small apertures with high shutter speeds. Keep in mind that Manual mode on the camera can be combined with fully automatic flash exposure, since the EOS-1N's metering systems for flash and existing light are separate and independently controlled.

### Flash Exposure Compensation

Just like ambient light metering, flash exposures are determined for a standard subject that reflects about 18% of the light. If the main subject to be illuminated by the flash is lighter or darker than this standard, compensation of the flash exposure is required.

Of the three factors that govern flash exposure—the aperture, the flash-to-subject distance, and the flash output—the correction is best controlled on the EOS-1N by varying the flash output. TTL flash metering makes it impossible to apply exposure compensation by changing the aperture or flash-to-subject distance.

Fortunately, the EOS-1N makes the input of a correction factor for flash exposures as easy as applying a correction factor to an ambient light exposure. Simply press the flash exposure compensation button when a Speedlite is connected to the EOS-1N. The symbol for flash exposure is displayed on the LCD panel's exposure compensation scale and you can use the quick control dial to select the correction factor in a range of +/-3 stops. The increment, in third or half stops, is determined by the setting you have chosen using Custom Function 6.

***Note:*** When the Command Back E1 is attached (remember, it has no quick control dial), use the main dial to input the flash exposure compensation value.

## Speedlite 540EZ

The 540EZ is the flagship of EZ flash units. With the zoom head in the telephoto (105mm) position, this flash features a maximum guide number of 177 feet (54 meters) at ISO 100. The light output can be reduced as much as eight stops (to 1/128 of the total power).

The zoom head provides flash coverage appropriate for seven different focal lengths ranging from 24mm to 105mm. By using a wide-angle diffuser, super wide-angle shots covering a focal length of up to 18mm are possible. When you activate the flash unit in the Auto Zoom setting, "Zoom" will appear on the LCD panel. This mode will automatically adjust the flash unit's zoom head to the appropriate setting for the lens in use. A manual zoom setting is also available, but it is easier and safer to set the flash for Auto Zoom most of the time.

In dark situations the 540EZ emits a near-infrared auxiliary light in order to allow the camera's AF system to work. All five of the EOS-1N's AF sensors can use the 540EZ auxiliary light for focusing. (If other Speedlites are used with the EOS-1N, only the central AF area works with the auxiliary light.) Though the reflector for the auxiliary light is fixed, the flash head can be rotated and tilted for bounce flash.

The 540EZ has several features for creating special flash effects. Up to 100 flashes per second can be emitted to create stroboscopic shots. The flash can also be synchronized with the second shutter curtain to produce properly exposed images of moving subjects with motion blur behind them.

## Speedlite 480EG

The largest and most powerful member of the Speedlite group, the 480EG is clearly intended for heavy-duty professional use. The flash has a guide number of 223 feet (68 meters) at ISO 100, more than any other Speedlite.

The "G" stands for "grip" because this is a classic "potato masher" flash unit. The flash does not mount in the camera's hot shoe. Instead, a dedicated cord connects the camera and flash. The camera mounts onto a bracket attached to a clamp on the handle of the 480EG. The "bracket-and-clamp" design makes it easy to separate the camera and flash, positioning the lighting precisely. For additional lighting control, the flash head can be tilted up to 90° and rotated up to 295°.

The 480EG offers a choice of exposure control methods, including two types of autoexposure. With the EOS-1N, A-TTL flash metering is available with the camera's Program, Shutter-Priority, and Aperture-Priority modes. The 480EG also offers variable ratio manual flash control, which allows the photographer to set the flash output directly.

## Speedlite 300EZ

With a guide number of 98 feet (30 meters) with the zoom head set for its maximum lens coverage (70mm), the Speedlite 300EZ is also a powerful option. Even with a relatively slow zoom lens, the 300EZ provides enough power for most situations needing flash.

The 300EZ also offers an array of features: The zoom head automatically adjusts to a range of lens focal lengths from 28mm to 70mm. A powerful AF auxiliary light allows the camera to focus accurately in low-light and/or low-contrast situations over the entire flash operating range. The 300EZ features both A-TTL and standard TTL metering, second-curtain flash synchronization, and a limited rapid-fire (strobe) capability.

## Speedlite 200E

This is the Canon system's small, low-cost flash unit. It is generally used with EOS Rebel-series cameras. It has a guide number of 66 feet (20 meters) at ISO 100. The angle of coverage is suitable for lenses as wide as 35mm, or 28mm with the optional Wide Adapter 200E, but there is no zoom feature, as signified by the lack of a "Z" in the model designation.

The 200E features TTL, but not A-TTL, exposure control and it lacks the bounce capabilities of more sophisticated units. These limitations make the 200E an unlikely main flash unit for use with the EOS-1N. However, it should not be overlooked as a secondary flash unit for more complex lighting setups.

## Macro Ring Lite ML-3

Unlike the general-purpose Speedlite models, the Macro Ring Lite ML-3 is a highly specialized flash unit dedicated to close-up photography. In fact, it is intended for use only with the EF 50mm f/2.5 Compact-Macro and EF 100mm f/2.8 Macro lenses.

The ML-3 has a guide number of 36 feet (11 meters) at ISO 100. Since this flash is used with subject distances of a few feet or closer, power is not the most important feature of this flash unit.

The ML-3 consists of two components, a control unit and a flash unit, connected with a coiled cord. The control unit contains the batteries and controls. This mounts on the camera's hot shoe. The flash unit is a ring that attaches around the front of the lens. It contains two curved flash tubes and two miniature focusing lamps, all behind a frosted panel.

When fired together, the ML-3's two flash tubes create even, shadowless illumination of flat subjects, such as postage stamps or artwork. However, either tube can also be fired separately for a more dramatic effect with three-dimensional or textured subjects. Continuous illumination from the two lamps aids focusing and allows you to preview the lighting setup.

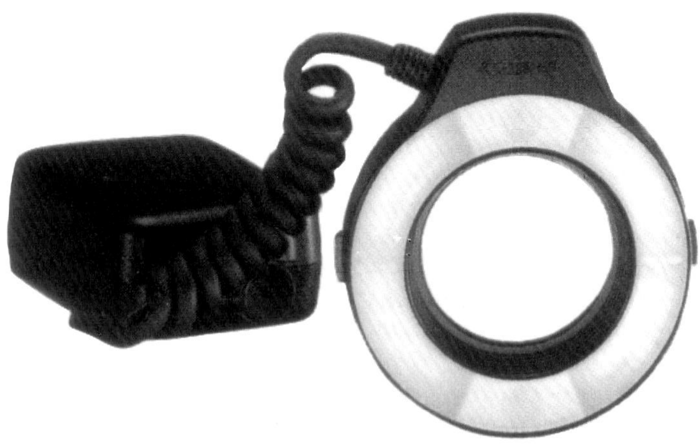

**The Canon Macro Ring Lite ML-3 is specially designed for close-up photography.**

Canon recommends the use of Aperture-Priority AE for optimum control of image sharpness and depth of field. Manual exposure selection is also possible, but this is only advisable for experienced macro photographers. TTL metering automatically accounts for the ambient light level, flash-to-subject distance, filter factors, and lens extension. The results are not only faster but also probably more accurate than could be obtained with tedious manual calculations.

**Hint:** Successful flash exposures are certainly easy with the EOS-1N and a dedicated Speedlite. But your EOS-1N and the Speedlite 540EZ (or other Canon Speedlites) offer such a multitude of imaging options that it is impossible to discuss all of them in this book. For additional information, refer to the *Magic Lantern Guide to the Canon Speedlite 540EZ.*

# EOS-1N Accessories

## BP-E1 Battery Pack

Because 6-volt lithium batteries are expensive and not always easy to come by, an accessory BP-E1 Battery Pack is available for the EOS-1N. The BP-E1 Battery Pack is simply a convenient power source and does not enhance the performance of the camera.

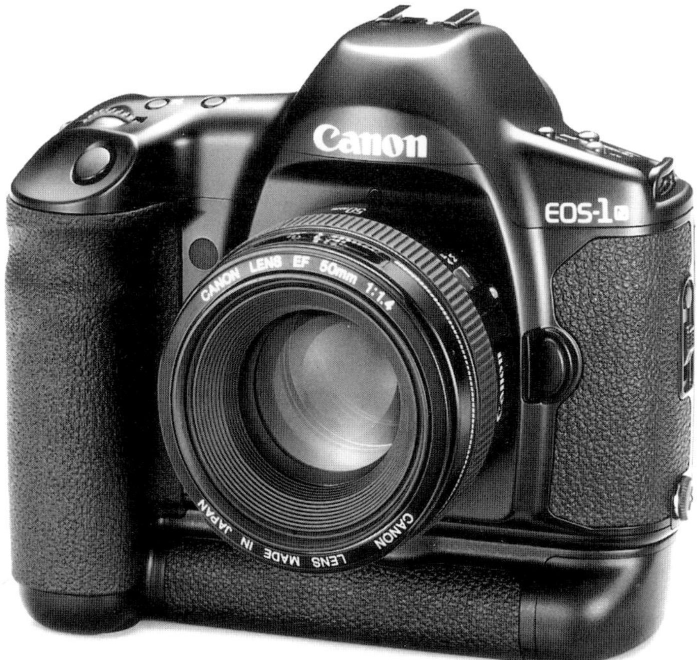


**The BP-E1 Battery Pack offers you the option of using lithium, alkaline-manganese, or NiCd batteries as a power source for your EOS-1N.**

Its L-shaped construction consists of a vertical handle resembling the standard hand grip and a horizontal battery holder that fits flush with the camera's base. The BP-E1 is inserted into the space where the camera's grip/battery chamber is normally installed. It screws firmly into the camera's tripod socket by turning the attachment knob. The grip portion of the BP-E1 unit holds the same 6-volt 2CR5 lithium battery as the camera, while the lower part holds four 1.5-volt AA alkaline-manganese or NiCd batteries. These are housed in a slide-in magazine that can be removed from the battery compartment with the touch of a button. Once the batteries have been loaded, the power source selector on the base of the grip section must be set to determine whether the camera is to receive power from the 6-volt lithium battery ("2CR5" setting) or from the four AA cells ("LR6" setting). The camera does not need to be switched off while changing from one power selection to another, however the camera should not have a function (such as film transport, self-timer, or long exposure) actively operating at the time because errors could result.

***Caution:*** *The Battery Pack BP-E1's compartment should never be loaded with AA-size lithium batteries because their high initial voltage could damage the camera's and the EF lens' electronics!*

## Power Drive Booster E1

The Power Drive Booster E1 is powered by eight 1.5-volt AA alkaline-manganese batteries or rechargeable AA NiCd cells, or a rechargeable NiCd Pack E1, which contains eight rechargeable 1.5-volt NiCd batteries. (The NiCd Pack E1 can be charged within 90 minutes.) The camera's 6-volt lithium battery cannot be used in the booster.

With this amount of energy, the Power Drive Booster offers more power than a standard 6-volt lithium battery can deliver. As a result, when the booster is attached to the EOS-1N, it increases the film transport frequency from a maximum of 3 frames per second (fps) to a maximum of 6 fps. However this top speed is possible only when One-Shot AF is set, ensuring that focus is constant for each exposure. If AI Servo is set, the camera can reach a continuous shooting speed of only approximately 5 fps.

Even in AI Servo AF mode, the EOS-1N is very fast with a Power Drive Booster E1 and a USM (Ultrasonic Motor) lens. The booster allows various functions that normally run in sequence to run

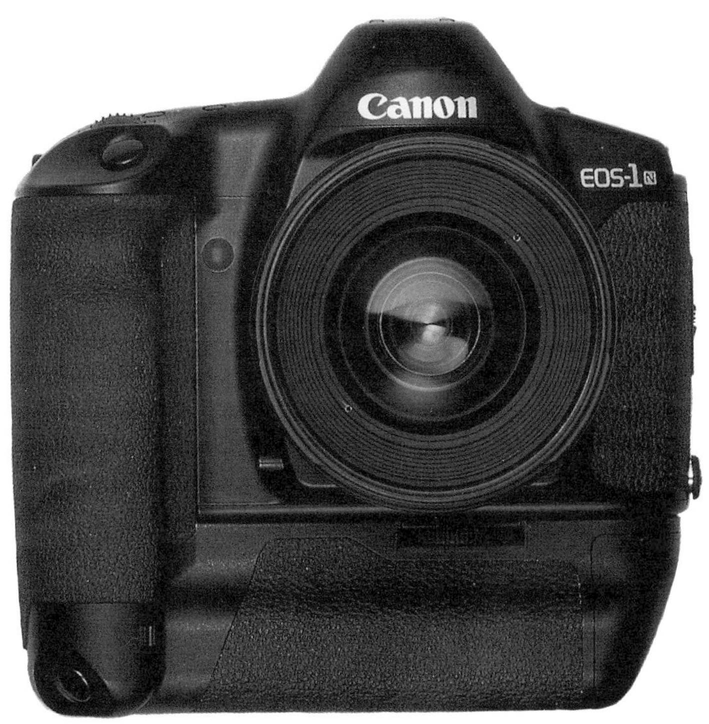


**The Power Drive Booster E1 converts the EOS-1N into the faster EOS-1N HS (High Speed), which can shoot up to 6 frames per second.**

simultaneously, for instance, focusing, aperture adjustment, and mirror movement. Up to 4.7 fps can be shot in AI Servo mode (with Focus Prediction Control). (The only non-USM lenses that can achieve this speed are the EF 80-200mm f/2.8 L, EF 20-35mm f/2.8 L, and EF 100 f/2.8 Macro lenses.)

Because taking a series of images at high speed is not always required, the EOS-1N can be switched back to single-frame advance mode with the booster. In low-speed continuous advance mode ("L"), values of approximately 3 fps are attained with One-Shot AF set and approximately 2.5 fps with AI Servo AF set. You can switch between low-speed and high-speed continuous advance mode by pressing the film winding mode selector behind the palm door and turning the main dial. The blue-framed window on the LCD panel will then display the symbol for continuous advance mode, indicating next to it either an "L" for low speed or "H" for high speed. If the battery power is no longer adequate for high-speed transport, the unit will automatically switch to the lower speed.

The Power Drive Booster E1 offers another advantage in addition to its improved power supply. The booster incorporates a vertical grip equipped with its own AE lock button and a shutter button, both conveniently located for easy access. The AE lock button falls directly under the thumb, and the shutter button under the forefinger when the camera is held vertically.

***Caution:*** *Alkaline-manganese batteries and rechargeable NiCd AA batteries are very common. Recently 1.5-volt lithium batteries of this size have been gaining a market share because they offer improved shelf-life, as well as superior performance at low temperatures. These batteries can be used only in conjunction with the Power Drive Booster E1 with an AE lock button marked with an asterisk (*). This particular model was designed specifically to be compatible with the EOS-1N. These batteries can also be used with the EOS-1N RS, which has a booster permanently attached.*

*Do not use AA lithium batteries with the Power Drive Booster E1 if it is attached to the EOS-1 camera.*

## Filters

If perfect images are your goal, you will want to use filters sooner or later. If you want to give your pictures that special touch, you will want to purchase a few special effects attachments.

### Polarizing Filters

Standard filters that enhance your images without changing their content include polarizing filters (although different people take different views on this point). The fact that only polarized light (light waves traveling in only one plane) passes through this type of filter, allows reflections to be removed from non-metallic surfaces and colors to be intensified. Water and panes of glass become more transparent because reflections are eliminated, the blue of the sky becomes more luminous, and distance shots become

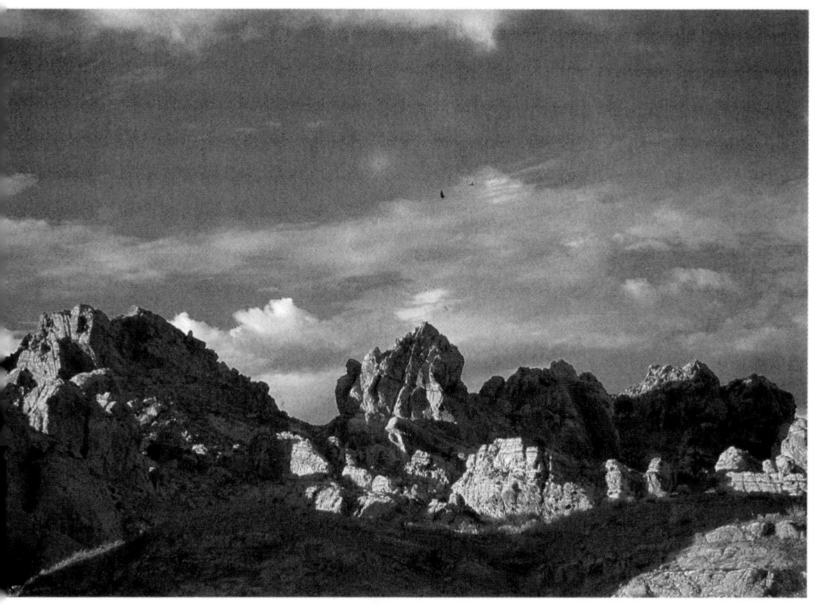

**The deep sky, white clouds, and striking contrast in the rocks were achieved by using a polarizing filter. Photo by Bob Shell.**

clearer because rays diffused by humidity are filtered out. Remember to make sure that when you use a rotatable, mounted polarizing filter, the main light source is at a right angle to the optical axis. Also, when using a polarizing filter on your EOS-1N, use only circular polarizing filters. Linear polarizing filters produce inaccurate metering results with cameras equipped with a semitransparent mirror, such as those used in all EOS model cameras.

**Graduated Neutral Density Filters**

Another type of filter found in many camera bags is the graduated neutral density filter. These filters are very useful in landscape photography, bringing the contrast between the sky and foreground into an exposure range that can be reproduced by the film—for example, to capture a brilliant sunset while retaining detail in the skyline.

To accurately position the location of the transition between the dark and the clear section, you must be able to slide and rotate the filter, which can be done with system filters such as those made by Cokin®. If the filter mount can be rotated, the filter can be positioned as desired.

### Ultraviolet Filters

UV-blocking filters (UV filters for short) and skylight filters are important if the light does in fact contain a high percentage of UV radiation—for example in high mountains or at the ocean. Many photographers leave a UV skylight filter on a lens at all times to protect the front element from being scratched or damaged.

### Monochromatic Filters

Colored filters are often used in black-and-white photography. A filter of a given color will lighten like colors and darken dissimilar colors in a black-and-white photograph. Yellow filters increase the contrast between clouds and a blue sky; red filters darken a blue sky with fluffy white clouds, creating an ominous mood; green filters improve the balance of light skin tones when they are converted to shades of gray on black-and-white film.

Working with daylight film in artificial light or with tungsten film in daylight requires conversion filters to correct the color bias. Blue filters will convert daylight film to correct the color balance for subjects under tungsten light. Amber filters convert tungsten film for daylight use. The exact color temperature determines exactly which filter is required. (Conversion filters usually have an alphanumeric reference, such as the 80A, which adapts light of 3200°K photoflood lamps to daylight film).

### Other Filters

Straddling the line between standard filters and special effects filters are warming filters, which elicit attractive skin colors and magical evening moods.

Soft focus filters remove harsh edges and reduce lines and blemishes. They are used most often for portraits, but give any subject a pleasant, dream-like quality. They come in various levels of diffusion. The effect of soft focus filters varies with lens aperture and is greatest when the aperture is wide open. Use the stop-down (depth-of-field preview) button to find the right aperture for the effect you want.

Cokin offers a wide variety of special effects filters, including star filters, rainbow filters, and assorted others, none of which will improve the technical quality of a picture but will merely change its appearance. When employed cleverly, with restraint, and when the effect is suitable to the subject matter, these special effects filters can produce interesting and successful pictures.

***Note:*** When a filter is mounted to a lens, two additional light-reflecting surfaces are added to the lens' optics. This is not taken into account in computing most lens' optical formulas, and therefore, a loss of sharpness and contrast could result. Exceptions to this rule are Canon's larger EF lenses, which come with a filter already in the filter drawer. Using a filter (either the one supplied with the lens or one selected by the photographer) with such a lens is integral to its optimum performance because a filter is factored into its optical formula.

## Viewfinder Accessories

### Magnifier S

Because the EOS-1N's autofocus is extremely accurate, the viewfinder's Magnifier S is really only required for extreme close-ups (using a bellows) with manual focus. This magnifier makes focusing highly reliable and enlarges the center of the viewfinder image by 2.5x. This image area is more easily viewed without eyeglasses than with eyeglasses, therefore Canon has designed the magnifier's eyepiece to be adjustable by up to +/- 4 diopters to accommodate the photographer's eyesight.

### Angle Finder B

A photographer who frequently takes exposures of flowers or small animals close to the ground or does copy stand work should consider acquiring the Angle Finder B, which allows you to look into the viewfinder from a 90° angle. The image is displayed upright and unreversed, just as it would be through the camera's viewfinder. The Angle Finder B offers built-in dioptric adjustment from +2 to -4 diopters. Although it can be rotated, the Angle Finder B does not provide as large an exit pupil as the rotating Speedfinders made for the F-1 and F-1N cameras. Still, it makes work incredibly easy.

### Ec-Series Focusing Screens

Canon offers eight user-interchangeable Ec-Series focusing screens (a screen-changing tool is provided with the purchase of these accessory focusing screens). Particularly useful is the D screen, which is engraved with a grid pattern. This allows you to align your EOS-1N precisely for shots of buildings, landscapes with super wide-angle lenses, and in copy work. The H screen has vertical and horizontal measuring scales, and the I screen has cross-hairs, making them both suitable for photography with a microscope or telescope. If you frequently focus manually or refocus USM lenses, consider the following screens: A (microprism circle), B (non-darkening, split-image rangefinder), or L (cross-split image rangefinder). The C screen is the standard focusing screen supplied with the EOS-1N. The EOS-1N RS is supplied with the R screen.

***Note:*** The focusing screen of the EOS-1N RS must be changed by an authorized Canon service technician.

### Dioptric Adjustment Lenses

Dioptric adjustment lenses allow photographers to take pictures without having to wear their eyeglasses. However, this applies only to farsightedness, because farsighted individuals can easily recognize their environment. Nearsighted individuals who take off their glasses to take pictures must put their glasses back on after each shot to avoid seeing their environment as a blur.

Canon makes ten Dioptric Adjustment Lens E corrective lenses that range between +3 and -4 diopters. The EOS-1N viewfinder's internal magnification is -1 diopters, and the dioptric adjustment dial can be adjusted between +1 and -3 diopters. When these variables are combined, these lenses can correct vision in the range of +5.4 to -5.6 diopters.

The use of a dioptric adjustment lens requires that the standard eyecup (which is also available as an accessory if the original one is lost) be exchanged for a special eyecup, the Rubber Frame Ec, which accepts the Series E Dioptric Adjustment Lens.

## Command Back E1

The Command Back E1 is attached to the EOS-1N in place of the camera's standard back. Note, however, that it does not have a quick control dial. The Command Back E1 is easy to use and has not changed significantly since the Command Back 70 (for the T70) was introduced.

To attach the Command Back E1 to the EOS-1N, first remove the camera back by pressing in the back cover lock release button and sliding down the back cover latch. Then, push the chrome stud on the top of the hinge down, toward the base of the camera. This releases the hinge. Now place the camera on a steady surface and hold the camera's palm door open with your right thumb. Place the bottom post of the Command Back E1 in the corresponding socket on the EOS-1N body. Press down on the part of the Command Back that retracts its spring-loaded top post. Align the top of the Command Back with the corresponding socket on the EOS-1N body and release the top post.

The Command Back offers data imprinting and timer control options. Because imprinted data can be distracting, we suggest you include it in pictures only when absolutely necessary. Data is imprinted on the bottom right of the picture. For ordinary situations, it is usually sufficient to imprint the date on the first picture of a roll or series in order for you to be able to organize them at a later date.

The following information can be imprinted:

- The date, in three different formats.
- The time and day.
- Sequential four-digit numbers that change automatically as pictures are taken.
- Six-digit codes consisting of numbers and/or letters that do not change during film transport and can be used to identify entire picture series.

The calendar takes into consideration leap years, but time changes between summer and winter (Daylight Saving Time) must be input manually.

With the Command Back attached, the self-timer countdown can be set from 1 second to as long as 23 hours, 59 minutes, and 59 seconds. Automatically controlled time exposures are possible from 1 second to 23 hours, 59 minutes, and 59 seconds. This range also applies to the duration of intervals possible between automatically controlled series. A series can be set to shoot from 2 to 99 frames. During a series, settings are maintained in the Command Back if film is changed between exposures. If extended breaks occur between individual exposures and a flash unit is active, it will be deactivated five minutes after an exposure is made and reactivated one minute before the subsequent exposure is made.

It features an LCD monitor and six buttons for setting data imprint or timer functions. The FUNCT button allows you to switch between the two functions. The MODE button is used for choosing one of the above-mentioned options in the selected function. (It does *not* set the camera's operating mode!) The SELECT button is used to change the LCD field in which information is to be changed (it will blink on the LCD), and the SET button is used to change the value within the selected LCD field. The START button is used to activate a function or to erase an erroneous entry in Program mode. The LEVEL button is pressed to select one of three brightness levels for data imprinting.

## Wireless Controller LC-3

The two-part infrared, strobe-type Wireless Controller LC-3 consists of a transmitter and receiver. The receiver is fitted onto the EOS-1N's hot shoe or, if a flash unit is attached, it is mounted with a bracket (which is supplied with the controller) that fits between the camera baseplate and the tripod head. A 16-inch (40.6 cm) cable, which plugs into the small socket on the left side of the camera, is used to connect the receiver to the camera. The receiver takes in signals emitted by the transmitter, which can be located a distance of up to 328 feet (100 m) away. This maximum range is available only when the transmitter and receiver are positioned at no more than a 10° angle, facing one another. If the triggering signal arrives at an angle of between 10° and 20°, the maximum distance possible between the transmitter and the receiver is reduced to 66 feet (20 m). This relatively narrow angle of reception is not a great restriction, though, because the receiver's head can be turned 360° in order to be aimed toward the transmitter.

The compact transmitter runs on four 1.5-volt AA alkaline-manganese or NiCd cells. By pressing the two-stage switch partway down, the exposure meter and the EOS-1N's automatic focus are activated. Completely depressing the switch fires the shutter. The Wireless Controller also allows you to delay the shutter's release by 3.5 seconds. If you want to get into the picture yourself, after pressing the release you can quickly put the transmitter in your pocket or hide it behind your back.

The LC-3 can control single exposures or series. In continuous advance mode the camera will take one picture after another as long as you keep the transmitter's shutter release pressed.

If the remote control release itself is to be triggered from a distance, the Remote Switch 60T3 (see below) can be attached, or the receiver of a second LC-3 can be connected with the transmitter of the first pair. This theoretically allows an unlimited distance between the receiver and transmitter. Still, there would be a release delay of slightly more than one second if nine relay stations were located between transmitter and receiver (range: 3,280 feet, or 1000 m).

Three transmitter channels are available. One transmitter allows the independent control of three units. Of course, several units can be operated simultaneously by remote control, provided all the receivers are set for the same channel. (Watch the receiving angle.)

A camera operated by remote release is not always required. The receiver socket can also be used to connect a handle-mount flash unit, while the transmitter can be connected with the camera's flash socket. As a result, off-camera flash exposures are possible without a tangle of cables.

**Other Remote Accessories**

The Cable Release Adapter T3 allows a mechanical cable release to be used with the EOS-1N. It connects the camera's remote control socket and accepts mechanical releases such as the Canon Cable Release 50 (20 inches, or 50 cm) and Cable Release 30 (12 inches, or 30 cm).

The Remote Switch 60T3 allows the EOS-1N to be triggered from a distance of 2 feet (60 cm) and can be plugged into the socket on the left end of the camera. This distance can be increased by connecting the remote switch to the 33-foot (10 m) Extension Cord 1000T3. Several 1000T3 cables can be combined to bridge even greater distances.

# EOS-1N RS

In 1995 Canon introduced a "sister" model to the standard EOS-1N camera, the EOS-1N RS, which features a pellicle mirror and an "RS" mode. This pellicle mirror design offers the photographer a continuous view of the scene, unobstructed even during the actual exposure. A big advantage to sports, wildlife, and news photographers, the pellicle mirror also enables the camera to operate at faster drive speeds in RS mode, up to 10 frames per second, and with less delay when the shutter button is pressed.

## The Evolution of the RS Model

### TLR vs. SLR

Designing a single-lens-reflex camera with a pellicle mirror was the answer to the photographer's desire to have an SLR camera with the advantages of the twin-lens-reflex (TLR) design. TLR cameras have two lenses, one for taking the picture, and a second with a reflex mirror that provides the view through the viewfinder. The TLR camera has several advantages over the SLR: the image is always visible in the viewfinder even during exposure, and because the mirror (located behind the viewfinder screen) does not have to move out of the way for exposure the camera is quieter, the vibration is reduced, and the delay is minimized between the moment the shutter button is pressed and the shutter actually fires.

### Canon and the Pellicle Mirror

In order for an SLR camera to feature the advantages of TLR design, the reflex mirror must stay in place during exposure. For this to work, the mirror must be both reflective and transparent. It must reflect a portion of the light to the viewfinder screen *and* allow the rest of the light to pass through to the film. This is made possible by a semi-silvered, or "pellicle," mirror. It stands to reason that if only a portion of the light reaches the film plane, some of the effective speed of the lens would be lost. This is true, in principle. But even if half the total light passes to the viewfinder, only one stop of light traveling to the film is lost. And if a camera can be designed so that even less light travels to the viewfinder, the loss of light to the film plane is that much less.

Canon offered cameras of this type quite early on, the Pellix in 1965 and its Pellix-QL ("Quick-Load" system) in 1966. The name of these cameras is derived from their pellicle mirror design. Unfortunately, these models did not enjoy great success and, due to difficulties in manufacturing sturdy and durable mirrors, six years passed before Canon again incorporated the pellicle mirror into a camera design. The next Canon cameras featuring pellicle mirrors were expensive specialty models manufactured for action photographers. The Canon F-1 High-Speed Motor Camera (based on the old F-1) was introduced in 1972 (for the Olympic Games in Sapporo, Japan) and the Canon F-1 High-Speed II (based on the new F-1) was introduced in 1984.

In the field of AF SLR cameras, it was the EOS RT, the sister model of the EOS 630 (EOS 600 outside North America) that was the first AF SLR designed with a pellicle mirror. The 630 was introduced at the turn of 1989–90 and was closely followed by the RT version. And now the current EOS-1N RS, a professional camera, also features this special pellicle mirror.

## The EOS-1N RS

### Pellicle Mirror

The EOS-1N RS's pellicle mirror reflects 35% of the light into the viewfinder, and 65% of the light passes to the film plane; hence the loss of light corresponds to about 2/3 of an f/stop. The viewfinder image is only slightly darker than that of the EOS-1N, so the camera is fitted with an Ec-R focusing screen that is designed especially to optimize viewfinder brightness.

The camera's stationary, pellicle mirror works best with the aperture wide open. If you are using a lens with a small maximum aperture and you find the image difficult to focus despite the relatively bright viewfinder image, the Magnifier S can be attached to the eyepiece to aid in critical focusing. This applies particularly to pictures containing many small details.

Most of the advantages of the pellicle design are based upon the fact that the subject can be observed uninterrupted during

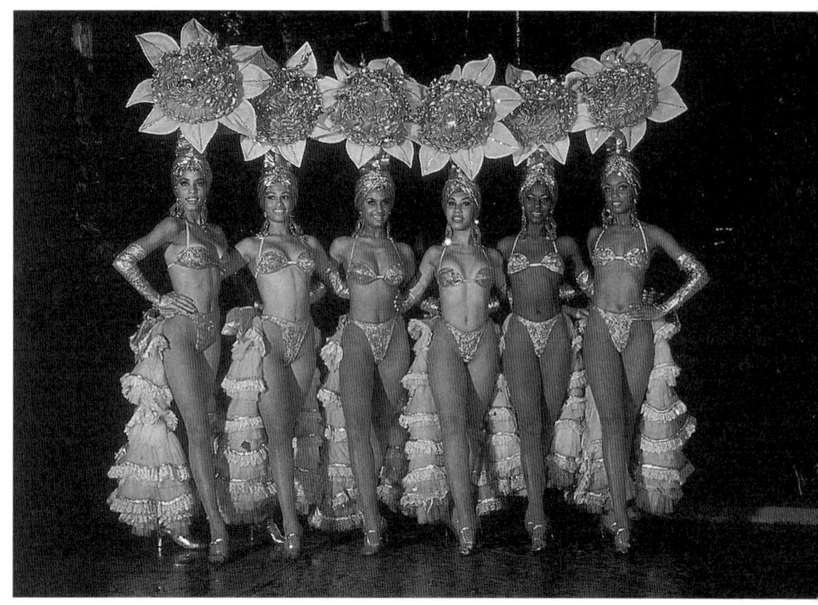

**With the EOS-1N RS's pellicle mirror, there is never a question as to whether the flash has gone off or not. You can see the scene through the viewfinder exactly at the moment of exposure!**

exposure. An individual's undesirable facial expression during exposure, for example, can be quickly reshot. The uninterrupted view is of particular value when a subject is being tracked. Because the view is never impaired, the photographer is assured that the target is in view so that one of the AF metering areas and the tracking speed can be adapted accurately to the moving subject. And finally, in flash photography there is never a question as to whether the flash has gone off or not.

**RS Mode**

Another feature of the EOS-1N RS is its built-in high-speed motor drive. By switching the camera's main power switch to "RS" and selecting continuous advance mode, you can shoot up to 10 frames per second. To achieve this speed, autofocus is automatically set to One-Shot mode, which does not allow focus tracking. (That would be asking a little too much considering the camera's

10 fps film advance!) Other limitations of RS mode are that auto-exposure bracketing (AEB) is not available and depth-of-field preview is achieved by lightly pressing the shutter button rather than using the depth-of-field preview button.

Also, because the stationary pellicle mirror has eliminated any delay during exposure (which occurs with conventional SLRs), the time lapse between the shutter's release and actual exposure is shorter than that of standard SLR cameras—reduced to 6 milliseconds! Whether this feature results in better pictures is mainly a function of the photographer's response. If he or she misses the "decisive moment," even the fastest camera cannot get the shot!

**EOS-1N RS vs. the EOS-1N**

Features that distinguish the EOS-1N RS from the EOS-1N are: the AF working range is reduced from EV 0 to EV 1, the exposure metering range is shifted from EV 0 to EV 1, and Depth-of-Field AE mode is unavailable. The EOS-1N RS's focusing screens are not able to be changed by the photographer and must be replaced by a trained technician.

In summary, compared with the standard EOS-1N, important advantages of the RS model are: continuous view of the viewfinder image, fast exposure response time, and rapid frame sequences. The first feature, in particular, could become addictive.

# EOS•DCS 3 and EOS•DCS 5

At PMA (the Photo Marketing Association trade show) in February 1995, Canon Inc. and Eastman Kodak Co. presented two digital cameras that combine the EOS-1N with a Kodak DCS digital imaging back, the EOS•DCS 3 and EOS•DCS 5. Based on an agreement between the two companies, the EOS•DCS 3 is initially being offered only by Canon and the EOS•DCS 5 only by Kodak. (This is subject to change in the future.) Both the EOS•DCS 3 and EOS•DCS 5 use the EOS-1N body fitted with a digital imaging back that looks like a large Power Drive Booster. The EOS•DCS 3 and EOS•DCS 5 modules each come in three varieties: DCS 3c/5c (color), DCS 3m/5m (monochrome), and DCS 3IR/5IR (infrared).

EOS•DCS cameras are compatible with all Canon EF lenses, including the tilt-shift and high-speed lenses, which can be used at their rated aperture values. The DCS models also retain most of the EOS-1N camera features and functions. But because the digital back replaces the EOS-1N's standard camera back, the digital cameras do not feature the quick control dial. Therefore, exposure compensation, flash compensation, and adjustments to the aperture in Manual exposure mode must be set using the following methods:

***Exposure compensation:*** In automatic modes, press and release the exposure compensation (+/-) button and turn the main dial.

***Flash compensation:*** Hold down the flash exposure compensation button and turn the main dial.

***Adjusting aperture in Manual mode:*** Follow the exposure compensation procedure (above).

## The Digital Back

At the heart of the digital imaging back is the CCD (Charge-Coupled Device) chip. The chip (which determines the effective image

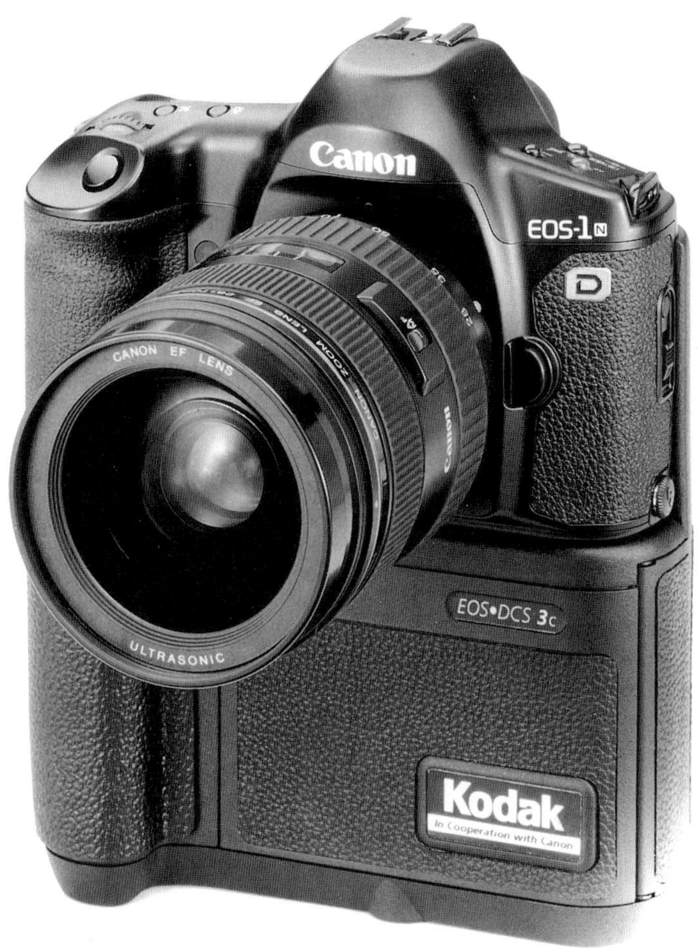


**An EOS-1N body and a digital imaging back made by Eastman Kodak Co. are combined to create the EOS•DCS 3c, one of the digital SLRs in the EOS•DCS series.**

area) in the EOS•DCS 3 measures 16.4 x 20.5 mm (approx. 0.6 x 0.8 in.)—comparatively large for digital cameras. The aspect ratio is approximately 4:5, not quite as narrow as the 35mm film format. The DCS 3 chip is 1012 x 1268 pixels, for a total of 1.3 million pixels, each having a size of 16 x 16 µ. The chip in the EOS•DCS 5 is smaller, measuring 9 x 14.3 mm (approx. 0.4 x 0.6 in.), and maintains the 2:3 aspect ratio of 35mm film. It has approximately 1.5 million (1012 x 1524) pixels, each having a size of 9 x 9 µ.

The smaller image area is outlined on the camera's focusing screen. The edge of the image appears shaded but can still be viewed well enough to see the surrounding information, which is helpful in anticipating the entry of a moving subject into the digital image frame.

Neither one of these chips fulfills the dream of having a full-size digital imaging format. But because of the reduction in image size, there is an effective increase in the focal length of the EF lens in use. The EOS•DCS 3 has a focal length extension factor of 1.6x, the EOS•DCS 5 has a factor of 2.5x. This means that with the DCS 3 an EF 100mm f/2.0 lens has the effective focal length of a 160mm lens, and with the DCS 5 that of a 250mm lens. The focal length range of an EF 80-200mm f/2.8L lens is extended to approximately 130 to 320mm with the DCS 3 and to 200 to 500mm with the DCS 5. This effect might at times be welcome because it offers super telephoto focal lengths without having to purchase the large, bulky super telephoto lenses. On the other hand, a 20mm ultra wide-angle lens can produce only the effect of a 32mm or 50mm lens!

The smaller image area also affects exposure metering. With evaluative and center-weighted average metering, the entire image area of the EOS•DCS 3 is metered (unlike in standard EOS-1N use, in which the outer edge of the image frame is not metered). The partial metering area is also effectively increased, covering 23.1% of the image area. Spot metering covers 9%, and fine-spot metering covers 5.9% of the total image area. In addition, the outer autofocus sensors effectively become closer to the image edges! With the EOS•DCS 5, the size of the effective image is reduced in the viewfinder so much that the two outermost focusing points are outside of the image area entirely, and the fine spot metering area comprises a large proportion of the image frame.

Both chips feature a color depth of 36 bits, 12 bits per RGB (red, green, blue) channel. This means that each pixel is capable of creating 4,096 different shades of red, green, and blue (at various levels of color saturation and brightness). And by mixing red, green, and blue, all other colors can be generated producing naturally colored imaging. The quality of color reproduction is a function of the monitor or printer used, and of course whether and how the image has been processed by one of numerous image manipulation programs such as Adobe Photoshop®.

EOS•DCS 3c (color) chip offers a sensitivity range from ISO 200 to ISO 1600, and the DCS 3m (monochrome) and 3IR (infrared) models have a range of ISO 400 to ISO 6400. For EOS•DCS 5 models, these sensitivity values range from ISO 100 to ISO 400 for the DCS 5c, and ISO 200 to 800 for the DCS 5m and 5IR models. ISO values can be changed for each shot, but cannot exceed these values.

## Memory and Image Storage

Both EOS•DCS models come with an internal buffer memory. The EOS•DCS 3 can store up to 12 image frames; the DCS 5 can store up to 10. If a series of exposures is desired, 12 frames can be shot in about 4.5 seconds (at a maximum frequency of 2.7 fps) with the DCS 3, and 10 can be shot at a rate of 2.3 fps with the DCS 5. Of course, you can also make single exposures and shorter series. The number of frames that have been taken (up to 39) will be displayed on the LCD frame counter on the top of the camera. The number of frames that can yet be stored in memory will be displayed on the LCD panel on the camera back.

Stored data can be downloaded from the camera's buffer memory onto a PCMCIA disk or compatible computer during shooting breaks. The size of each image file can be compressed from about 4.5 MB to about 1.6 MB. This process takes approximately 15 to 20 seconds per image. If all 12 frames are shot in a series using continuous mode, the images' data are automatically downloaded onto the disk following the last exposure. While this is occurring, an LED marked "CARD BUSY" on the digital back will blink. (The "CARD BUSY" LED will blink whenever the card is being read or written to.)

***Caution:*** *Do not remove the disk from the camera while the "CARD BUSY" LED is blinking.*

To delete images from the buffer memory before they have been transferred to the disk, press the DELETE button on the digital back.

Compatible disks for the EOS•DCS system are the PCMCIA-ATA hard disk cards. The PCMCIA-ATA Type III disk cards have a capacity to store 170 MB of image data, holding more than 100 images. The card is inserted on the left side (as seen from the rear) of the digital back.

The camera can be used as a drive for the PCMCIA card to transfer images to a computer. In this case, the camera is connected with the computer by means of a SCSI cable (a direct connection is possible with the Apple® Macintosh™ computer, however an adapter is required when transferring data to IBM PC or compatible units). It is possible that a computer might be equipped with a PCMCIA compatible drive, and in that case, the card can be used directly in the drive. This connection works not only for transferring data. You can also connect your EOS•DCS 3 or EOS•DCS 5 camera with a computer. In the studio each shot can be viewed immediately on the monitor, appraised, and stored or deleted using the computer as the control panel.

Power for both the EOS-1N camera and digital back is supplied by a built-in, rechargeable nickel-metal hydride (Ni-MH) battery pack. It is loaded in the bottom right-hand side of the camera. It can be fully charged in one hour and furnishes enough power for up to 1,000 exposures.

**Sound Capability**

A built-in microphone on the DCS back can be used for recording comments or other information associated with each photograph, and each sound file can last up to 25 seconds. This feature is particularly appealing to photojournalists. Each sound file is linked to the image last recorded. In continuous advance mode, however, only one sound file can be recorded for the series, and it will be attached to the last image in the series. Sound files cannot be played back on the camera itself, but must be played back through a compatible personal computer. And finally, be aware that sound files take up disk storage space, reducing the number of images that can be stored. A 2.5-minute message requires approximately 1 MB of disk space.